Policymaker's Journal

Policymaker's Journal

From New Delhi to Washington D.C.

KAUSHIK BASU

SIMON &
SCHUSTER

London · New York · Sydney · Toronto · New Delhi

FSC
www.fsc.org
MIX
Paper from
responsible sources
FSC® C016779

For
Avaaz Austen Basu,
Sky-Aria Basu-McCleary
and
Ivy-Page Basu-McCleary

Contents

Preface

This is a diary. It consists of notes and jottings, and of events and encounters, during my seven years in the world of policymaking. I wrote them erratically and intermittently, with no real purpose in mind, maybe with the hope of leafing through the pages in later years, and for my grandchildren to discover them. The idea of publishing it as a book came much later, but I have tried to stay true to the original spirit of a diary. It is a record of impressions of the moment. This means that some people whom I met and liked then, I now wonder why; and some, with whom it was a fleeting encounter, I wish I had made more effort to get to know them better. I have not made corrections in the text to the judgements of the moment, though now, in retrospect, I wish I could meet some of them again to ask if I got them wrong or *they* have changed. Aung San Suu Ki, for instance, belongs to this category.

The two parts of the book—Delhi and Washington—are rather different. In Delhi, the shock and awe of moving from the ivory tower of academe to the world of politics and policy was so overwhelming that I kept copious notes. This became sparse after I moved to the World Bank in 2012. As a result, the Washington years are not as comprehensive. The reader has to put up with the fact that what is recorded here actually happened and is true but there were events and encounters with people and organizations that I kept no record of, and they do not appear in the book.

Once I began transcribing my sometimes-illegible diaries, I took a lot of help from research assistants at Cornell. I would like to record special thanks to Grace Lee, Sylvia Blom and Haokun Sun for their help. They went beyond the call of their job descriptions so many times that I am grateful to them. I have been lucky in general, in being surrounded by colleagues and students who are brilliant, warm and friendly.

As I worked on this diary, I had to reach out repeatedly to my World Bank friends for help with finding documents and records. I would like to thank in particular the people who comprised my so-called Front Office Team: Vivian Hon, Laverne Cook, Bintao Wang and Grace Sorensen. By the time I was working on this, they were no longer part of my front office. But their prompt response to all my requests reminded me of their warmth and helpfulness.

I also worked with relatives and family to have them read bits and pieces and to discuss the style and content. I am grateful to Karna, Shabnam, Diksha, Mikey and Alaka for their advice and suggestions and also for the conversations and laughter. In addition, Shabnam read a large part of the manuscript when I was still vacillating about the value of this project, and shored up my confidence. Finally, Alaka, as always, read it all, and, as always, kept getting shocked at my grammar. I am grateful to her that readers will not get those shocks.

Finally, I am grateful to my editors at Simon and Schuster, Sayantan Ghosh, Megha Mukherjee and Himanjali Sankar.

Introduction

On 9 August 2009, I got an unexpected phone call. The call came as I packed my suitcases in our home in Hauz Khas in preparation for the long journey back to Ithaca the following evening, after the usual summer months in Delhi, to resume my job as chairman of the Economics Department at Cornell. Introducing herself as Vini Mahajan, a joint secretary in the office of the Prime Minister, she quickly got to the point. The prime minister wanted to ask me if I would be willing to serve as chief economic adviser to the Indian Government, a job that the prime minister himself had once done. I told her that this was too big a decision for me to answer off the cuff. Minimally, I needed to speak to the prime minister to know what he had in mind. The only catch was, I told her, I was leaving for the USA the following evening. She said she would call me back and did so ten minutes later, and asked if I could come to the prime minister's residence the following evening, maybe on my way to the airport.

The conversation I had with Prime Minister Manmohan Singh the following evening changed the course of my career over the following seven years, as I moved out of the cloisters of academe to the frenetic world of policymaking, first in India, and after that at the World Bank in Washington. Perhaps because I came into this world so suddenly and with so little background experience, while there was a lot of fumbling and learning, I took it all in with a sharper focus and with some of the outsider's objectivity that a jaded bureaucrat would not have. I realized early that it would be an experience worth recording, though I had no idea how long it would last, since I had to wrestle the frequent urge to fly back to Ithaca during the first several weeks. I began keeping a diary from 8 December 2009, the day I began my new job, in my grand office in the North Block, in Lutyens' Delhi, perched on the majestic slopes of Raisina Hill.

This book is a revised version of my diary, revised because I often wrote the diary in a hurry at day's or even week's end with scant attention to grammar and readability. Also, I have now taken the liberty to insert some reflections in retrospect, without altering any description of what actually happened. These later additions are amply clear and, where there is any ambiguity, they appear either in parentheses or as footnotes.

I have occasionally omitted a name or blurred a person's identity in trivial stories in order not to cause embarrassment to a junior staff in my office. There are one or two passages and conversations I decided to leave out because they contain sensitive material. But nowhere did I rewrite to alter the meaning or change a description of what had happened.

For some readers who will wonder after reading this book why I do not describe any act of corruption or bribery, I should add that this is because I never witnessed a corrupt deal being struck during my nearly three years in the Indian government. There are two reasons for this. First, while there is a lot of corruption in government, its incidence is not as high as many outside observers believe. Secondly, the corrupt ministers and bureaucrats—and I am sure there were some—would not cut a corrupt deal in the presence of someone like me, who has come to government from outside and will return to the outside world, and might even publish a book on his experiences someday.

My Indian government years were a period of high inflation, growth challenges (as the global financial crisis arrived ashore in India), and also a remarkable growth recovery; with India moving past China's GDP growth rate, corruption scandals breaking, causing widespread street protests, a lot of late night decision-making, which you knew would rock the stock market the next day, and getting to know politicians who were outstanding as statesmen in the midst of all this, and also many who were not.

The World Bank years were never that close to actual policymaking, but nevertheless breathtaking in their scope. They ranged from interacting with policymakers in tiny remote countries like Samoa, to gigantic nations with comparable heft, such as China, through sitting down with leading researchers to compute and announce global numbers on extreme poverty and rankings on how easy it is to do business in different countries (fully aware that there would be calls from irate finance ministers as soon as these were published), to handling politics within the World Bank, which could actually be as challenging as any global economic problem.

The book is a record of this experience with my own thoughts on policymaking, on the meaning of morality in public life, on how to handle stress in public life, and much more woven into it. It covers the India period comprehensively and has snatches of my four years with the World Bank. My diary writing became quite sparse during my four years in Washington. I tended to write up descriptions when I travelled and there were also some of the Back-to-Office Reports written after my travel. I drew on some of those for this book. I should clarify that this is not a book on economics or policymaking. I recorded the professional side of my policy years in India in the book *An Economist in the Real World: The Art of Policymaking*. Maybe one day I will write a similar book about my Washington years. The present book is more on life and musings in the world of frontline policymaking.

I hope that the book will be not just interesting reading, but serve as some sort of history—pop, personal, biased, no matter what pejorative adjective one may wish to use. I am aware that different cultures respond differently when they hear the words: 'It is history.' For some, like the French, it signals the need for people to listen carefully in order to understand their own predicament. For others, such as for those in the fast lane in USA, the response it elicits is: 'Good. So we can ignore it.'

I write this book with both the American and French attitudes in mind. This book will have much that is to be relished but eventually tossed out of one's head, but also some musings and ideas to be carried along, mulled over and hopefully used to shape a better world, for better lives.

PART ONE

The Delhi Years

2009–2012

1

Initiation

Personally, 8 December will go down as a marker date—the day I took up office in the Ministry of Finance to serve a two-year term[1] as Government of India's chief economic adviser, or CEA, as he is commonly known. My choice of pronoun is merely a reflection of the fact that no woman has been CEA, up to this 14th one. I have come to this job never having worked in the government. All my thirteen predecessors had had some experience, either as full-time civil servants or having served some years in the government in advisory or bureaucratic work.

It felt sufficiently momentous that I have decided to maintain a diary of my two years in or till I get thrown out of government, whichever is earlier.

This first week in office as CEA may well have been the most bewildering week of my life. It was a week of welcome celebrations

---

1. I later agreed to a small extension, which meant I was in this job for nearly three years.

and greetings, of briefings and meetings, of learning names and forgetting them, of a stream of individuals walking into my office to tell me that they will be reporting to me or reporting to someone reporting to me. It was a week of a relentless twelve hours each day in office.

I find it difficult to believe that until two weeks ago I was working as chairman of Cornell's Department of Economics, on the fourth floor of Uris Hall, occasionally looking wistfully out of my office window at the long winter shadows of trees and towers on those days when the clouds were kind enough to absent themselves, and taking walks along the banks of the beautiful Lake Cayuga, and complaining to myself of the pressure of work.

The changes I would have to adjust to were apparent the very first day I arrived at my office in the North Block within the imposing ramparts of Lutyens' New Delhi, built by the British sometime in the early 20th century, on the slopes of Raisina Hill, to celebrate the shifting of the capital of their prized colony, India, from Calcutta to New Delhi.

As I got out of my official Ambassador car with my weather-beaten briefcase and cheap laptop, two persons emerged seemingly from nowhere and whisked these out of my hand. My first instinct was to run after them and recover my belongings.[2] My usual experience, for instance when going somewhere with my wife and family, is to have heavy objects thrust upon me, not taken from me. The only times I have had things taken from me have been in mugging incidents, such as the one in Venice.

Relieved of my bags, I walked jauntily into the high-ceilinged building. As I approached my office and reached out to push open

---

2. The diary entry of this day was published in *Hindustan Times* on 18 December 2009. I decided that, now with me working in government, it was time to stop my popular writings; and I treated this as my last column. An edited version of this essay was later published in my book *An Economist's Miscellany* (Oxford University Press, 2010).

the huge wooden door, my men Friday did it for me. In these five days, I have not once touched the office door when getting in. It is like those airport doors with sensors that open automatically when people approach them.

The hardest learning that I am expected to do is not about these mechanical and, in some ways, trivial customs, but concerns speech. The problem stems from the fact that I speak clearly. The art of political speech is to say things that sound meaningful but are impossible to pin down. No one can say what you said is wrong because no one can understand what you said. You hear such speech from master politicians in not just India but the United States, the United Kingdom, China (if we knew what they were saying) and just about everywhere.

Since I mentioned the Venice mugging incident, let me complete my diary entry by recording the story because it is an achievement I am proud of. Also, it illustrates the art of translating theory (in this case, game theory) to practice, something that I will have to do a lot in my new job.

My wife and I had bought ice-cream from a road-side stall just outside St Mark's Square. The best time for a mugger to strike (I realized later) is when both hands are occupied juggling cones and coins. And indeed, within minutes of buying ice-cream, I realized that my wallet was gone. It had money, credit cards and travel documents. Alaka wanted to rush to the nearest police station. I felt that would be useful service to Venice but of no use to us, and I was not feeling charitable. I reasoned there were two possibilities. Either the thief had run into the milling crowds in the main square or was still in the small cluster of people buying ice-cream. If it was the former, the wallet was lost; if the latter, there was hope.

Just then a young couple walked away from the group enjoying their ice-cream. There was some probability—somehow they fitted the age-profile of pick-pockets in my head—that they could be the culprits; so we began tailing them. If they were guilty, they would soon check if we were still behind them, I thought to myself. Soon they paused to look into a shop window and casually turned back.

So we also turned back. I told Alaka I was now almost certain they had taken it. Alaka did not believe me, but, being more intrepid than me in these matters, promptly walked up to them and asked (and the accusation was evident in her tone) if they had seen anybody suspicious near the ice-cream vendor since we had lost our wallet there. To this, the man turned his pocket inside out and said, 'Check my pocket if you think I have taken it.' Alaka and I spoke in Bengali that that unexpected response confirmed his guilt; and I insisted that he allow me to check his back-pack. He agreed and said that since we were in the middle of the street, we should move to a side. As we did so, his girlfriend moved away. The readiness with which he opened his bag made me signal to Alaka not to let the girlfriend out of sight. Alaka was clearly now persuaded for she literally held the girl physically. As the man rummaged in his bag, I threatened to call the police. The game, he realized, was up. He asked me to speak softly and called his girlfriend. The wallet emerged from her back-pack.

Late that night my wife and I walked to the same vendor to have another round of ice-cream to make sure that we did not get scarred for life with a phobia of street-corner ice-cream.

16 December 2009, Wednesday

The new challenges I would face in life as a result of my new job became evident early enough. Last evening, I travelled with Alaka and our daughter, Diksha, to Kolkata. I had some meetings to attend and also I had flown in from Ithaca directly to my job and wanted to catch up with my mother, who had turned ninety earlier this year and lived alone in Kolkata. I boarded the flight with a draft copy of the *Mid-Year Review of the Indian Economy*. The *Mid-Year Review* had been started by one of my predecessor CEAs, Ashok Lahiri. It provided a quick summing up of how the economy had done during the first six months of the fiscal year (April to September, in India) and some forecasts of where the economy was headed. It was to be placed in parliament three days later by Finance Minister Pranab Mukherjee, and, as always happened in India with such events, would attract a lot of media attention. Till then it was a strictly confidential document.

Never having handled anything more confidential than the salary list of faculty and staff in the Economics Department of Cornell, where I had been department chairman for a little over a year, I was quite callow in these matters. I worked on the draft, making minor corrections, placed it in the magazine pouch in front of my seat, took a nap, and on reaching Kolkata, got off the plane without the *Mid-Year Review of the Indian Economy, 2009*. After reaching my mother's home, chatting with her for a while, as I opened my bags, I realized what I had done.

I panicked. The airplane was headed to Mumbai from Kolkata. True, most passengers would have no idea what that boring document was. But in case it was an economist or a corporate person, or, worse, a journalist, who got my seat and found the manuscript, it would be a coup for him or her. All the numbers would be out in the media before the finance minister presented it to the parliament. Who says democracy doesn't have its downsides?

What should I do? I wondered. Calling the airport and saying this was a confidential document would be exactly the wrong thing to do. In addition to the numbers leaking out, some airport official could make some money selling it to a newspaper. I decided I would describe this as my research paper which was of great value to me as an academic document. So I began phoning, starting with an old friend, Kishore, who worked with the Airport

Authority of India. He was vacationing somewhere and could not be of much help. I mustered up courage and phoned the Kolkata airport, without knowing anybody there, and pleaded about my life's research having been left behind on a flight. Could some cleaning staff have found it? Alaka phoned the airline company to make the same plea on my behalf. People were surprisingly nice, but all to no avail.

I was now reconciled that there was a probability that it would leak out; and I realized, in case that happened, I would have to offer my resignation and I was sure the government would have no choice but to accept it. The only plus was that it would be the shortest term a CEA had held and I would have left the government with a record which in all likelihood would never be broken. Diksha said she was getting a headache from all this.

Around midnight, I told myself this was a trial, a trial to see if I had the mental capacity to take this in my stride. I reasoned, that I had not done anything wrong deliberately; and I had done my best to resolve the problem. Yes, this was a crisis but no one (excepting me) would get hurt by this. So I must go to sleep, tossing it out of my head. And to my surprise I discovered I had the capacity for that. I went to sleep peacefully. [This capacity has helped me all through my seven years in the world of policymaking.]

A few hours later, while it was still dark, the phone rang. It was the Kolkata Airport Authority saying that a sweeper had found the document and it was in their safe custody and we could come and get it in the morning. A sense of joy coursed through me, not only because the leak was prevented, but at the thought of how much goodness there is in the world. People who had no stake in my 'research', looked for my papers, found them, and had the decency to phone me at night, knowing that I was worried about this.

25 December 2009 Friday

It feels like the most eventful month of my life drawing to a close.

On 13 December, there was our son Karna's wedding reception at the Delhi Flying Club. He and Shabnam, his classmate from Yale, had got married formally in New York earlier but we wanted a nice event in Delhi. Friends and relatives came from Kolkata, Mumbai, and some from America. And, given my current job, there was a lot of Delhi's *eminence grise*.

On 14 December, the prime minister, Manmohan Singh, met me for a one-on-one meeting in his office. We discussed India's main policy challenges and what he hoped I would be able to do. The prime minister also invited me to a lunch on 15 December. It was in honor of Lee Kwan Yew and was to be held at the prime minister's residence, 7 Race Course Road, or 7RCR, as everybody called it. It was arranged for twenty people. Shashi Tharoor was there, as were Nandan Nilekani, Jayanthi Natarajan (very friendly), and Chidambaram (in a slightly dour mood). At dinner, I was seated next to Lee Kwan Yew's daughter, Lee Wei Ling, who is a distinguished neuro-physician. She, it was quickly evident, is a remarkably intelligent woman. She kept asking me politically incorrect questions about India's caste system and language-group politics in India. I tried to hush her up, but without success. She was unbelievably knowledgeable about India, Kolkata, Bengalis, Cornell University, and the town of Ithaca. She even asked me about Beebe Lake on the edge of Cornell.

My interactions with politics before this had been minimal. My father was briefly in politics, having served as the mayor of Calcutta and then as the speaker of the West Bengal Assembly. So I did meet some political figures then, but not too many and certainly did not get to know anybody well. My father himself was an apolitical politician. He had grown up poor and had studied law late in life because that was the easy thing to study those days in Kolkata. It was against all odds that he became one of the city's most celebrated lawyers. I always felt his going into politics and becoming the city's mayor was not because of any deep political passion but really to prove to himself (and, no doubt, to his street-corner friends from his childhood, with most of whom he had kept in touch) that he could make it to the top. Even though he did not have a great interest in politics, there were stories suggesting he had a knack for it. In 1963, when I was eleven, he went to Ottawa representing the Indian government for a conference. Those were days of rare foreign travel and so there was a lot of excitement among his clients and in the family. At that time, the controversial Barry Goldwater running for the US presidency was the big North American news. On the sidelines of the Ottawa conference my father gave an interview to a local newspaper in which he was asked about his views on Goldwater. His long answer, not giving out his hand, was praised by the Indian officials who travelled with him, and reported in a local newspaper as shrewd Indian diplomacy. We later learned from him, in the safe confines of our home, that he had no idea who or what Goldwater was. From the question he guessed it was either a contentious scientific invention or the name of a controversial politician. So he had to give an answer that would fit both.

However, since he was not 'into' politics, I got very little exposure to it.

I had met Manmohan Singh on several occasions, starting from before he joined politics.

[During the course of my nearly three years in his government I got to see him and talk to him regularly. Subsequently, after I joined the World Bank as its chief economist, I got to meet many politicians around the world. I am convinced that in terms of honesty, basic decency, and, in particular, lack of guile and intrigue, he has few peers in the world. There are, of course, human beings like that, but they typically do not make it to the top rung of politics. It is, I believe, indeed accidental that he made it to the prime minister's post and India was lucky for that. Sonia Gandhi gets credit for this act of talent spotting and for the graciousness of pulling herself back from what was all but hers, to make way for Manmohan Singh.]

Two years ago, when I was not in public life, Chandrababu Naidu sent me a message, quite out of the blue, wanting to meet me. He had been one of India's most dynamic chief ministers, having persuaded Bill Gates to move a large operation of Microsoft to Hyderabad, and I was curious. I went to meet him somewhere on Pandara Road.

It was a strange hour-long meeting. I was impressed by his concentration, and by his zeal to do something for Andhra Pradesh. It was a one-on-one meeting, but for a lady assistant of his (I presume), who quietly sat in one corner. Some way through the meeting, a man came in with a tray, said 'Tea', placed two tea cups in front of me and Chandrababu, and left. Fifteen minutes later, the same man came in, said 'Soup', and placed two soup bowls in front of us. I felt like asking, 'What's going on?' but kept quiet, and had my soup instead. I couldn't figure out why Chandrababu met me. Was he really interested in ideas concerning the economy? Was it some kind of atonement for having joined the BJP? Was he just interested in building up some intellectual network? He did talk about Amartya Sen. Did he want to get to know him, through me? And, also, did he always have tea and soup in quick succession? I did not get any of the answers but it was an early 'political' experience I cherished.

As it happens, Amartya Sen came to our home in Hauz Khas earlier today for dinner. We also invited Pulin and Nalini Nayak. It was a very pleasant evening. Sen was, as always, Socratic in conversation. A fine mixture of philosophical depth and humor. He told us that, because of his strong position in support of feminism and the letter 'a' at the end of his name, which suggested a woman's name, some people—this was before he shot into prominence with the Nobel in 1998—assumed he was a woman. The most memorable letter he received was from a woman, who, exasperated by men, and wanting to support Amartya in some of his public debates on feminism, began the letter with: 'Dear Ms. Sen, They will never understand...'

Amartya Sen has been quite a celebrity right from 1972 when I first got to know him as a teacher and later as my PhD adviser, but his stature has grown, especially because he straddles both economics and philosophy in a manner that has few peers. He is arguably the greatest living economist-philosopher in the world. He is also the greatest conversationalist I have known. People talk about Isaiah Berlin as the great intellectual conversationalist. I never met him but I have difficulty imagining a better conversationalist.

Having watched Amartya Sen's growing band of admirers around the world I feel it is likely that one or two hundred years from now, he will appear to people looking back at history, as a personality as prominent as Rousseau or Voltaire. This leaves me with a quandary. I think of the period of Enlightenment and the intellectuals who lived and wrote then as representing one of the greatest human achievements, second maybe only to the rise of the Greeks, four and more centuries before the Christian era. The Enlightenment was a period of big strides in philosophy and mathematics—calculus came out of the works of Newton and Leibnitz, religion was jettisoned for a secular morality. During the rise of the Greek thinkers, we again saw the flourishing of philosophy and mathematics—there was the birth of geometry thanks to Thales and Pythagoras.

Amartya Sen is one of the finest minds of our time but can we really place him on the same pedestal as Rousseau? Let me clarify. What I am asserting is that he will likely end up there a few hundred years from now. For me this raises an interesting question about evaluating philosophers in their lifetimes and in retrospect. If it is true that Sen will rise to the stature of Rousseau over time, this begs the question whether we have a propensity to underestimate intellectuals in their lifetimes or overestimate them in retrospect. It is possible that Rousseau is great but not as great as he appears to us now a few centuries after his time. He, in his life time, was like Sen in his, and neither of them as great as Rousseau in retrospect.

One of the most remarkable traits of Sen is his wide interest. He is interested in economics and philosophy, of course, but he is also interested in mathematics, in contemporary politics (his knowledge of the nitty gritty of what is happening in India always surprises me), in ancient Indian history, and in everyday gossip. Seeing Sen today, mellowed by time, I remembered so many past meetings and occasions. The first meeting with him (which he will not remember) was in 1970, when I was an undergraduate student at St Stephen's College. My dear friend, Sanjay Hazarika, and I were walking in the Delhi University campus when we saw a man sprawled on the pavement just outside the Delhi School of Economics. With the idealism of youth and upset that none of the pedestrians were doing anything, we ran into the Delhi School of Economics and saw Amartya Sen outside the main office. Sen was then (I believe) department chair and already a mini-celebrity. We barely said hello to him but insisted that he should call an ambulance or some help for the man in the street outside. He asked some questions about who the man was, whether he was unwell or just sleeping there. In our hurry, we had not garnered any information but rushed to call in help. Sen said he would send some of his staff to check out the person but we had better go out and be with the man. When Sanjay and I ran back to the same spot the man was gone. In retrospect I think he was a man who may have had a peg or two too many, slumped for a while, and then pulled himself up and walked away. In any case, Sanjay and I looked at each other about what we would do when Sen came out with his Delhi School entourage. It was obvious to both of us that there was only one course of rational action, since Sen had no idea who either of us were. We ran from the scene of the crime.

That was my first meeting with Sen. I should also add that Sanjay, who was one of the kindest persons I knew, got more and more disenchanted with the grave inequalities and injustices in our society, joined the revolutionary Communist movement and quit college before getting his degree to help usher in the revolution, which never happened.

Talking to Sen today I also got a flashback of maybe fifteen years ago, when Alaka and I, with Diksha (our daughter, then three or four years old) in tow, visited him at India International Center (IIC). He was visiting Delhi and staying at the IIC. Always up for a conversation, he invited me, Alaka, and Professor Anjan Mukherjee from JNU to visit him. We did not have a baby sitter at home and so took Diksha along and made her sit in a corner with paper and crayons, while we had a long conversation, ranging from economics and philosophy to gossip about economists and philosophers.

28 December 2009, Monday

The prime minister and Mrs Gursharan Kaur (his wife) invited me to a dinner at their residence held in honor of Japanese Prime Minister Yukio Hatoyama, and his wife, Miyuki Hatoyama. I arrived punctually at 8:30 pm—the joys of unpunctuality are clearly behind me now. Among the twenty dinner guests were L. K. Advani, Sonia Gandhi, Mukesh Ambani, Nirupama Rao, H. K. Singh (India's Ambassador to Japan), and Deepika Padukone. I was surprised to see Deepika in that group but realized later that she was there for Miyuki Hatoyama, who was an actress, once upon a time.

Deepika looked stunningly beautiful. I introduced myself to her. She seemed visibly uncomfortable in this political-policy gathering (and must have been wondering the way I wondered why she was there at all). I liked the fact that she seemed a modest and sweet person. I talked with her a little but one of the visiting Japanese bureaucrats took to me more than her, and I was, much to my regret, whisked away to meet others. This was my first meeting with Mukesh Ambani. He seemed agreeable and we talked quite a bit about several matters, including higher education. I said hello to Sonia Gandhi, but not much else. The food was excellent and, as always in Indian political dinners, there was no alcohol.

1 January 2010, Wednesday

As another new year dawns, I look back at the last few crazy weeks of my life. Inflation is raging, there is effort to rein in the fiscal deficit, which had been deliberately raised to battle the global financial downturn since 2008 and, as always, every new expenditure creates new interests that refuse to let go of the money and so returning the deficit to where it was is turning out to be hard. Add to all this, the super-energetic Indian media is always around, watching and reporting on everything we say or do. This is maddening but in the long-run a strength that forces our leaders and bureaucrats at the top to be more transparent than they would be otherwise. The media, ever ready to contest and quiz the leaders, is India's strength. Few nations outside the advanced economies have this kind of media and this raises India's global stature and also its long-run growth prospects.

In the midst of fighting inflation, unemployment and hemorrhaging finance, I was involved in another battle—to get access to the large, well-maintained bathroom on the first floor, meant for the secretaries to the Government of India. The bathroom had three towel racks with three nicely laundered towels marked 'Finance Secretary', 'Revenue Secretary' and 'Expenditure Secretary'. My two senior personal secretaries, and also the peons and ever-loyal driver, Manbir Singh, were upset by this. They reminded me that though I was called chief economic adviser, I had the rank of a secretary. In fact, I was the only other secretary in the Ministry of Finance, apart from the three who have 'secretary' attached to their title: Finance, Revenue and Expenditure. So instead of just using the VIP bathrooms on the ground and first floor, accessed by additional and joint secretaries, I should, they insisted, have access to the even better bathroom. It was their pride that was being hurt. I told them flatly that I did not see myself, amidst discussion of inflation control and deficit management, slipping in a request to the finance minister that I be given access to the special first floor bathroom.

So my personal secretaries, led by the chief of my administrative staff, the outstanding Mr Somanathan, took it upon themselves to wage the battle. And they won, they gleefully informed me this morning. Indeed, I was pleasantly surprised to see a fourth rack with a fresh towel marked 'CEA'.

There was only one downside to this bathroom. It was fairly far away from my office; and along the corridor, the peons, security guards, and other officers sat on flat benches outside the offices of various senior bureaucrats. As is the custom in India, when a senior adviser or bureaucrat walks down the corridor, they all stand up and salute. As I left the bathroom today, to my dismay I found them all jumping to their feet to salute me. It is an uncomfortable thought that for the next two years I would get a salute for my performance.

2 January 2010, Thursday

Amartyada, as I and many others call him, invited Alaka and me to lunch with him and some friends at Taj Palace. The other guests were Chitra Sarkar (of Air India) and her husband Partha Sarkar, Anuradha Luther (Maitra), one time Delhi School student, with whom I shared many common friends but I had never met her before, and, surprisingly, also Vikram Seth. I instinctively liked Vikram, and since I am a great believer in instinct, I decided he must be a good human being, though there is no hard evidence of that, unlike for the fact that he is a great writer, one of the greatest in fact. I was terrified he would ask me if I had read *A Suitable Boy*. He did not. We discovered a common interest in art. He showed me pictures of his recent sculptures and I told him about my interest in painting sarees and T-shirts and we agreed to meet some day and see the real stuff.

I spent most of the day in my North Block office. It is such an ample and lovely office that the long hours are beginning to feel effortless. Today I began working on the Budget speech that Finance Minister Pranab Mukherjee will deliver in parliament at the end of February. I got totally absorbed in this. It is strange that it is possible to get absorbed in another person's speech.

3 January 2010, Sunday

Relieved by the arrival of Sunday, Karna, Shabnam, Mai (mother-in-law), Alaka and I went to the renovated National Gallery of Modern Art. It is very impressive. What an art heritage India has. But it is sad that it gets so few visitors. The guards seemed quite annoyed that they had to keep their eyes open while we were there. India ought to make a greater effort to get Indians and especially school-goers interested in the creative arts. It will help the country be more innovative and even have higher GDP growth, in case art for art's sake does not interest us.

Alaka and I had dinner at the home of Montek Singh Ahluwalia and Isher, with Narayana Murthy, Sudha Murthy, Nandan Nilekani, Rohini Nilekani, Amartya and Emma Rothschild. Montek's home is such a gracious place and the conversation is always good. Feels a bit Renaissance-ish.

Amartyada's presence in Delhi means more dinner and lunch invitations for me. These invitations are a welcome break since the days are now endless quantities of work giving shape to the Indian Budget. We are also now working full pace on the *Economic Survey of India*. As an economist I used to read these annual surveys, maybe the most important yearly round-up of the Indian economy one could find anywhere. The Indian government may not be good at implementing economic policies but it has few peers in the quality of writing about economic policies. British colonialism is clearly not without its legacies.

It is exciting to be on the production side of the *Economic Survey*. As an academic I had led a perfectly selfish life. I hear so many economists say that they became an economist to help make a better society. That always made me feel a bit guilty because the only reason I became an economist was because the logic and puzzles of the economy seemed so fascinating. As a researcher I did nothing but indulge in that fascination. I like to believe that I am a good human being, who wants a better society and people to be better off. But I kept those concerns for after-work hours and for weekends. My work hours were time for self-indulgence. My only justification for this—not that I needed a justification—was that the finest research needs this, just as the production of finest art relies not on the artist's desire to help society but the obsession to produce good art. I can see that this kind of obsession, as I had during my research career, can bring you face to face with moral conflict, for instance, if you realize that you have discovered how to make an atom bomb. Do you go ahead or stop? Luckily, I never had to confront such a dilemma. And, if I did, I feel certain, I would take the moral option.

Friends often asked me why I returned to India immediately after my PhD and did not work in England or the United States as most Indian PhDs did. Was it patriotism for India? Fortunately, or unfortunately, that was not the case. I think of patriotism—if by that we mean the propensity to think of one's people as special—as immoral, like racism. I try hard not to be a patriot. The right way to live life is with human empathy for all, irrespective of race, religion, sexual orientation or nationality.

My return to India, after my PhD, was almost an unthinking decision. I had gone to England to study and I came back after that. It is possible that subliminally I was concerned about my aging parents and wanted to be close to them. Money has never been a major driver for any of my decisions (though I try not to let my employers know this) and so the fact that by returning to India I was taking a big salary cut was of little concern; I wanted to work for the innate pleasure of the work. Also, I loved India and that is where my cultural roots are. The somewhat anarchic, laid-back lifestyle of India appeals to me.

When I took up the job as CEA, I told myself that I had had enough of self-indulgence and I was going to do this in order to help create a better society, a better economy. I could have worked for any country but India is still a nation with vast numbers of poor people, and, given my roots and instinctive understanding of India, I was likely to be more effective here.

My ethical objection to nationalism finds comfort in the fact that two of India's greatest minds, Tagore and Nehru, took a similar position. Both of them were instinctively against the stridency of nationalism, even though they loved India. Nehru is truly impressive on this because as prime minister he had to, of course, espouse the cause of the nation—his nation. But he was always uncomfortable with this. There must be few prime ministers or heads of states who could write, as Nehru did, that we have to live by our national identity now since that is the way the world is organized. But we must also strive to go beyond this and eventually create a world where our primary identity is that of citizen of the world.

This is pretty much the spirit in which I decided to enter the world of policymaking. I had had enough fun doing research as an end in itself. I would now work single-mindedly to try to raise the standard of living and well-being of the nation that was in my charge. That was the resolution with which I came to the government; and these last few weeks I have worked hard. Fortunately, I have a tendency to get hooked to whatever I do (once I have got over that initial hurdle of starting to do it); and I am finding the work quite exciting. The work on the *Economic Survey* is especially enjoyable. I also have a wonderful team of officers from the Indian Economic Service, totally dedicated to their job. In short, it is turning out to be enjoyable work but also quite exhausting.

So much so that the invitations I am getting by virtue of Sen being in town are turning out to be most welcome. There was lunch yesterday at Manmohan Singh's residence, 7RCR, with Amartya, Emma, Montek, Isher and a few others. I met Daman Singh, the prime minister's daughter, and her husband, who is a civil servant, for the first time. It is quite a remarkable family, where there is absolutely no pomposity involved by virtue of being the prime minister's family. This is rare anywhere in the world and especially in developing countries.

Dinner last evening was at Vinay Bharat Ram's home. It was a relaxing evening with Lord Skidelsky, the biographer of Keynes, whom I had read extensively but not met before and Lord Meghnad Desai, who was one of my professors at the London School of Economics (LSE). I don't think I have ever met two lords in one room before.

My first meeting with Meghnad was quite a jolt to me. In 1972, when I was finishing my undergraduate studies in St Stephen's College, I recall going to the university Coffee House one day with a bunch of college friends (I did that with more regularity than I care to remember) and we all commented on a man with a huge afro hairdo, wearing a shirt with shocking brightly-colored stripes. Several months later, after I joined the LSE, I was told to go and meet the person who would be my tutor. I knocked on his door, was asked to come in. The first sight was of piles of books on a table. Then from behind a pile emerged first the afro, then the man in the Coffee House.

It was a proper working lunch today with Nandan Nilekani at the Taj Chambers, mainly to discuss his unique bio-metric identification system.[3] I think it is a transformative scheme that can help vault India ahead. Of course, much will depend on how much use it is put to. Nandan and others often emphasized that it is basically a technology to make sure that 'you are you'. This is an inadequate way of explaining this. The right approach would be to describe this with a little bit of set theory. There are zillions of transactions and activities taking place in India— people buying goods, cutting deals, boarding trains, joining clubs. The unique identification system is a way of associating each individual with a subset of this universal set of transactions. In other words, the person who withdrew money from a bank in Chennai and the person who bought a train ticket in Delhi are the same person. This has meaning and can be contested, whereas 'you are you' is tautological. If transaction or activity is defined in such a way that each of them is performed by one person, then the unique identification system helps create a partition of the set of all recorded transactions and activities in India. Bio-metric identification is basically a platform for partitioning all the activities occurring in a country. The richness of the information will of course have its risks but all technological advances come with their own risks. We simply have to develop safeguards against them and try to get the benefits, which in this case can be very large, I believe.

---

3. This would later become India's famous but controversial Aadhaar program.

6 January 2010, Wednesday

I went for my routine medical check-up, mandatory on joining the government (to make sure, I suppose, that you were not bringing some exotic bacteria into the government) to Ram Manohar Lohia (RML) Hospital, state-run and designated for use by government officials. It was a dreadful experience. I was instructed to come by 9 am on an empty stomach, and I did as advised. I soon discovered that the first task was being shunted from one room to another and even from one building to another, filling forms and signing my name in various places. I counted I signed in six different registers in different rooms. Since the keepers of the registers were often difficult to locate, this took an enormous amount of time.

After some time, with no X-rays, no blood tests, no medical examinations still done, I asked irritably, 'When can I eat?' The hospital official smiled genially and said, 'You can eat now.' It was never clarified why one needed an empty stomach to sign. After a lot of time I was directed to the office of the head of the division, Dr Chaturvedi. On my complaining to him that I had just filled forms and signed and no tests had yet been done, he said calmly that everything would be taken care of. I tried to chat him up a little, addressing him graciously as 'Dr Chaturvedi' hoping to energize him into quick action. But to no avail. I was later told by a nurse that Dr Chaturvedi was not there that day. The person occupying his seat was Siddhu. In retrospect, I was very impressed by Siddhu's equanimity; he was completely comfortable with my addressing him as Chaturvedi and he even nodded as I tried to chat with him. Kafka should have been here. Siddhu told me to be in the waiting area and I would be taken care of.

Around 11:30 am a junior staff explained to me that a patient feeling harassed by the hospital had beaten up a radiology staff member and, as a protest, all his radiology colleagues had gone on strike, and it seems the wave of sympathy was so great even some staff from other departments had (he added the word 'understandably') stayed away from work. Hence, the hospital was somewhat chaotic today, he explained.

Seeing this junior staff member's inclination to at least talk properly and explain, I asked him, if the whole process would have been faster on another day. He replied, 'No, it would take the same amount of time.'

I suppose I should have cheered up that our government has created a system which is impervious to strikes making any dent to its working.

I eventually left without any tests being done.[4]

8 January 2010, Friday

Yesterday I sent a letter to Mrs Sonia Gandhi, saying that I have just joined the government and would, at some point, love to meet with her and share some of my ideas for India. I also mentioned that Alaka wanted to discuss her ideas on gender, women and health; Mrs Gandhi may want to save time by seeing us together.

When I came to office today my chief assistant, Mr Somanathan, came in to say that Sonia Gandhi's office had called; she would see both of us at 4 pm. Alaka and I arrived there ten minutes before 4. There was heavy security, and we were ferried in her car from the outer gate to her home. She was waiting in a large, windowless (I seem to recall but I may be wrong), beautiful study. One wall was lined with books. Another had lovely photographs of Nehru, Indira Gandhi, Rajiv Gandhi and others.

At first, she seemed to be puzzled why we wanted to see her. She eased up when she realized that we had come with no special

---

4. My colleagues in the North Block berated me for going to the hospital without having someone high up in the Health Ministry call up first. I returned later after first speaking to the secretary in the health ministry and have her call in. My experience was a little better.

interest but just to chat and bounce off a few broad ideas. Then onwards, she laughed and talked easily, and was full of grace and charm. She talked about her mother-in-law, art in India, politics in Bengal. She spoke very warmly about other politicians. She said she liked Mayawati even though she made it difficult for all people with any Congress allegiance, including petty shopkeepers, in the state. She said this with a certain warmth and understanding of human foibles. I asked her about Mamata Banerjee. She seemed fond of Mamata, but added how she can at times be volatile, and then laughed and said, 'Like so many Bengalis.'

My first assessment of her is that she is a good person on whom more power has been thrust than she would care for. When I told her that both Alaka's mother and my mother were excited that we were going to see her, she looked genuinely puzzled and asked, 'But why?'

There was a sense in her demeanor and even in the décor of her home of loneliness at the top. I kept remembering Rabindranath Tagore's play, *Raja*.

As I got comfortable, I talked freely, asking her questions about Katherine Frank's controversial (but eminently readable) biography of Indira Gandhi. We talked about the last night in Indira Gandhi's life. I asked her if it was true that Sonia Gandhi was not feeling well that night and Indira came and chatted with her in the middle of the night and comforted her. She said that that was true. The next morning Indira Gandhi was assassinated as she crossed over from her home to her office to give an interview to Peter Ustinov.

Our meeting had begun at 3:55 pm. At 4:30 pm Alaka, feeling guilty that we were taking up too much of her time, said 'We'd better leave. You must be busy,' and we got up.

13 *January 2010, Wednesday*

This was one of the more eventful days since I joined government on 8 December. At 10 am I went to the prime minister's residence for a Cabinet Committee meeting on prices. All secretaries had gathered in a cavernous waiting room, and I sat down with them. But soon an orderly came and told me that I was asked (I presumed by the PM) to go to the main room, where the meeting was taking place. This, I later learned, was the custom. The advisers and bureaucrats wait to be called in and join the cabinet meeting to answer questions or make a presentation.

The prime minister was at the head, flanked by the finance minister and the cabinet secretary. All senior ministers were there—Sharad Pawar, A. K. Anthony, P. Chidambaram, Ghulam Nabi Azad, Ambika Soni, Mamata Banerjee. Mamata smiled at me; I reciprocated. Warm nod from Chidambaram. The cabinet secretary, Chandrasekhar, was, as always, friendly and courteous. As I entered the room, he was in fact explaining my note on inflation to the cabinet committee who evinced not the slightest interest.

I entered the room amidst a friendly banter of exchange between Mamata Banerjee, Pranab Mukherjee, Ghulam Nabi Azad and others on the causes of inflation. After this subsided, the prime minister asked me to explain my views on how to control inflation. I explained that since at this time it was a strangely skewed inflation with the bulk of the rapid price rise taking place in the food sector, we needed to work on the architecture of food release; and gave them some specific ideas of what to do. The overall inflation, raging at about 10 per cent per annum, needed monetary and fiscal policies for its containment and that would take time. But the food inflation, at about 20 per cent per annum, could be quickly brought down by releasing food from our reserves in a well-designed manner. But the design was, I stressed, important.

At the end of the meeting, as we walked out, Mamata Banerjee, the maverick politician from Bengal, whom I had never met before, paused to talk to me. She was very friendly and assured me she will come to our home in Hauz Khas just for a chat one day.[5] She has other flaws but pomposity and hierarchy is not one of them.

From there, I headed straight to the meeting of state finance ministers in Vigyan Bhavan. The meeting there went on and on. Asim Dasgupta spoke very well, as did the Punjab Finance Minister Manpreet Singh Badal. His principal secretary, Karan Singh, is a PhD from Michigan University and had worked with Ennio Stacchetti. During a coffee break, both the Punjab finance minister and the principal secretary invited me to Chandigarh. The meeting lasted till 5 pm, when I had to rush again to the prime minister's residence, this time for a discussion of how NREGA was doing.

I returned to my office at 7.15, worked till 8.15 and went home feeling drained.

I have decided I have to, some day, write a book on my Government of India experience. *Triste Tropics: Notes from my Years in the Indian Government,* I would call it.[6] The first week in my job I felt miserable and had to tell myself that if Malinowski could spend months on end among the Trobriand Islanders, surely I could take life in the North Block among politicians and bureaucrats for two years. I must treat this as my anthropological excursion, like that of Levi Strauss or Malinowski; or a scientific exploration to the tropics to collect flora and fauna, such as by Darwin.

I am indeed collecting a lot of impressions and learning a lot. I am now convinced that economic policy is so poorly crafted because it is developed by consensus among politicians. If an

---

5. This never happened but she is the kind of politician who actually meant it.

6. I did write something like this but the title was different—*An Economist in the Real World: The Art of Policymaking in India* (MIT Press, 2015).

airplane was designed by this method—the wing should have an upward tilt because that is what seemed right to a majority, the nose should tilt left because that is what the majority wants—it would, in all likelihood, not fly.

Indian democracy has the disadvantage of a vertical structure. Everybody gets involved in every decision. You can see this from those ubiquitous government folders which travel from desk to desk, gathering no-objection signatures, before anything is approved. It is often felt this is what democracy is all about. Everybody or a majority has to be in approval for a decision to move. This is best described as a 'vertical democracy'. But there can be another kind of democracy. Everybody has a say but not on all decisions. All the decisions are partitioned so that you get to have a voice for only the ones in your domain. India needs to shift from its relatively vertical structure of permission system which slows down decisions to a more horizontal, partitioned democracy.

When it comes to economic decision-making, it is a pity that it is not recognized that economics has a technical, engineering-type side to it. While economics is indeed open-ended and nebulous in some ways, in some areas it can be used with as much sharpness as in engineering projects. Auctions are a good example. Government can do vastly better if it sells resources not by evaluating them by themselves, setting price and selling it off, but by selling it off through well-designed auctions, which would endogenously determine what the price is.[7]

Another thing that I have learned is that in the Indian bureaucracy—and maybe this is a feature of bureaucracies everywhere—to any question that you may be asked, you never say you don't have an answer. If you don't have an answer to the

7. The Government of India would eventually do this, for 3G spectrum auctions, with huge success in fund raising but also drawing attention to the fact that it raised much less than it could have in earlier 2G auctions.

question asked, then give an answer to a question for which you do have an answer, never mind no one asked that question.

15 January 2010, Friday

Marathon day. It began with a jog at 7:30 am in Lodhi Gardens. At 10 am I participated in a meeting on food grain release strategy of the government. 11:30 am: pre-Budget meeting with economists. At 1 pm, I went to the prime minister's residence for a working lunch. There were twelve of us, including several functionaries of the Reserve Bank of India. The PM told me that he was keen to get a note from me where I spell out 'how' to release food grain from the government's granaries.

So after lunch I worked almost continuously (interspersed with some previously fixed meetings), and at 7:30 pm sent the note to the prime minister, the finance minister, Montek Singh Ahluwalia, and the cabinet secretary. Dinner was at Taj Hotel, Man Singh Road, hosted by Dr Subbarao, the Governor of the Reserve Bank of India.

19 January 2010, Tuesday

The last two days were spent in Neemrana, the magnificent princely home, half-way between Delhi and Jaipur, for the annual economic policy conference organized by NIPFP and Brookings Institution. Alaka came with me. Manbir drove us there. Manbir has become my man Friday, a totally dependable person. He takes great pride in the fact that he is the driver for India's chief economic adviser. And we get along well. The first weeks were a period of adjustment for him because of my relatively informal style, he being used to driving career bureaucrats. Two weeks ago, when I got into the front seat next to him (which I normally don't) and reached for my seatbelt, he looked uneasy. Then turning to me, Manbir gently admonished me, 'Now that you are not a professor but the Chief Economist of India, you don't need to wear a seatbelt.'

Neemrana is such a beautiful place that the two days of conferring seemed blissful. So much so that I did not mind coming down with food poisoning on the last day. We drove back home yesterday, and I had no choice but to take the day easy.

Thanks to my absence from office for three days—the Neemrana conference and its aftermath on the stomach—today turned out to be a day of unprepared meetings. I was told I had a meeting at the Planning Commission at 3 pm and, on arrival, I was ushered into the office of the Planning Commission member, Saumitra Chaudhuri. Trying not to reveal my ignorance, I asked him the 'details' of the agenda. He laughed and said, 'It's the usual useless stuff.' I tried to change my tack, because I had come so poorly prepared that I really had no idea what the meeting was about, and asked who else was coming for this meeting. He said, 'With the Planning Commission you can never be sure,' and burst out laughing. It struck me much later that may be he did not know what the meeting was about either.

I returned to my office in North Block to be whisked off to a meeting in Room 131A. I had no clue what the meeting was about but I thought I would sit in a corner and gradually figure out and maybe then make a remark or two. As I walked in to the room, everybody jumped to their feet. I had been long enough in the government to know what that meant. I was the chairman of the meeting. And that meant I was about to chair a meeting, without having a clue of what it was about.

It turned out that the meeting was about GBS. Since I had no idea what GBS stood for, this was a major handicap. Contrary to my hope that someone would say it in full, no one did. Clearly, it was such an important acronym that it had become a familiar word to all bureaucrats in the Ministry of Finance.

I was impressed by my ability to chair and participate vigorously in the meeting that lasted forty minutes, without managing to find out what GBS stood for. (GBS would later become an important part of my life. It stood for Gross Budgetary Support, which referred to the budget allocated by the Ministry of Finance to the Planning Commission for a variety of social expenditures around the nation, and it was a matter of much bargaining and soul searching in the Indian government.)

24 January 2010, Saturday

I came to Kolkata two days ago and spoke to the Kolkata Amcham (American Chamber) at the Park Hotel. They presented me with a beautiful paper cutter, an object I had forgotten existed. It's interesting how certain gadgets fall out of use. In this case, the bigger puzzle was why every home needed a paper cutter once.

This morning Brigadier Bhattacharya, who hails from a non-descript village outside of Kolkata called Arbelia (which also happens to be my ancestral village) came to see me. He is quite an amazing person in terms of energy and ideas. He is ever full of them. He held forth today about the Society of Logistics Management that he was active in and, given the importance of this topic, he was trying to get even the village folks of Arbelia interested in this. As he talked at length on this, my mind drifted off wondering what exactly logistics management meant, when I heard him chortling, 'The villagers, of course, have no idea what logistics management means.' I joined him in the hearty laughter.

25 January 2010, Sunday

My life has been an *intellectual* rags to riches story. While a lot of appreciation is shown for rags to riches stories in terms of wealth and money, not enough is shown for my kind of achievement. I was born into a family remarkably devoid of intellectual achievements and aspirations. Especially the lack of intellectual aspirations is quite unusual among middle class Bengalis, who all seem to aspire to be poets, writers and mathematicians. The standard refrain for Kolkata school boys who refused to study was: if you carry on like this you will have no choice but to be a businessman—the ultimate failure.

My parents were not typical Bengalis in this sense. My father was one of the highest IQ persons I have known. He reasoned seemingly with perfection. He also had some freaky abilities, such as that of being able to read and listen at the same time. It was a common sight to see him in his chamber reading some document with some of his familiar clients speaking to him. New clients would often pause seeing him reading. He would impatiently tell them to continue speaking. But he was not an intellectual in any sense. He was not a scholar; not well-read in history or philosophy.

He grew up mostly very poor. His father had moved to Calcutta from a life of agriculture in Arbelia and then died early, plunging his twelve children and wife into a life precariously perched on the border of poverty. My father was the one who had to pull the large joint family out of this vulnerable predicament, through intelligence and hard work. He and my mother wanted me to be a man of the world. I was never told to study hard and do well in school, and I did not disappoint them. There was shock and awe at home when I once came 4th in class—it happened in Class 8. The only time I would beat that record would be for my MSc in Economics at the London School of Economics. My problem has always been that unless I find something very interesting, my mind switches off. Hence, good teachers have been critically important for me. In Class 8, there was Mr Vianna (or Vienna—there is a dispute among my school WhatsApp group about the spelling), who got me interested in studies. My interest in mathematics I owe to my father and Mr Bhaumik in my school, when I was in

Class 11. The irascible Mr Bhaumik loved maths and infected me. And during my MSc in London, Amartya Sen, Ken Binmore and Maurice Perlman were teachers who inspired me hugely.

Intelligence was valued at home. My father loved mathematics and logic and was an admirer of Euclid. And his ability to reason in everyday life seemed flawless. I remember when I was very small, I must have told a lie and my mother was admonishing me for this. She told me how I should never tell a lie, because that displeases God. My father, who was passing by, stopped, and said, 'You must try to never tell a lie so that on that rare occasion when you have to, you can get away with it.' But he was not a scholar, and clearly he did not care for that. After a well-known Indian linguist and litterateur, Suniti Kumar Chatterji, came to my father for legal advice, my father spoke to him at great length and with respect for his stature. But after he left, I remember my father telling me—and I don't know if it was his conversation with Dr Chatterji that prompted this: 'Never do a PhD.' I was in middle school then.

It was quite a break from my family tradition that I did do a PhD and did well by it. My decision to do a PhD was a decision on a whim in London. I wrote and told my father of my final decision, sparing him the agony of deliberation. All through my childhood my parents' (and my) plan for me was that I would become a lawyer. Since I had an obsessive interest in logic from when I was small, I used to think of a lawyer's life as one of endless indulgence in the joys of reasoning. A year or so after completing my PhD and seeing me despondent and worried as to whether I had been wise in chucking up a career as a lawyer (I never regretted the decision thereafter, in fact, I consider myself lucky I made the career switch) my father, usually a laconic person, consoled me with two observations which are etched in my memory. He said maybe I had done right by my decision. As a lawyer, my life would be tied to a handful of wealthy clients in Kolkata, whereas as an academic the world could open up to me. Working as a teacher in India then, I took this as a father's comforting words and never imagined this could be true in any sense. In retrospect, the world did open up in ways beyond my wildest expectations and I feel so fortunate for that.

The other observation was not verifiable; so I do not know if he was right. He said, since I wanted to be a lawyer in order to indulge in a life of logic and reasoning, I should have no regrets. If I did become a lawyer I would soon discover that I would have to hold back on the best arguments in order to make sure the judge followed my reasoning; and that usually meant quite a low bar.

Reminiscing about the past, I described my ancestral village, Arbelia, as nondescript. It may be worth digressing to point out that Arbelia has one great achievement. It is the birthplace of the founder of the Mexican Communist Party, in fact the world's first communist party outside of Russia. M. N. Roy, born in Arbelia, led a colorful life as an intellectual involved with the international Trotskyite movement. He lived in Moscow, California and Mexico (and Arbelia of course). It was when he was living in Mexico with his American wife that he, along with a small group of Mexicans, founded the Socialist party in 1917, which would two years later become the Communist Party. I do not know what the Mexicans think about the fact that having founded Communism in Mexico, he changed his mind about Communism and became a radical humanist.

6 February 2010, Saturday

Today was the meeting of all chief ministers, 10 am to 5:30 pm, at Vigyan Bhavan, to discuss the raging inflation. Sharad Pawar was conducting it. He, the prime minister, the finance minister, Montek Ahluwalia—deputy chairman of the Planning Commission, and K. V. Thomas from Pawar's ministry were on the dais. The room was full of chief ministers, senior bureaucrats and representatives from various states. I chatted briefly with Nitish Kumar and Shiela Dixit.

Pawar opened the meeting, giving a catalogue of the various actions that have been taken. For such a powerful politician, Pawar has an unusual speaking style. Like a somewhat jaded historian, his speeches are always a detailed compendium of things done or ought to be done. The prime minister spoke and then the chief ministers were called upon to speak.

In terms of pure oratory, in my opinion, the two best speakers by a wide margin were Nitish Kumar and Narendra Modi. If I had to rank the two I would put Nitish at number one spot. His Hindi was lyrical; so it was good oratory with a literary flair. Modi's speech had a rabble rousing quality that was unmatched.

This kind of a meeting, a first for me, was fascinating. It was a melee of cultures, accents and languages. What a fascinating country India is. The Uttaranchal chief minister spoke in Hindi, the ones from Punjab, Bengal and most other states spoke in English, the political head of Pondicherry spoke in Tamil and there were a few chief ministers who spoke in what language I could not be sure.

Lest anybody equates my praise for the two speeches with the speakers, I should hasten to add that I like Nitish Kumar. He has made mistakes but on the whole (and yes, admittedly, by the standards of politicians) his intentions seem good.

The preaching of hatred against groups—be that of religion, caste or race—should have no place in the modern world. Growing up in a traditional Bengali Hindu household, I was always taught that the one basic moral axiom by which we must try to live is universal love.

I would grow up to reject a lot of what I was taught in my childhood. By the time I was fifteen, I was clear that a kind and powerful God who created everything, which includes so much human suffering, was a logical impossibility. Either he is not kind or he does not have the power to eliminate human suffering. And if you insist he has both these qualities the only way to reconcile that is by the conclusion that he does not exist.

My parents were traditional but open-minded enough not to object to my atheism. In fact, my hunch is that my father was a skeptic. He was too clear-headed a person not to be so. He would every Tuesday go to the Kali temple but I heard him say on more than one occasion, as he got into the car to go to the temple, 'I don't really believe, but I don't want to take any chances.' There should be a caveat to this argument. Since we don't know anything about God, we should allow for the fact that God may not like those who pray regularly and disturb Him. So it is not obvious what 'not taking chances' should prompt you to do. I virtually never pray and have been so lucky in life that I am tempted to conclude that not only does God not exist but He loves me.

I must here record that, despite being a non-believer, I share the value of universal love and inclusion taught by many religious leaders. I believe that the killings and violence directed at the minority Muslim population that took place in Gujarat in 2002 should be condemned by all human beings, be they Hindus, Muslims, Christians, Jews, agnostics or atheists.

11 February 2010, Thursday

Today I sneaked off to see the film *The Japanese Wife*. Since everybody in the Ministry of Finance has been working relentlessly on the Union Budget, I gave the impression I was leaving the meeting to do some work alone. I felt guilty leaving office at 9 pm. However, I felt better seeing Pranab Mukherjee also leave just before 9, seemingly to do some quiet work. Then the terrifying thought struck me of bumping into the finance minister at the cinema. I wonder who would be more embarrassed if I saw him at *The Japanese Wife*.

It was a soothing film—lyrical, and gently romantic, with light humor and lovely photography. After several days of 12-hours a day of office, this was a much-needed break.

16 February 2010, Tuesday

I came to Kolkata last night to deliver the convocation address to the Bengal Engineering and Science University (BESU), Shibpur. I agreed to do this because of my admiration for BESU's dynamic Vice Chancellor, Ajoy Ray. I had never worn a convocation gown before but had my fill today, as I sat on my chair on the dais for a full three and a half hours, trapped in my gown. They came in swarms to collect their degrees. I remembered the 1964 film *Haqeeqat*, with Dharmendra in the lead, depicting the India–China war of 1962. Every time a line of Chinese soldiers were mowed down, another wave appeared on the horizon. You hand over degrees to those graduating in mechanical engineering and the software engineers are up waiting to be called for their degree.

My lecture went off surprisingly well. I spoke for half an hour. At one point where interest could have sagged I told them the story about the hat seller that I had published in an essay on game theory in *Scientific American*. For those who don't know the story, on a journey to sell hats, this hat seller decided to take a short nap under a tree. When he woke up, he found all the hats were gone. Monkeys had come down from the tree and taken them. In desperation, he flung off his own hat. Monkeys, being excellent imitators, started flinging off their hats. He picked them up and cheerfully continued on his journey. Forty years later, his grandson, going the same route, made the same mistake and when he woke up he saw monkeys sitting on the tree top with the hats he planned to sell. Then he remembered his grandfather's story, and confidently flung off his own hat. But now one monkey came down, picked up this last hat, put it firmly under his arm, walked up to the hat seller, gave him a tight slap and said, 'Do you think only you have a grandfather?'

As we walked out at the end of the function, a lady rushed up to me, thanked me for the lovely story and said she had not realized monkeys were so clever.

19 February 2010, Friday

All other activities in life have gone sparse as the work on the *Economic Survey* and the Union Budget is guzzling up my waking hours and making them longer than I would care for.

It is fascinating watching the government from within. I earlier took Keynes' remark on the greater importance of ideas than vested interests in the shaping of the world as nice but a bit self-serving for an academic. I spouted it often as a professor because it raised my status, but I didn't really believe it. Now, having taken leave from academe and come into the world of policy, for the first time I believe that Keynes had hit upon a fundamental truth. It is the lack of imagination and the grip of stale ideas on political leaders and career bureaucrats that have a tendency to stall good policy.

I also now feel convinced that economics as a discipline is not just a stunning intellectual achievement but it is, in practice, a very useful discipline. Admittedly economics has many areas where policy has to rely on little science and a lot of judgement and common sense. But there are also fields, such as the design of auctions, the fine print of antitrust laws and the methods of giving food or other subsidies, which are beginning to resemble engineering. Ideas from these fields can be put to great use. One has to see them not being used to realize their value.

India's food procurement policy is riddled with such obvious fallacies. I have been in numerous meetings on food price inflation where bureaucrats insist that the Indian government must at all times hold on to some minimal food reserve because food is such a vital need. What they miss out on is that if a certain amount of reserve is held at all times, as a rule, they may as well not hold that reserve. But it is very difficult to make seasoned minds see this.

There are many other ideas that can bring some quick relief but it is a battle to make people change tradition. I regret that I am not pushy enough to get my ideas into practice. I feel some of them are so obviously good that any clever person would want to use them once they hear about them. As it happens, only the prime minister seems to see clearly some of these ideas that I bring up in meetings.

The more I see the prime minister alongside other politicians, the more I am convinced he stands head and shoulders above them. Like Nehru, he is truly passionate about India. My conversations with him are almost never about politics and everyday political machination. It is always about what we can do to enable India to do better. I am aware that this may not be of much value since political intrigue is such an important ingredient of political life.

Only if voters were a little more sophisticated to understand this, we would have a more successful nation.

20 February 2010, Saturday

Diksha called from Mumbai to say that not only am I appearing repeatedly in the business pages of newspapers, but I am beginning to look like the people who appear in the business pages of newspapers. I better not be in this job for too long.

26 February 2010, Friday

Today was Budget day. I do not know if this is so in any other country but the day of presentation of the Union Budget has all the festivities of a major sporting event. People gather in front of televisions to listen to the budget being presented in Parliament by the finance minister, cheering some proposals, castigating others. I had for many years watched this from outside, and never imagined I would witness this from the inner sanctorum.

I arrived at my office before 9 am and at 9 assembled at the entrance to the North Block with the finance minister and others of the Budget Team for a photo session. Then the core team trooped over to the presidential residence, the Rashtrapati Bhavan, to discuss the central proposals in the Budget with the president and to get her signed approval. The finance minister and six of us were ushered into her magnificent office-cum-drawing-room, with large paintings of Ajanta Ellora caves decorating the space. The walls and large doors let in ample natural light. Books are lined up to the ceiling—I wonder if anyone knows what there is in the top shelf.

Pratibha Patil, in traditional sari and *ghomta*, greeted us warmly with a *namaste*. She flashed a second glance at me. Maybe there was a faint memory of the Padma investiture ceremony of 2008 when she awarded me the Padma Bhushan. She was polite and gracious and, more than that, sweet. She reminded me of *mejopishima* (my father's second sister). Pranab Mukherjee began to explain the Budget and the intricacies of economic policymaking to her. She listened with as much interest as *mejopishima* would evince in economics. There is something almost school-boyish about Pranab Mukherjee that he can go on explaining the intricacies of the Budget despite no behavioral manifestation of interest on the part of the listener.

Soon the president's approval was signed and off we were in our fleet of white Ambassador cars to the parliament, to share the Budget documents with the cabinet ministers. After a short discussion of the main content of the Budget with the ministers it was time for the formal presentation in Parliament. The finance ministers go to the well of the parliament, as do the other ministers, and the rest of us are seated in the VIP gallery, overlooking the well. As the finance minister began to read the speech, which I and the other five or six main advisers knew almost by heart, it was difficult not to get an adrenalin rush. A few minutes into the proceedings a young man in pajamas, somewhat resembling Rahul Gandhi came into the well and took his seat. I realized later I was wrong about the 'somewhat', because he was Rahul Gandhi. The Budget speech is an excellent occasion for many members of Parliament to sleep and several make good use of the opportunity. Sleep notwithstanding, as is mandatory during all Budget speeches, at some point the opposition stages a walk-out. It is done for no other purpose but to show passion and concern for every line of the Budget.

After the Budget the evening is a time of media interviews. When I go home for a quick shower they are there for a line on the new tax rates, a word on inflation control and so on. I am then rushed to a series of interviews being held in makeshift camps of various television channels and newspapers. The whole atmosphere is that of the end of a sports competition. There is a festive air all over.

Much to my pleasant surprise I have discovered during the last few months that I have no fear of public speaking and media interaction. This is not because I am confident of my knowledge or intelligence but because I genuinely do not have any anxiety about messing up. I keep feeling that if I mess up, I mess up. That's it. It can happen to anyone and I will never lose a good night's sleep for that. This is a self-help tip for readers planning to go into public life. A few weeks ago I was also given a useful advice by Pranab Mukherjee. He said that once you are in prominent public life you will hear a lot of criticisms and even some vile, senseless attacks. The trick is to master the art of taking such information in through one ear, quickly processing it and then tossing it out through the other ear.

2

In the Belly of North Block

For government housing in India, more important than spaciousness, comfort, the amount of light and the several standard things one looks for in a home is whether or not you got it 'out of turn'. A house got out of turn shows power and connections. So people in Delhi rattle this off almost like an address. 'Where do you live?' you ask a civil servant, and he answers, 'I live in Rabindra Nagar—I got it out of turn.' Or 'X-123 Motibagh. My minister got it for me out of turn.'

This is also the problem with corruption and politicians. An act of corruption, far from being a source of embarrassment, to be kept secret, is in many circles a source of pride. It shows how powerful you are that you can get away by being egregiously corrupt. Hence, in such circles, the more corrupt you are, the more respect you command. Social sanctions and social approval, contrary to what many economists and sociologists believe, can bolster rather than deter bad behavior.

10 March 2010, Wednesday

It happened again. A careless statement of mine, optimistic about India, made the stock market indicator, the SENSEX, move up. It was widely reported how Basu's statement about inflation coming down soon—I wonder where I got that from?—made the stock markets rise. For the first time, I understand the effectiveness of the orchestra conductor. Just move your baton around and different sounds emanate from different corners of the room.

One of these days, I must conduct a test to see if I can bring the stock market down by making a morose comment about the economy. I will, of course, have to put it back again by making a bullish remark.

11 March 2010, Thursday

Somanathan had told me, *sotto voce*, that government gives senior officers briefcases worth up to Rs 6,000. More than anything else, in order not to disappoint him, I urged him to get me some samples. A sardarji showed up today with six unsightly to tolerable briefcases and set them up on my table top, like grooms in a *swayamvara*, for me to pick one. Somanathan, of course, came in; then my other personal secretaries and assistants, and even my normally shy peons came in to witness this grand event.

Whispered suggestions floated up to me and various suggestive fingers were pointed shyly at various briefcases. The one I picked cost Rs 2,500. The audience gasped and pointed out that my allowance was Rs 6,000. But I insisted I liked the one I picked. One of my assistants must have had a background in economics. He suggested, 'Then, sir, you should take two.' The approving murmur suggested that everybody thought that was a brilliant idea.

I protested that I did not need two. Another peon stepped forward and said, 'But what is two and what is one? Two briefcases together is like one briefcase with two compartments.' Everyone cheered and many slapped him on the back for his brilliant philosophical intervention.

Weighing the pros and cons of hurting the feelings of my staff by ignoring their brilliant idea, and the pain of overconsuming briefcases, I went with the latter: 'Okay, I will take two.' Then, turning to the salesman I said, 'Since the two add up to Rs 6,700, and the government allowance is for Rs 6,000, please take the remaining Rs 700 from me.' My staff was aghast and turned to him, 'You came to sell one. He is taking two. You can surely give him a concession of 700 rupees.' The salesman, a man of genial disposition, thought for a moment and saw merit in this argument; and I am now the proud owner of two ugly briefcases.

23 March 2010, Tuesday

I arrived yesterday in Shillong by a propeller plane from Kolkata. I am received by Prasenjit Biswas—classic Bengali intellectual and a very charming person. It is fascinating being in Shillong because I had heard so many stories in my childhood from my parents of their visit to this magical town inhabited by the beautiful *khasi* people. But the program on this short, two-day visit is so packed I will not get to see the town at all.

One of my tasks in Shillong is to address a gathering of students and professors at the North-Eastern Hill University (NEHU), which I did last evening. I am introduced by Joshua Thomas, a scholar and senior office bearer of the Indian Council of Social Science Research (ICSSR). He is a wonderful human being, full of warmth. I knew this from an earlier travel with him to Imphal, Manipur. Clearly, my liking for him was fully reciprocated, because Joshua Thomas introduced me at great length, elaborating on my research and the impact of my policy work. And then, without a pause, he added that I would be getting the Nobel Prize this year. The tone was the same as someone announcing that a person has got the Nobel Prize. The audience broke out in applause; some people rushed up to shake my hands and congratulate me. I had no choice but to smile and accept the congratulations.

28 March 2010, Sunday

It has been a hectic few days since Shillong. From there I travelled by road to Guwahati, flew to Kolkata and on 24th evening to Mumbai, where I delivered the convocation address to the Indira Gandhi Institute for Development Research on the 25th, and flew to Delhi in the evening. I was told I would have to go back to Mumbai for the HLCCFM meeting of the Reserve Bank of India on the 27th. As soon as you see the letters HL in a Government of India meeting, it is clear you cannot miss it. HL, as I learnt, soon after joining the government, stood for 'High Level'. In this case, the fact that the HL applied to Coordination Committee on Financial Markets made it even more critical.

The governor had a dinner party at his home in the evening. Diksha came with me to the dinner. And this morning, I took the Emirates flight to Cairo via Dubai.

I feel a bit tired on arrival but nevertheless go to a dinner, hosted by Magued Osman, a distinguished statistician. Also present at the dinner are Tarek Moursi, professor of Economics at Cairo University and some other faculty members, men and women. It turns out to be a wonderful occasion—Egyptians are so friendly. I love Egypt.

29 March 2010, Monday

I had breakfast with the Indian ambassador, Mr Swaminathan, a remarkably energetic and enthusiastic man. It never ceases to surprise me how much talent there is in the Indian bureaucracy.

I delivered a keynote address at a conference organized by the university, with lots of students, professors and policymakers in the audience. It went down very well. Egyptians are exceedingly warm and pleasant people and the women are beautiful. I am very impressed by the women. Some are in hijab, some in western clothes, but all seem to be comfortable and confident in their own attire and styles. Both men and women ask questions and contest what you say but are, at the same time, friendly and cheerful. In so many ways Egypt feels so much like India. Not rich, but happy, cheerful, chaotic, and stable, all at the same time.[8]

In the evening I went to see the *son et Lumiere* show at Giza and then to the Khan el-Khalili market.

30 March 2010, Tuesday

After breakfast I did a press conference in my hotel with representatives of three newspapers. One of the journalists asked me, quite out of the blue since this was meant to be an interview on economic policy, how India's relations are with its neighboring countries. I am now seasoned enough to know what the politically acceptable answers are to questions which go beyond dry economic policy. I vacillated for a moment. To go for the usually safe 'No comment; this is not my area of expertise,' might have sounded as if I was hiding something. On the other hand, I didn't want the PM calling me up for ruining India's neighborly relations or his party's electoral prospects. I decided it is better to be on good terms with our neighbors than bad. So I started telling the journalists about how smooth the relations have been among nations in South Asia. They did not react much, whether from surprise or lack of proficiency in English, I do not know. But, as happens in such situations, one tends to repeat with greater emphasis what one has said in order to be intelligible. Soon I was overdoing the wonderfulness of our neighborhood. As I spoke more to cover up these ridiculous remarks, the more stupid they sounded. It appeared that India and Pakistan have so much love

---

8. Little did I know then that this was virtually the eve of the Arab Spring. It shows how instability can happen suddenly and unexpectedly. All societies need to be careful.

and good vibes between them that we should be upheld as the model of good neighborly behavior.

It was too late to say this was not my area of expertise. I felt glad I would be away from Egypt by the time this gibberish is published along with the photographs taken during the press conference.

The Indian ambassador had organized for me to meet the minister of investment. So from the press conference I was rushed to meet the minister, Dr Mahmud Mohieldin. I was ushered into an ornate room with two throne-like chairs at one end, facing the room with a slight tilt towards each other. To my surprise I was asked to sit on one of them. The minister, immaculately suited, came in, shook my hand and sat on the other grand chair. Four of his assistants came in to take notes while we spoke. Three of them were women and the fourth was a man.

Just behind us, between the minister and me, was a large picture of president, Hosni Mubarak. I realized I was in for a more formal meeting than I had anticipated. What added to my discomfort was my footwear. I had gone wearing sandals, and tried to intertwine my legs to prevent them from being caught on camera. I doubt if I succeeded for there was a cameraman taking photographs of the two of us from all angles. The grand style of the occasion and the attention on me made me wonder if they had made a mistake and thought I was the finance minister of India. It was beginning to feel like a meeting between Henry Kissinger and Zhou Enlai (with one of them wearing sandals).

I was tense to start with but end up not performing badly. I began by thinking of what Kissinger would do at the start. He would probably ask about how Mao Zedong was doing. I began by asking after the health of Hosni Mubarak given his recent surgery. We dwelled a minute or two on how, luckily, he was faring well. Then we discussed foreign direct investment flows into Egypt and India; and our mutual foreign and economic policies. He said Europe has now become redundant for the world. Seeing no reason to incur his wrath by disagreeing on a matter which would have no effect on him, me, Egypt, India or Europe, I nodded and showed my approval by paraphrasing his remark. Much to my dismay, the note-taker wrote this down. I invited Mr Mohieldin to come to India. He answered me that he would soon. I escaped unhurt.

Later in the day, I visited the Information Decision Support Center (IDSC), a think tank to support the Egyptian cabinet, saw the Citadel and left for the airport, feeling quite happy.

During my few months in the government I have discovered I am good at handling difficult situations with a certain *sang-froid*. I feel lucky to have this temperament. Unlike some others I do not have to perform to *appear* comfortable. Deep down in me there is a feeling that life is, in the end, a meaningless charade. Also, I am not completely sure that others exist. If the world can be complex, my mind can be complex enough to create the complex image of an otherwise non-existent world. Of course, I lead life like most people and, in fact, I enjoy meeting and interacting with human beings (and hope they are not figments of my imagination). But the feeling deep down inside me that life is a chimera has a calming effect. In fact, it allows me to enjoy life more than most others do. To an outsider seeing the photographs and reports on the meeting, it may appear a grand event. Of course, I know it was not Kissinger meeting Zhou Enlai, but even that meeting may not have been quite as momentous as it appears to us in retrospect.

[That so much is chimera would be reinforced a few years later when I joined the World Bank as a senior vice president, and discovered that among the five or six senior vice presidents, who were second-in-command at the Bank was Mahmud Mohieldin, who had moved from Cairo to Washington a few months before I joined the bank. At that meeting in Egypt, he had appeared a grand, pharaonic character; and I had felt that, while I had relished the meeting, I had wasted his time from all the precious work he was doing. During the World Bank years Mahmud would become a valued friend. He was a wonderful, normal human being, like you and me. The thought strikes me that there may be no one pharaonic when viewed up, close and personal.]

2 April 2010, Friday

Dinner was hosted this evening by the prime minister in honor of Venkatraman Ramakrishnan, who won the Nobel Prize for Chemistry last year. He seemed a modest person; he made it clear that he was a scientist at heart and did not really understand political sophistry. At dinner I got to chat with Rajat Gupta, with whom I had interacted earlier when he was setting up the Indian School of Business in Hyderabad. Others at the small sit-down dinner included Prof. Samir Brahmachari, Jyotiraditya Scindia, P. Chidambaram, C.N.R. Rao, and Barkha Dutt. I decided that the occasion deserved my stealing the menu card.

3 April 2010, Saturday

I met the prime minister at his residence at 11.45 am for a one-on-one meeting. We talked about India's role in BRIC and, at length, about India's export strategy. He also mused about the prime ministerial job. I got the impression that he would be glad to be relieved of it. He had done a lot. The reforms he led as finance minister in 1991 would leave a legacy on India's economy as important as the legacy Nehru left behind on India's politics and democracy. From 2005, he had presided over the fastest growth India had ever seen for three consecutive years. As we spoke I looked out at the lush green lawns outside, all quiet, guarded and secure. Being a prime minister is like living in a grand prison.

6 April 2010, Tuesday

The last few days we worked feverishly to prepare for Tim Geithner's visit. USA does have a special place in the world today. For no other country's dignitaries is there so much preparation.

It turned out to be an exciting meeting that began at 11 am at the Taj Palace Hotel. We had the finance minister, finance secretary, Shyamla Gopinath, me and three or four others on one side of the table and Tim Geithner and five or six US officials and policymakers on the other side. The finance minister, Pranab Mukherjee, has the most staggering memory I have seen in any politician in any country. That skill was on display but, overall, I thought our performance was poor. There were rather dreary, bureaucratic statements. I attempted to lighten the atmosphere by making some frivolous remarks. It had Geithner laughing and Pranab Mukherjee suppressing his laughter. But I do hope I played a useful role in easing up the conversation flow. For two hours we spoke, mainly Geithner and the FM with occasional remarks and interjections from us. Most of the discussion was around the financial crisis. Geithner seemed like a nice person.

Overall I continue to feel that momentous though these meetings and discussions may seem, a lot of policymaking is groping in the dark. Hence, on some days I feel that no one should worry too much about making the right decisions, since we have so little clue about what the right decisions are. And the public position one is expected to take is always the same. When the economy does well you say this is a consequence of our policy initiatives and when it does poorly you point to how this is a fall-out of what is happening elsewhere in the world.

8 April 2010, Thursday

Today was a marathon meeting, from 4 pm to 8 pm, at the prime minister's residence with ten key chief ministers, a bunch of top union ministers and a few senior bureaucrats. I met Buddhadeb Bhattacharya, who heads the communist government in West Bengal, for the first time. Ever the *bhadralok*, he spoke very nicely and said he knew of my work. I believe him because he has a reputation for being cerebral and well-read. But his speech was disappointing. He had done no homework and gave out some trite party-line remarks on inflation. Nitish Kumar was excellent, speaking in eloquent Hindi, showing both commonsense and commitment.

And here is a virtually verbatim transcript of the speech of one minister, whom I actually like, that I jotted down rapidly: 'You have to worry about agriculture also. Otherwise food also will be short, as we have seen in many states. We need subsidy also; and another problem I have seen is that we need cheap fertilizer. We need technology also. But to solve all these problems we have to make calculations also.'

The chant-like quality of the speech—returning repeatedly to the same word (like a name in a prayer or an invocation in a *mantra*) clearly had a soporific value. Several ministers fell asleep or, maybe, got into a trance.

10 April 2010, Saturday

On Friday 9 April evening, I left for Kolkata. Mother is clearly fading. The intensity of her desire to have her children, especially me, around at home with her is more intense than I have ever seen before. She has always been a strong person, never letting love and sentimentality get in the way of anybody's work—what she considered the larger calling. To see her asking me to stay back and miss office is so uncharacteristic, and knowing that it is a wish almost impossible to fulfill, is painful. All I can do is remind myself what she herself always taught us—to treat work as the most important commitment in life and not to give in to sentimentality.

I take the evening flight to Mumbai, where I have a series of meetings. I meet Diksha in Bandra and head to the Taj President Hotel.

15 April 2010, Thursday

On 13 April evening I took the evening flight from Mumbai to Mangalore. The good thing about smaller towns is they come with flowers to receive you. It is indeed a very warm welcome and I have been in a senior government position long enough now to be able to take it in my stride.

Late at night I visited the beautiful, old Kadri temple and also the modern temple built by Janardhan Poojary.

Yesterday I spoke at Corporation Bank—huge auditorium, packed with seemingly 400 people. In a small town, I suppose I am worth coming for. The lecture, the visits to the temples and, in fact, the whole town exudes a R.K. Narayan-esque atmosphere. There is something very charming about the town. When asked at my lecture what I thought of Mangalore I felt tempted to crack the joke: 'I always thought Mangalore was a spelling mistake.' But nowadays with newspapers ever ready to quote me, I had to hold back. If this was quoted in the local newspaper, I would have to leave hurriedly.

I visited the beautiful Krishna temple at Udupi, saw the Manipal campus and this morning flew to Delhi.

16 April 2010, Friday

We had a rather charged meeting this evening in the finance minister's chamber, with the governor of RBI, Dr Subbarao, Omita Paul, the Finance Secretary Ashok Chawla and Financial Services Secretary R. Gopalan to discuss monetary policy. It may be because monetary policy is such a hush-hush matter that these meetings and decisions give me an adrenaline rush.

All the discussion was on different options for monetary tightening. We—mainly the Reserve Bank—do a huge amount of research to back these decisions but the 'science' of monetary policy is still so rudimentary that one shudders at the major, life-affecting decisions we take with so little understanding of the consequences of these actions. This is a problem without escape since not taking a decision is also a decision.

17 April 2010, Saturday

Home alone. It is a rare evening when that happens. Sanjay and Bhaskar—both Banerjees—came for lunch. Post-lunch I sent Mai, my mother-in-law, off to her home and went to office for a few hours of work. Alaka is in the U.S.A., and I am on my own at home. And, as always, in such situations, as mysteriously to me as to any outside observer, I wallow in self-pity and feel acutely lonely. Unless someone has this strange affliction, he or she would not be able to understand this. This is all the more puzzling because in all other ways I am psychologically such a normal—rather boringly so—person. Mercifully, I get this kind of a feeling and anxiety rarely and with age it has become even more rare. I remember how in Helsinki many years ago, maybe in the late 1980s, when I was spending some weeks at World Institute for Development Economics Reasearch (WIDER). For some reason, maybe the children's school year starting, Alaka, Karna and Diksha had to leave a week before me. The day they left, I went for a walk alone and returned to my apartment feeling forlorn and lost beyond measure.

It is nowhere nearly as acute now. In fact, being alone now is often an occasion to introspect. These last few months have been a phenomenal time for me, and I have met more remarkable people—both good and bad—than in all previous years. I knew that Indian civil service jobs are highly coveted and so India's top bureaucrats are exceptionally smart people. Some of them are so intelligent that I feel inadequate. That is, in terms of IQ and knowledge. The feeling of inadequacy is deep but it does not trouble me because there is another yardstick of intelligence by which, rightly or wrongly, I have never felt handicapped. When it comes to creative, analytical thinking, I try not to, but I do feel disdain towards most people, including successful academics. I keep feeling I am seeing through problems much deeper, much more transparently, than they can. This may be folly on my part but it is a fact I cannot deny. My mother was, in an unobtrusive way, an overconfident person and I may have inherited this from her.

Writing all this, with Debabrata Biswas' soulful Rabindrasangeet in the background, has lessened the intensity of aloneness. I had better get down to some work now.

20 April 2010, Tuesday

I get more 'respect' now than I did in my academic incarnation. But I can't help being aware that this *ex officio* respect is mostly a sham. A lot of the time it is a case of people knowing that I can get things done that makes them fake respect, and then, occasionally, come to believe that they truly do. What one got as a researcher, writer and lecturer was much more genuine. I, in turn, have to admit that I have true respect for few individuals in India's political and policy leadership, though when I meet prominent people I too fake respect. But I draw a line. There are unsavory politicians for whom I would not even fake respect. I would rather just walk away.

I wonder whether I will become less happy if I stay on in government much longer. I feel I am less happy now than I used to be when I lived the life of the mind. But making these inter-temporal comparisons of one's state of mind at different phases of life is difficult. We often delude ourselves into believing that we were happier then or sadder then.

An American friend of mine, afflicted with severe manic depression, once told me that he sensed in me 'a touch of manic depression, without the depression'. We agreed that that's the best kind of manic depression. Indeed, it is true that I am generally happy and occasionally intensely so. One psychological trait that helps me is my total inability to feel guilt about anything. This I inherited from my mother. Once we were all discussing guilt. I said I had little of it; one of my sisters said she had quite a bit; Alaka said, as I knew, that she had a lot. Then my mother, much to our surprise, said she was like Alaka. If she thought she had done something wrong, she would have huge pangs of guilt. But, she went on to add, she had never had to deal with this because, luckily, she had never done anything wrong in her life. She was eighty-three years old then.

                                        11 May 2010, Tuesday

This is strictly not a diary entry. I mean it may or may not be about what happened today, yesterday or recently. My not writing a diary the last several days has been weighing on me. So now that I have boarded a long flight, from Toronto via Brussels to Delhi, this seems a good time to ruminate about the last few days, weeks, and more generally about life in the belly of North Block.

I have just finished a two-day meeting of G-20 countries in Toronto. It seemed like a futile meeting in which representatives from twenty nations quibbled over what should or should not go into a document on the G-20 nations. To me, much of this seems inconsequential though I also joined in the discussion vigorously, slipping in an occasional joke for comic relief. It must have been for my own comic relief because no one laughed. To these people the meeting was too serious a business for frivolity. I cannot see anything good or, for that matter, bad coming out of the meeting. And here we were—some eighty of us who had travelled great distances, staying in 5-star luxury, leaving yeti-footprints of carbon. And this was just one meeting. We were told how there will be other meetings—the sherpas in Berlin, the deputies in Calgary, the finance ministers in Busan and the prime ministers later in Toronto. This is what much of life is about, I suppose. I am also aware that I am more cynical than others. Maybe you do need to leave this carbon footprint for an overall better world. If nothing else, the meeting up with people and the camaraderie, does make for greater understanding among nations. Luckily, I don't have to take that decision.

During these two days we had a lot of serious discussions on monetary and financial economics, with the Greek sovereign debt crisis looming in the background. I am amazed at how much we human beings can talk when we have little to say. The ploy is to take cover behind nice-sounding statements. Take economic recovery. Some economists agree we are about to see a V-shaped recovery. Others say it will be U-shaped, whereby we will stay at the bottom for a while. Then there are the proponents of a W-shaped recovery, which involves a second dip. Some agree it will be a J-shaped recovery where we will ultimately rise beyond where we were, unless of course we have an L-shaped recovery in which we have to be reconciled to there being no recovery. Think of literally any letter of the English alphabet and there is some economist who believes we are about to see that letter-shaped recovery. What all this shows is that we have little idea about the nature of recovery but will not admit to that.

A lot of these monetary policy discussions occur nowadays by slipping into health analogies which sound nice, but mean little. When a person who has bad health refuses to exercise, we don't allow the person to sit on the couch and die, we try to coax the person onto the treadmill. So we hear experts saying, 'We must get Greece on the treadmill; otherwise its economy will die.' The audience nods sagely. But what does 'getting Greece on the treadmill' mean? Moreover, it is not at all clear what the death of a nation means.

If I am right that much of what these monetary policy experts say has little content, how do they understand one another? After all, they do agree, disagree, discuss, and debate. My hypothesis is that this is like the twitter of birds. Birds do not understand one another (admittedly, that is our presumption) but still they have seeming conversations.

To test this out, in the middle of the Toronto discussion on monetary policy in G-20 countries, I decided to offer a meaningless comment which used the right words and had the right soundbites. But the comment had no meaning—at least no meaning to the person making the comment. It was fascinating to see my audience agree and disagree with me. Judging by the animated discussion that this gave rise to, the group clearly found it meaningful and deep.

I write this in a light vein but I am serious about this aspect of some parts of economics. I do not for a moment think this is true of all economics. There is a huge amount of meaning to what Ken Arrow wrote, John Hicks wrote, Paul Samuelson wrote. There is Euclidean elegance and meaning in what Gerard Debreu did. There are some stunning, almost magical, insights in some of the theoretical works of Joe Stiglitz and George Akerlof. But many policy experts, especially in the area of macroeconomic policymaking, take advantage of the core of economics which is deep, and talk, whereof one should be silent, to sort of quote Wittgenstein.

But there is one puzzle. If my hypothesis is right, how come central banks do their job reasonably well, as they seem to? I believe the answer has to do with evolutionary behavior. Central banks use rules of thumb regarding repo rates and various policy rates. The reasons they give for their choice of particular rules are not compelling, but the rules of thumb they follow (and the actions that these rules lead to) work because the bad rules of thumb, which led to adverse reaction, have over the years been dismissed. So the policy rules actually used are not the ones we can demonstrate will work, but they nevertheless serve some purpose by the laws of evolution. The bad rules have, in effect, gone extinct. You do not need any special understanding to get to this just as the giraffe does not have to understand the value of a long neck in order to have one.

Now that I have expressed my views on international policy meets, it is time to turn to the Indian bureaucracy, my home turf for the last five months. As I noted earlier, one amazing trait I have been observing across bureaucrats is that, when asked a question, they never admit to not having the answer. The technique is to give the answer to the question for which you have an answer.

'Is there a good reason why the Reserve Bank keeps policy rate changes a total secret till the change is actually announced?' the minister asks.

If you don't have a clue why that is so, you will say, 'But, sir, the policy rate changes seldom remain secret. Our journalists are so good, they always manage to find out the policy rate change in advance. I don't know how the blighters do it.'

Brussels Airport. I am waiting for the second lap of my journey. Thanks to Jet Airways, Brussels airport seems like an outpost of colonialism—Indians colonizing Europe. This is what Sutanuti must have looked like when hundreds of Englishmen docked there in the eighteenth century. With four Jet flights coming in from India and four leaving for USA, this terminal is chock-a-block with Indians, which automatically means a disproportionate supply of rowdy kids. The entire airport has a faint fragrance of After Mint so generously served on all Jet flights.

Back to the topic of India's bureaucracy. Its other problem is its hierarchical structure. Some of this is, I suppose, superficial, and so may not matter much, like the use of the word 'Sir'. But it does increase verbiage. In one meeting I decided to keep tab. A secretary in the Ministry of Commerce was saying 'Sir', on average sixteen times every minute (there was a minister present). Assuming it takes her half a second to say each sir, 13 per cent of her speaking time was spent saying sir.

A lot of these matters of form are quite innocuous. I don't, for instance, think there is anything wrong in using such salutations. However, I personally find it impossible to say 'Sir' because when I went to LSE as a student, it was dinned into my head by my professors, Lord Meghnad Desai prominent among them, that 'Sir' was a colonial left-over and should be abandoned.

In the firmament of Indian politics and bureaucracy, the person who stands out is the prime minister. I believe history will judge Manmohan Singh the way I do—bigger, or more correctly, more enigmatic, than society currently judges him. Just as by the traditional laws of aerodynamics the bumblebee should not be able to fly, by the laws of politics, Manmohan Singh should not be able to plough through the thicket of Indian politics to become prime minister. If nothing else, his total honesty, should ensure that he would not survive for long in politics. In my one-on-one conversations with him, I get taken in by his completely honest assessment of Indian politicians, his disapproval of how some of them are prone to crony capitalism, and how he wishes he did not have to see some of them.

During my first meeting with him, after he became prime minister, some twenty minutes into our conversation, his assistant came in and handed him a slip, with a name. This was standard practice; it had the name of one of his government's ministers, who was waiting to see the prime minister. The prime minister got up, looked resigned, showed me the slip for me to read the name, and said, 'This is the kind of people with whom I have to spend time now.' The name will remain confidential even from my diary.

If a young person sought advice on how to become a prime

minister, a safe advice to give is not to be like Manmohan Singh. If despite this Manmohan Singh became PM, much of it has to be put down to luck—the luck of his being close to Narasimha Rao and Sonia Gandhi, who had the good judgement to choose him.

In the end, having become, what the laws of society and politics would not have predicted, prime minister, he has been, I think, outstandingly successful. Unlike other politicians, he has not given an inch to building up his own image and legacy. Freed from this burden, he has managed to do more than most other traditional politicians have. I know that a nation's growth depends on much more than what the prime minister says or does, but India's outstanding performance of growing each year above 9 per cent from 2005 to 2008, which made it an international story owes a lot to Manmohan Singh's professionalism which influences all those who work with him. India today is a more professional and science-based nation, and this is giving dividends.

But thanks to his modesty and focus on work rather than publicity, Manmohan Singh is thought of by many people as ineffective.

I am convinced that the best politicians are ones who are willing to lose elections. They are the ones who can bring about the deepest and best changes. By definition, one rarely sees such politicians.

12 May 2010, Wednesday

I have been attending to matters of national emergency for the past five months, from inflation flare-ups, to challenges of subsidized food distribution, to dealing with the aftermath of the global financial crisis. As a result, I have been shying away from a brewing rift among my secretaries—three of them and their assistant. Don't ask me why so many.

Yesterday, Mr Somanathan, the chief of my staff, a man always reserved and dignified, was telling me in hints and suggestions how it was impossible working with a 'Ms K'. This had happened earlier and was brought to my attention, but we human beings are, or at least this human being is, often prepared to face global problems and national challenges head-on, but shirk from wading into and trying to resolve minor in-house rifts. But yesterday, as Mr Somanathan spoke, the peon, Satbir, came in and said that on the previous day Ms K had told Somanathan she did not talk to 'small people', which in these bureaucratic circles is a big insult.

I decided I could no longer ignore this and so called Ms K in. She lumbered in, smiling benignly as always. I told her that she has to have better behavior with Somanathan and, also, used the opportunity to catalogue a few other complaints like her frequent absence from work. Regarding the later she made it clear the fault was mine since I relied on Somanathan so much that she had little work and so felt no need to come in regularly. And as far as Mr Somanathan went, she said there were many things to complain about, but the main problem was, 'Woh muskarata nahi'—'He does not smile.'

I decided there was no way I could ask Mr Somanathan to smile at Ms K. So the in-house rift would have to be left where it was. I turned my attention to India's food inflation and the appreciating rupee.

14 May 2010, Friday

How varied my life as CEA is. Two days ago I was attending to the woes of Ms K, and today I am drawn into India's federal woes. I am in Kolkata and gave a keynote address to the Exim Bank and was told that Chief Minister Buddhadeb Bhattacharya is eager to see me. Buddhadeb is a doyen of the Communist Party of India (Marxist), a great intellectual and a *bhadralok*, and I am keen to meet him.

I arrived at the Writers' Building sharp at 5 pm. To my surprise the police outside knew I was coming and rushed to open the door for me and take charge. Despite my bewilderment at their behavior, I acted nonchalant (and also enjoyed the treatment). I was taken to a wood-paneled inside-the-coffin-like room with no windows and gaudily done up twenty-odd sofas with red covers. One special chair was a bit like a throne, and next to it was a rare photograph of Rabindranath Tagore. The chief minister came in his crisp dhoti-kurta and occupied the throne. I sat on his left and facing me was his principal secretary, Subesh Das. Subesh looked familiar, and he reminded me he was in my Development Economics class at Cornell. Buddhadeb Bhattacharya is a PLU (people like us), and it was easy for me to relate to him. He had read my essay on Bankura and told me he liked it. It is rare for a minister to have read anything of mine.

He clearly enjoys a good *adda*—told me how he ushered in the last new year chatting with Amartya Sen at the Taj Bengal Hotel (he also told me what Sen told him about Prakash Karat). We chatted for about forty-five minutes—part adda, part economic policy.

On policy, he said he wanted (1) the finance minister to spell out a definite plan for the 400 crores he has allocated for Eastern India. He felt (2) there should be much more effort to boost agriculture and, (3) there should be some special help for jute products since there is fresh global demand for jute as an ecologically desirable product but he was worried about competition from the synthetic fibers lobby. (4) He wanted subsidized food to be given to all. While saying this, he could sense my unease. I believe this is not feasible, at least not without large collateral damage to the economy.

While talking about policy he said, 'Where there is a will, there is a way.' I believe this widely quoted saying has hurt a huge number of people all over the world. On the contrary, it is important for us to realize that there is many a plan in life for which no matter how much the will, there is no way to bring the plan to fruition.

20 May 2010, Thursday

Mukesh Ambani came to see me at 12:15 pm. We had a very nice chat till 12:45, mainly on higher education in India. I was pleased by his interest in this and also by the fact that he did not waste my time by asking for tax reductions, which so many business persons do.

In the afternoon, I organized the first Finance Ministry roundtable (on Balance of Payments and rupee valuation) with, among others, Ajay Shah, Ila Patnaik, Surjit Bhalla, Ashok Desai, Urjit Patel, and Roberto Zagha, of course in a dhoti. As the dhoti goes out of use in India it is good to have a Brazilian carry the burden of this tradition.

25 May 2010, Tuesday

I came to Mumbai yesterday for the High Level Coordination Committee on Financial Markets (HLCCFM) meeting and for a meeting on the management of foreign exchange reserves at the RBI today. I enjoy these reserve management meetings because I have some novel ideas on how this can be done better than any central bank, including what the People's Bank of China, has done. This is, of course, the mandate of the Reserve Bank and I can do no more than present my ideas and try to persuade the central bankers.

The basic idea is that the Reserve Bank of India can appreciate the Indian rupee without having to off-load US dollars. The trick is to twist the demand curve for dollars appropriately, which the Reserve Bank has the capacity to do. It is not easy to explain this because my argument relies on a little bit of algebra and try holding a bureaucrat's attention over algebra.

In the evening, I cut the ribbon and gave an opening address to a large gathering of mainly CFO's organized by the Standard Chartered Bank. BBC's Mishal Husain, intelligent and charming, in equal measure, compered the event. I got to chat with Joseph Stiglitz before and after that about designing economic policy. It is refreshing to talk to someone who is such a deep thinker. I get too little of this nowadays.

26 May 2010, Wednesday

Back in Delhi, I received a very nice—slightly personalized—letter from Sonia Gandhi, regarding the Indira Gandhi Conference in November. The personalized touch was her warm remarks on my forthcoming book, *An Economist's Miscellany.*

During the day I met with the CPWD engineers who are renovating the government home Alaka and I will get to occupy, AB-83, Shah Jahan Road. Trying to get the engineers to do the things you want is quite a job. I wished I was better at leaning on people.

5 June 2010, Saturday

Yesterday was a light-work day. We now know that petroleum product prices may be decontrolled as early as next week. This will immediately mean an increase in the prices of all fuel products and that will cause a furor in the country. It could also give a short-term upward nudge to inflation. So I spent a part of the day with a few advisers computing the effect of this on the overall price level in the nation.

Last evening, just before leaving my office, I had got a message saying that the prime minister would like to see me at his residence today.

I came to my office today at 11 am for some light work but got up soon to meet the prime minister at 12. I was not too sure why he had called me so I carried some papers on inflation and G-20 matters. As always, he really seemed pleased to see me and, I was pleased to see him. We had a thirty-minute, one-on-one meeting. He asked me questions on G-20, and what India can do to get more out of the G-20 engagement. After that I brought up the topic of inflation and how it is often misreported. He asked me to call a press meeting and do a briefing.

We went on to discuss petroleum prices and the Parikh committee proposals. He asked me to send him my recommendations on Monday.

We then talked about China, Pakistan, and the USA. I have an interesting idea about Indo-Pakistan political relations. Stepping beyond my remit as economic adviser, I told him about this, and got the impression that he did not take it seriously, which made me feel good about the fact that on most matters he does take me seriously.

19 June 2010, Saturday

I arrived yesterday in Xiamen (Air India to Hong Kong and Dragon Air to Xiamen). I am staying on the 21st floor of my hotel, overlooking the lake formed by a seawater inlet. The beauty of the place is somewhat marred by being excessively built up.

Yongmiao Hong treated us to dinner, Japanese style. In a small room in a restaurant where some eight of us sat—seven men and Ye Guo. Women served food and drinks, which included multiple small dishes.

Today I gave the opening keynote address to a mega-audience. I had planned on giving a technical paper on the financial crisis but, seeing the size of the audience, I decided to taper down the technicalities impromptu. Making adjustments while speaking meant I gave a rather disappointing lecture.

Lunch was hosted by the regional Communist party chief in grand style. Eric Maskin joined us—it is always a pleasure to talk to him.

25 June 2010, Friday

These last two weeks, I had worked on and off on decontrolling petroleum and diesel. Today at 1 pm the Empowered Group of Ministers (EGoM) met and in less than an hour decided to decontrol petroleum and diesel—though diesel would still get a per-liter subsidy. For kerosene and LPG there is just a one-shot price increase. I spoke a lot, uncharacteristically so, at the EGoM to make sure we were getting the finer details of the decontrol right. Montek Singh Ahluwalia was not there at the meeting and I felt I had an added responsibility for that reason, since Montek would usually do the explaining of the more technical matters at the EGoM.

There was a lot of media gathered outside the Ministry of Finance because they had got wind that there may be major breaking news coming. At the end of the EGoM there was light-hearted banter among the ministers about who would go out and give this news since that could do big damage to the person's political career.

In the end the ministers broke the news with a brief statement and then I spoke at length to several newspapers and TV channels explaining why India badly needed to de-control petrol prices. I genuinely believe in this and so it was easy for me to explain this with all sincerity. By keeping petrol price artificially low even when global prices rose, we were blocking out a major market signal. Ordinary consumers of petrol would continue to use more petrol, which would mean more subsidy being provided by the government, creating fiscal strains and this was also bad for the environment. Soon after my interaction with the press, I heard

a strike has been called in Kolkata and more are likely to follow
around the country.

Late at night I suddenly felt strangely disturbed. In one fell
swoop we took a decision that would affect millions of lives. For the
twelve or fifteen of us involved, it was several days of deliberation
but, finally, just one decision. Yet it can be momentous for the
nation. How strange life is.

27 June 2010, Sunday

The last two days we, and especially Alaka, have been busy
organizing our move to AB-83 Shah Jahan Road. All this time we
have been staying at our own apartment in Hauz Khas. Our new
Shah Jahan Road house, which is part of government property,
is a lovely two-storied home with a sprawling lawn in the front
and back, in Lutyens' Delhi. I think no one should have such
ample homes when so many people have no homes. This may
seem like a contradictory thought on the eve of moving into
such a home. But it is not. What I am saying is that if there were
a vote on whether anybody should have such sprawling homes in
today's India, I would vote no. There is no contradiction between
this and moving into one such home. As Paul Samuelson wrote
in an autobiographical essay entitled, 'My Life Philosophy': 'I
have generally voted against my own economic interests when
questions of redistributive taxation have come up.' He was saying
that he would not give up his high income but vote for a system
where everybody with such high incomes is made to give up a
substantial part of it. Indeed, there is no contradiction in doing
well in a free-market capitalist society and wanting such a system
to be replaced by something more humane. The world's biggest
example of this kind of attitude is probably Frederich Engels.
Contemporary America has several such billionaires. And, in fact,
hope lies in such people. Indeed, the common view, that it is

hypocrisy to argue against wealth inequality if you do not give up your own excess wealth first, plays an important role in stalling radical thinking and silencing many people from speaking up.

I spent some time today with the economists Jacques Dreze and Arunava Sen discussing the School of Economics and Economic Development (SEED). As founder of CORE in Belgium and one of the world's greatest economic theorists, Jacques has a lot of credibility. He is keen to set up SEED in India. How valuable this will be to India is however not clear.

11 July 2010, Sunday

Late at night on 6 July, Alaka and I traveled to Lausanne. Jet Airways to Brussels, then Geneva, and finally by train to Lausanne Gare, with all its old-world charm. Finally, we took a taxi from Lausanne Gare to Hotel Château d'Ouchy. It is a beautiful old hotel on the banks of Lac Leman or Lake Geneva. Lac Leman on the map looks like a dolphin's leap and we are located near the tail.

Both Alaka and I are to lecture at Ecole Polytechnique Federale de Lausanne or EPFL for a day and a half each, and we have tossed in a few free days into the trip. Europe, with a light work schedule, is bliss.

On the 7th we met briefly with some of the organizers to discuss our lectures, mine mainly on the Indian economy, Alaka's more on social and demographic matters. Then the rest of the day we spent strolling around town and lounging and reading. The only dark spot was the horrible pizza we ate in an unknown restaurant near the station.

On the 8th, I headed to the EPFL for my lecture in the morning. As one comes out of the railway station and walks down the wide paved vista, with buildings with high arches, mostly empty because it is vacation time for most students, it reminds me of the paintings of Giorgio de Chirico. Deserted grand buildings can be strangely evocative and sad. Maybe it is a reminder of our own impermanence.

I lecture to a motley group of some thirty students, civilized and generally quiet. They are keenly interested in India; so the discussions are of a high quality and engaged. Our hosts, Hans-Peter, Florence, Christine and Vivian, are such charming people that the entire experience is wonderful, aesthetically and intellectually.

I gave my second talk on the 9th. In the evening, Alaka and I went to the Festival of Food and Music going on around the main cathedral, on a hill near Riponne-Bejart. It was a beautiful long summer evening. You could see ordinary homes, with lighted windows, an occasional one silhouetting a person peering out like one of those characters in T.S. Eliot's poems. There are some cobbled streets, with old-style street lamps. And it is all wrapped in the lilting music, rolling down from the hill top. We returned to our hotel late, feeling blessed.

Talking about cheese, I had told Hans-Peter, I love to eat Gruyère. He either did not hear the word 'eat' or heard it as 'visit'. He began making detailed plans for Alaka and me to visit the town of Gruyere, and after that for us to meet up with him and his wife, Beatrix, in Berne. Since my life is a saga of not offending people, instead of simply eating Gruyère cheese, yesterday we ended up going to Gruyere.

It is a charming village atop a hillock, with the entire area exuding a faint aroma of cheese. It has a few hundred inhabitants and one million visitors every year. It must be the place with the world's highest visitor to inhabitant ratio, leaving out places where there are no inhabitants.

From Gruyere we headed to Berne. Hans-Peter and Beatrix picked us up at the station. We then went to their home, which is a small apartment on the fourth floor of a thirteenth century building, overlooking River Arne. With a beautiful balcony facing the river and old homes with artistic windows and wrought-iron verandahs on the other side, and with art decorating their walls, this is one of the most beautiful homes you can imagine. It somehow reminded me of David Hockney's painting, 'Mr and Mrs Clark and Percy'.

Hans-Peter and Beatrix are people of immense charm. Their friends, Susanna and Teresa Chatterjee (yes, Chatterjee), joined us for dinner. I was curious about Mr Chatterjee, and learnt that he was now married to someone else.

Today we went to the little town of Nyon, also on Lake Geneva. We had lunch with Vivian and her husband, David, and their two adopted Indian children.

12 July 2010, Monday

Alaka left early to lecture and I worked all morning in Chatteau D'Ouchy. At noon, I went to EPFL to meet the other lecturers and Alaka, and to have lunch in the post-modern Rolex building. As we were settling down for the meal, my cell phone rang. Apologizing that my phone was not on silent, I looked at the phone and discovered that it was the Indian prime minister's office. A stern voice said that the prime minister wanted to talk to me. The prime minister came on the line immediately and started asking me about India's inflation situation and wanted my views on petroleum decontrol. He was clearly presuming I was at my desk in office or at home. I felt a bit awkward and told him I was not in Delhi but in Lausanne. I didn't want to use the word 'Switzerland' because, with all the talk of corruption in India, it evokes images of a money laundering trip. If he was taken aback that I was away from India, he did not give any hint of that. He told me he would like to have my detailed views on petroleum de-control and its possible impact on overall inflation as soon as I returned to Delhi. It felt very show-offy to return to my lunch table and say the prime minister just called. But it was a choice between showing off and lying and I chose not to lie.

Today must be my day of giving advice. A little before the prime minister called seeking advice on the economy, a dear economist friend of mine called for advice on his teetering marriage.

13 July 2010, Tuesday

It was a free day for me. So I walked around town and drank coffee and read. It has been a blissful three days break for me and the two days of work was also indistinguishable from a vacation because I taught what I enjoy. And one has to toss into this the sun and the perfect summer weather. Additionally, Lausanne for me is sacred because it is a town associated with some of the great names in economic history—most prominently Leon Walras, the originator of modern general equilibrium theory.

With its little cafes, art shops, and winding by-lanes, lined with old homes with French windows, it is a beautiful town, with a long history that goes back to the time of the Roman Empire. The over-crowding of homes in the Riponne-Bejart area is supposed to have happened after the fall of the Roman Empire when insecurity drove people to huddling in and around the perch of the hill. It is interesting how some of the contemporary charm of cities and towns are rooted in the tragedies of the past.

I have changed my view of Switzerland ever since I began doing these Lausanne visits. I used to think of Switzerland as a clinically efficient and mildly boring country, with a population whose only excess was dairy consumption. But thanks to these visits and meeting lots of people, I have got to love the country. The people are friendly, the cities are romantic and beautiful, and it is a nation of great intellectual history and art. Over and above that, it must be a sign of my geographic infidelity that I invariably fall in love with the last place I have visited.

15 July 2010, Wednesday

Arrived back in Delhi last night, back to the world of inflation management, growth stimulus, exchange rate fluctuations and design of food distribution. With the finance minister I realize I do not have to feel awkward that I had gone off to Switzerland for a few days, since 'Switzerland' always sounds like a vacation, because he had misheard 'Lausanne'. I heard him telling someone, 'Kaushik has just come back from Los Angeles.'

I appeared on Karan Thapar's television show today to debate the petroleum de-control with the Communist leader Sitaram Yechury. Both Sitaram and Karan are aggressive debaters but at the same time, they are good, thinking individuals. And you realize they are not really aggressive at all because the aggression vanishes as soon as the TV camera is switched off.

16 July 2010, Thursday

I did a press interview at the press information bureau, PIB. It catches me by surprise how I have taken to this public life, despite having had most of my career in the cloistered groves of academe. In these PIB press briefings, you sit with three or four policymakers on a slightly raised platform, with some fifty excitable journalists flanking the platform in a semi-circle. Indian journalists are an impressive lot. They are well-informed, engaged, and they (most of them, that is) are dedicated to the cause of spreading information and have no hesitation in cross-examining the government. This culture of freedom of the press is such an asset for the country. Of course, this creates awkward moments for those of us who represent the government but this monitoring by the media is ultimately good for India's economy and growth. All this is helped by PIB's excellent Chief, Neelam Kapur—effective, friendly and unpretentious.

18 July 2010, Saturday

In the early hours, I take off from Delhi to Seoul by the direct Asiana flight, to attend several G-20 meetings, including the working group on development. I have to also attend the Sherpa meeting, which is a high-powered body, because India's G-20 Sherpa, Montek Singh Ahluwalia, is unable to come. Our host is Changyong Rhee. It's a very busy meeting, packed from morning until night. However, as it happens, I found the Sherpa meeting quite vacuous, more form than substance. It's a pity. In today's globalized world there is a lot for the G-20 to do, but the political forces girding the group make it virtually impossible.

However, the food was wonderful and we were treated to some very good modern Korean dance. I find South Korea a very romantic and beautiful place. What adds to its mystery and charm is the strange land that lies to its north, North Korea, a nation that is like a fictitious, surreal creation by Bunuel or Buddhadeb Dasgupta. I am so fascinated by the country that I have told the Indian prime minister that if he ever sent a delegation to North Korea, I would like to be on it.

30 July 2010, Friday

I took the morning flight from Delhi to Mumbai to speak to the World Presidents Organization (WPO) at the Four Seasons Hotel. Sid Khanna organized the event. Vikram Mehta was the chairman for the evening. It was a very St Stephen's evening. A rather westernized gathering, with the inevitable surface polish, which made for a pleasant, if superficial, evening.

31 July 2010, Saturday

I spoke at the Claridges Hotel in Delhi on the occasion of a Sage-NCAER-CMCR book release, where I shared the podium with the Tata group executive, R. Gopalakrishnan, my St Stephen's classmate and now chief statistician of India, Pronab Sen, and Rama Bijapurkar. Rama chaired the event. My lecture was a hit even though I had nothing to say. This is always a bit alarming. I decided to weave into my short lecture my discovery of government culture during the early 1990s when Pulin Nayak and I were trying to set up a new research institution, the Centre for Development Economics (CDE) at the Delhi School of Economics. CDE is now well-established but there was a lot of running around in 1991 and 1992. The main problem was we needed many permissions and clearances from the government and since neither Pulin nor I were familiar with the corridors of power, we were being given a run for our money. Finally, feeling desperate, I decided I would have to trouble the one person I knew a little—Finance Minister Dr Manmohan Singh. On the day of the appointment, trying to make sure I was not late, I landed at his office rather early and ended up idling in his waiting room for about forty-five minutes. During this time, several bureaucrats popped in and got to see me waiting to meet the FM. I never knew waiting to see the minister could be such a powerful signal. After that day the files started moving quickly and I could see senior bureaucrats more easily. This was so effective that I thought I should ask Dr Manmohan Singh if I could come once a week to his office. I would not disturb him. I would just sit in his waiting room for half an hour quietly and go away.

I think this did it. Despite any lack of content in my lecture, people said it was terrific.

3 August 2010, Tuesday

Amartya Sen lectured today at Vigyan Bhavan, with the prime minister in the chair. Sen spoke largely on the centrality of education and literacy for development. The cameras were almost equally focused on the podium, on Sen and Singh, as on the audience, where Sharmila Tagore and her daughter, Soha Ali Khan, both looking beautiful, were sitting. Being a movie icon clearly has huge value in India.

It was on the whole a disappointing lecture. Sen was nowhere near his usual scintillating self. The high point of the lecture was when he ticked off the PM for not taking a tougher stance on Myanmar's military. Some of the prime minister's secretaries and advisers in the audience looked distinctly uncomfortable by this public remonstration of the PM. But the prime minister himself took it graciously. This is a sign of Manmohan Singh's inner strength that he does not get ruffled by criticism. This is also so wonderful about India. One can freely criticize the political head of the nation and engage with him on important but critical matters. Outside of rich nations one finds few examples of such political maturity. I hope this will last.

After the event, we went to dinner to Poonam and Shiv's home where Sharmila and Soha also came. I chatted with Soha, who seems like a nice person. This is also true of Sharmila. For someone who was such a superstar in Bollywood and was one of the world's most glamorous actors, she is a surprisingly balanced, hang-up free person.

8 August 2010, Sunday

I came to Kolkata yesterday. It's a private visit. I thought the weekend was a good opportunity to see my mother. She seems to be doing fine. She is cheerful and more alert then she was six weeks ago. Not bad at ninety-one, but it still feels sad to see her old and vulnerable, given what an independent and feisty person she was. Till five years ago she was visiting us regularly in USA enjoying the visits and making new friends, not to mention embarrassing us by walking over to our neighbors' homes on Siena Drive in

Ithaca and, without forewarning, knocking on their doors to chat. Our neighbors were surprisingly friendly. We got to know many of them well because of her. When a few years ago a couple in our neighbourhood got divorced the person who was most upset was my mother in Kolkata. She knew them well and felt that if she had been in Ithaca, she would have talked them out of it.

Today is also the day of my completion of eight months in the government. If one needs an alibi to reflect on the government, let today, a Sunday, be it.

Two problems make the Indian government less efficient and less effective: Overwork in the top echelons of bureaucracy, and the culture of permissionism that pervades the government. At one level, it is impressive that virtually all civil servants who are fairly senior, or are striving to be so, work extremely hard. A slightly less charitable view of this phenomenon is that the senior bureaucrats often work as back-end, on-call workers for their master—the minister or some member of Parliament. And like the on-call workers in the feudal landlord's manor, once they are part of this system, they have no choice but to plod away fourteen hours a day, seven days a week. Whatever be the cause—ambition, diligence, drive or exploitation—the upshot is that they work to the point where efficiency and creativity suffer. These individuals, though initially very bright, come to acquire a parrot-like quality, with the ability to do a large amount of mechanical work. This does hamper creativity in the government.

The other problem is what can only be called the malaise of permissionism. For a newcomer arriving straight into the top echelon of government, as was the case with me, what is immediately noticeable is how everyone is always taking permission. The requests for permission generally get passed up the pyramidal structure of the government; and a surprising amount of trivia go all the way to the top, namely, to the minister. You want to go to Varanasi for a day to attend to an ailing relative, you want to change the brand of coffee served in the ministry, you feel there should be another attendant to keep the bathrooms clean. All such proposals move in a chain of hard cardboard folders, tied with strings, from one room to another acquiring notings from senior members of the bureaucracy.

This is such a far cry from the American University where senior professors are allocated budgets and can with a stroke of a pen get a visitor to come from New Delhi, Tokyo, or Istanbul, all paid for. The system there is not one of *prior* permission but periodic review to make sure that no one is misusing authority. I know that the switch over to such a system will initially cause some corruption and misuse. But the alternative is so inefficient that we have to try change the system. Moreover, being given some final authority on matters nurtures trust and a sense of responsibility and even honesty. There will be some initial misuse but that has to be treated as transition cost. We have to remember that even with all these cumbersome checks and balances we are not known for the absence of corruption.

13 August 2010, Friday

I used to initially get baffled by how politicians manage to speak and participate in discussions on so many diverse topics, many of which are extremely complex. I have now discovered their secret. The trick, if you listen carefully you will realize, is to speak freely and not hold back because of any silly principles like, when you say something, it must mean something. As long as the sentences are sufficiently convoluted for their content to be a blur of words, others will find meaning in what you say. I can vouch for this because I have sat in on meetings, where I, for one, could make no sense of what I was saying. I had to tell myself, if all others found my remarks so engaging, who am I to be so arrogant and claim that those remarks are meaningless.

The other thing that I am learning—this is not specific to politicians and bureaucrats, though—is just how poorly people argue. A prominent farm lobbyist, name omitted, came to see me a few days ago. He said that, contrary to what people claim, he was certain that India's agricultural output will grow at the rate of 7 per cent per annum at a sustainable pace. Then, as our discussion proceeded, he began to lay down a list of demands that was necessary for the government to attend to—subsidies, tax cuts, government investment in the agriculture sector, and so on, if the growth of 7 per cent was to be realized. I listened to him carefully and asked if he expected the government to give in to his demands. He snapped back that people in government were so useless, he had no expectation the demands would be met.

15 August 2010, Sunday

I woke up early to go to the Independence Day pageant, where the prime minister would speak from the ramparts of the Red Fort at 7 am. This was the first time I was seated on the speaker's side at the Independence Day event, looking down at the sprawling crowd spread at the foot of the fort. Manmohan Singh spoke well and clearly but, as is his style, there was no political hyperbole to stir the audience. It was full of facts, totally honest, but not one to get the audience riled up with delusional thoughts, as political orators do. With a sophisticated electorate this would be an asset but electorates are rarely sophisticated.

It was magnificent to see the dawn breaking over old Delhi, with the skyline gradually shimmering into visibility. One could see some segments of Chandni Chowk, and the grand domes and spirals of mosques, gurdwaras and temples gradually became brighter. India looked majestic, a celebration of its diverse history, the mish-mash of cultures and secular achievement. These ramparts of the Red Fort have seen so much history. From its construction in 1639 by the Moghul Emperor Shah Jahan, the premises of the Red Fort have been almost continuously in use. This is where Shah Alam II and his family must have wandered in the last days of the Moghul Empire, and witnessed the final collapse in 1803, with all of India ultimately coming under British control.

I have long maintained that patriotism is a morally wrong emotion, rather like racism, where you uphold a small group as special, but the beautiful lay of the land in front of me, a reminder of hundreds of years of history, war, conquest and peace, created an almost mystical ethos of history and, I cannot deny, patriotism.

As we sat through the event, the sun rose, and gradually became the scorching Delhi sun. Later in the day I got one of my worst migraine attacks, the sort I get once every one or two years. Luckily, it is a Sunday, so no office missed.

21 August 2010, Saturday

The prime minister gave me time at 10:30 am to see him at his residence. I bumped into B. L. Joshi, governor of Uttar Pradesh, as polite and courteous as always, in the waiting room. The PM's calendar is always well-managed; within ten minutes I was called in.

The two of us had a wide-ranging conversation, on India's representation in G-20, corruption in public life and, interestingly, on economic warfare between nations—I have some novel thoughts on this.

I told him he should do a big address, somewhat akin to an Independence Day speech, on television, maybe two or three times a year. He wondered if that would serve a purpose; and turned it on me saying that I should speak to the general public, explaining the inflation situation and other aspects of the economy.

He said he felt despondent about the quality of politics in

India. We sipped coffee; he seemed weighed down today. There was a regal peacock walking outside in his sun-soaked yard, with two peachicks in tow. I wondered if he had time to savor such sights.

24 August 2010, Tuesday

In most walks of life we have to worry about getting caught out for our ignorance. A few months into joining the government, I realized that this is one problem that we do not have to encounter in the government. This is because the lack of a comment or a confused statement is viewed as a sign that the person knows it all, but is holding his card to his chest. In the early days, it would happen that I spoke completely honestly. For instance, when asked what I thought of the narrowing of the 'policy rate corridor', I would say, feeling a bit ashamed of myself, 'I am afraid I know nothing on this subject.' To that the response invariably was, 'Sir, we assure you we won't report on this.' Or 'Sir, please don't be so diplomatic.'

Gradually, one learns, of course. Now, when asked such questions, I answer: 'At this time, I would prefer not to comment on this.'

2 September 2010, Thursday

It is Janmashthami today. All offices are closed. Shah Jahan Road, with an occasional car whizzing past, with the sun beating down on the tar, looks like a piece of abandoned history. I decide to settle down for a rare relaxed day at home; and just then the phone rings. It is from the prime minister's office. The caller is polite and tells me that the prime minister would like me to come to his residence, right away, for a meeting on sugar decontrol with the sugar barons. These meetings, with what are essentially corporate lobby groups, invariably have a tense under-current involving tricky political and legal matters. I know I am treated as a bit of an oligopoly and antitrust specialist in the government, and the prime minister likes to get into the thicket of such issues, when taking decisions relating to industry. But I feel reluctant, especially because I was looking forward to a day of untrammeled leisure, reading and some writing, something I do so rarely nowadays outside of making jottings on government memos.

I toy with the idea of pretending to be deeply religious and on a vow to spend Janmashthami praying and fasting, and say I cannot come. Religion does have its uses in the government.

An hour later, I am at 7RCR, going through detailed deliberations on sugar pricing and availability of sugar. Three hours later, I have been put on yet another committee—on sugar decontrol.

4 September 2010, Saturday

I deliver the 12th Dharm Narain Lecture at 11 am today on 'Does Economic Theory Inform Good Policy?' It is a packed auditorium. Lots of people are turned away. The lecture is a big success.

21 September 2010, Tuesday

I left Delhi early on 19 September by Gulf Air to get to Amman, via Bahrain. I am in Jordan for the HDCA conference. HDCA stands for Human Development and Capabilities Association, which was founded by Amartya Sen, in close association with Martha Nussbaum. The group of academics who do research on capabilities seem to include some with a cult-like allegiance to this approach. Listening to them, I get a sense of total, unquestioning devotion to the idea of capabilities and functioning. They get disturbed by anybody who feels these are not path-breaking ideas.

I wonder if I am seeing the birth of a religion? This must be the way new religions get formed. There has to be a germ of interesting ideas, propagated by a person of some exceptional qualities but beyond that it is luck (I am not saying good or bad). Herd behavior sets in, with some disciples acquiring a missionary zeal; and 200 years later we have the 'Sen religion.' I wonder how Sen, who is so rational, an atheist and against cults, would feel if he realized that he was headed to become the father figure of a future religion. My hunch is that, having a religion named after you would be such an exciting thought that while he would may be not abet it, he would not actively get in the way.

These thoughts play in my head as I spend much of the day visiting the astonishingly beautiful, historic city of Petra.

25 September 2010, Saturday

I have been doing a lot of G-20 work, pertaining to MAP—the Mutual Assessment Process. I have been leading the Indian team for these meetings and since India and Canada were the global leaders for this, I had a lot of responsibility on my shoulders. The Canadian team used to be led by Paul Rochon. We got along well and I put in a lot of effort to represent India ably and also to get the 20 of G-20 to coordinate their efforts. I had been feeling for a while that India has so much talent but we don't reflect this effectively enough in our G-20 work. We need to commission four or five background papers by Indian policy economists, which we would use for the G-20 MAP work. My calculation was if we sanctioned these papers, paying each author Rs 1 lakh 25 thousand per paper, we could get some useful intellectual back-up for the endless amount of talking we do in our G-20 meetings. Given the massive amount we spend on our G-20 missions this seemed well worth it. So I approached the finance secretary for this and also sounded out some other secretaries in the Ministry of Finance. There was a lot of foot-dragging. My impression was that the only reason for this is the bureaucrat's instinctive tendency to feel we can do it all; we do not need outside experts for anything. So, feeling a bit frustrated, I decided a few weeks ago, to bring this up with the prime minister and mentioned that this is not happening presumably because of budgetary reasons. He thought this was an excellent idea and should not be held up for any reason. He said he would get me the budget.

I do not know what happened after that but the finance secretary met me, visibly upset that I had taken this to the PM (I am presuming the prime minister's office called him). He said this kind of thing he would have sanctioned in a minute if I had gone to him. I wondered about the use of the 'if'. It was then sanctioned in one minute.

28 September 2010, Tuesday

Ah, culture! How varied it can be. It took me a while to realize that in Indian officialdom, to enter someone's room not only do you not knock, it is actually considered impolite to knock. Either you have the right to enter a person's office or you don't. If you have the right, the norm is to go right in. I remember, in my first weeks, some urgent matter concerning exchange rates came up for which I needed to see the finance minister immediately. So I ran up to his office and, as I was about to knock, his door-keeper, who knew me well, came charging, 'What are you doing?'

I said I needed to see the minister urgently. He looked baffled, 'Then go in.'

It has taken me a while to adjust to this custom, it being such a strict norm in the west to knock before entering. What made the adjustment harder is that, given the high humidity in India, many doors are swollen and jammed, and so one needs to push against them for them to open. The upshot is that not only do you not knock when entering someone's office, but you often end up entering the room like a cannon ball, as the door suddenly gives way.

Despite the initial adjustment problem, I have now come to believe there is merit to the Indian custom. If you have to go to some persons' office, why disturb them fifteen seconds before you have to disturb them?

3 October 2010, Sunday

I have just returned from Kolkata and have to head to Washington tonight. Two days ago I went to Kolkata and then by road to Falta to review what was happening in the Special Economic Zone (SEZ) there, which is run by the Ministry of Commerce. I was impressed by some of the businesspersons and senior managers I met. They seemed professional and sensitive to the needs of the workers and the buyers (and not solely to profits).

Then I took all of yesterday off to be with my mother, since I was about to travel abroad. My mother has not been feeling well and she looked visibly frail. My three sisters who live in Kolkata were worried. My mother kept telling me I should stay back with her for a few more days. This, as I recounted earlier, was uncharacteristic of her because she would always advise us—her children—against sentimentalism and about the importance of work and professionalism. I explained to her that the Washington mission was important and I could not miss it unless absolutely necessary. I had a strange, miserable feeling that I was being too tough. I returned to Delhi with a heavy heart earlier today, and will catch the Washington flight soon.

7 October 2010, Thursday

On 4 October I arrived in Washington for the IMF-World Bank Annual meetings. As is standard practice for senior members of the government I am staying at the magnificent Williard Hotel in a suite that is beautiful and absurdly large. It has been three hectic days with back-to-back meetings.

Today was the high point. It was a session where a couple of finance ministers, which included India's Pranab Mukherjee and South Africa's Pravin Gordhan, were addressing a large audience of experts in one of the IMF auditoriums. For some reason, Pranab Mukherjee had to leave and he gave an instruction to the attendant behind him, who came running to me to ask if I could take the FM's place. Government is a place of defined hierarchies and there were one or two more senior people there. So it was surprising that the FM asked me to take his place. I felt a bit uneasy but also excited and ran up to the dais. I had no idea if I was supposed to play mere placeholder or join in with the other ministers and opine about the world. I thought that since I had no instruction, I would go for the latter option which was greater fun. So I merrily held forth on the state of the world economy. Most ministers are so terrified that people will understand what they are saying that they speak without saying anything. I think the audience liked the fact that I spoke clearly about why the global economy was in this sorry state.

As I was completing my little oration, I could see there was a call coming in from Kolkata. After a while, as the Q&A session was going on, there was a call again, and then again. There was no way I could take the call. When the session ended, I walked out of the building and even before crossing over to the main building of the World Bank, I stood on the sidewalk of 19th Street and called the number. It was my niece, calling to tell me my mother had died. She died peacefully enough at 10:50 pm, Indian time. Unlike my father on whom I was dependent, my mother, certainly by this time, was dependent on me. It is much harder to take the death of a dear one who depends on you. She had seemed so frail when I left Kolkata about a week ago, I wondered if I did right by insisting I had to leave Kolkata and get back to work.

I did not go into the next meeting where I was anyway just an observer; I walked around Pennsylvania Avenue for a while, then met up with Pranab Mukherjee in Williard Hotel and told him I have to go to Kolkata immediately. He was kind and understanding. My mother followed very few religious norms. When my father died and according to Hindu custom I was supposed to shave my head on the twelfth day after his passing, my mother had whispered to me that no matter who said what, I should not shave my head because 'that looks awful'. But she had told me that when she died she had one request. She wanted me to be the person who touches the fire to her lips to start the process of cremation. I just had to go to Kolkata for that.

I managed to get an Air India ticket to leave for India tomorrow.

26 October 2010, Tuesday

An important chapter in my life in Kolkata is over with my mother gone. I feel sad but unlike some people who feel shattered by their parents' passing, I do not. I was close to my mother and also my father and treasure their memories but life goes on. I have been back in Delhi now for several days, back in the rough and tumble of politics and policy.

I came closest, at least by some metric, to resigning from my job today. Nirvikar Singh, close friend from my London School of Economics days (he was a few years my junior, and known in LSE for his extraordinary high IQ) and professor in USA, came to see me in my office. We were chatting when a note came from the finance minister saying there is an important meeting of the FM with the governor of the Reserve Bank of India on 29th in Delhi and that I was expected to attend it. I had been in the government long enough now to know that 'expected' by the minister means 'ordered to'. As it happens, I had agreed some months ago to give the Sarat Chandra Kagti lecture in Guwahati on 29th October and had taken the requisite permission, including from the FM. This was not a fancy, 5-star event but of great sentimental importance to Mridu Kagti, who has been seriously ill with Lou Gehrig's, and was organizing this in his father's memory. I knew Mridu from my college days. I felt I could not let Mridu down.

I reacted uncharacteristically strongly. Since Nirvi was sitting with me, I told him how I felt about this and said I was going to speak to the finance minister right away, and if he said I could not go for this, I would resign. Nirvi calmed me down and said I was overreacting, clearly spoilt by my career in research where one almost never has to take anybody's permission. I argued that I was not angry about this. It was a purely principled decision I was taking—I just would not cancel the lecture. So I ran up to the FM's office. It all ended non-dramatically. Pranab Mukherjee heard me out, sensed there would be a showdown, and said he fully understood. I lost my one *Mahanagar* (a 1963 film by Satyajit Ray) moment.

1 November 2010, Monday

We left Delhi on 28 October—Alaka and me—for Assam. I am to deliver the Sarat Chandra Kagti Memorial Lecture in Guwahati tomorrow. Mridu Kagti and his wife Seema invited me. I gather that the original idea to invite me was from Nilay Dutta, my dear friend from St Stephen's College. Nilay was among the two— the other being Rahul Khullar—in my batch in college whom I considered the most brilliant students, and by a wide margin. Nilay never finished college because he dropped out to join the Maoist revolution, served time in jail, and was now one of the most successful lawyers in Assam. I was excited at the thought of meeting Nilay again. To complete the story, Rahul is one of India's most brilliant civil servants and also fastidiously honest and principled. India needs more such people at the helm.

The non-stop Jet Airways flight from Delhi had Saugata Roy and Ranee Narah, a most-engaging personality, with us. I chatted a bit with them and then caught up with my reading. We were received at the airport by Mridu and Seema, and the police had come to escort me. Throughout our four days in Assam I am given a personal bodyguard and a truckload of armed security personnel that drives ahead of us. Alaka is uncomfortable. But this is a region with stray revolutionary movements that makes this necessary for all senior government officials.

We're staying at the Ashok Brahmaputra in Assam Bazaar. It is a lovely small-town hotel. Never before have I had an armed policeman stationed outside my hotel room. I am not worried at all about terrorists but the thought of the policeman having one crazy moment is not comforting.

On 29 October, we have breakfast at Nilay's home, with his wife Biju and Pranab Jyoti Das, a college friend settled in Guwahati. Nilay nowadays talks more freely about his underground days and time in jail than he did when I met him the last few times.

From there we were taken to what was described to me as an 'All-Assam Quiz Contest', held at Pragjyoti ITA auditorium, at Machkhowa. Mridu had clearly played a role in organizing the quiz. It turned out that for two questions concerning who the author is for two books, the correct answer was 'Kaushik Basu'. The questions made me feel proud and famous. But the fact that none of the contestants, nor members of the audience (to whom the questions were directed when the contestants failed to give the right answer), knew the answer, quickly brought me back to reality.

We then had lunch at India Club, Dighalipukuripar, and then we went back to Machkhowa for my lecture on governance and economic development.

After the lecture we went to Mridu's house, in Uzanbazar, for dinner with his extended family and friends. They are clearly very well off and the home has all the graciousness of a feudal home that is no longer at its peak. It reminds me a little of our own home at 29/1 Ballygunge Circular Road in Kolkata. The food was served elegantly with lots of helpers, who are clearly proud of the home. All family members were charming and friendly and we got to chat a lot. Mridu himself, despite his Lou Gehrig's illness, exudes warmth, kindness and a zest for life, which has almost a spiritual force. His mother, over ninety years old, reminds me of my maternal grandmother. My grandmother had lived a life of luxury and wealth with multiple villas in old Calcutta. In my adulthood, her income flow had diminished and the wealth had begun to fade. But she lived in an enormous home, with very few inhabitants—one son, his wife and their daughter, and several loyal servants. But my grandmother never lost her stately manners. Incapacitated, sitting in the middle of a large bed, she would order the staff around. When we visited her, she always greeted us with a vigorous handshake, which she had learned from the colonial British visitors they used to have at their home.

On 30 October we went to Kaziranga, staying at Jhupuri Ghar resort, which is just little cottages scattered over a large, forested area. We were given a simple but elegant cottage. The only time I got to use the armed security accompanying me everywhere was at Jhupuri Ghar. As night descends, Alaka discovered a frog in our hut-style bedroom. I refused to catch it and nor would Alaka; and we could not sleep with the croaking and the risk of stepping on it at night. So I had no choice but to call the security person sitting outside our cottage, gun in hand. I was handicapped because I have no idea how to say 'frog' in Assamese, and so I decided to use the Hindi word for it, adding a gentle Assamese accent. So I told him that he needed to throw the 'menduk' out of our hut. That to him must have sounded like 'memsab' because he looked alarmed at my request, especially since Alaka did not seem to be giving any trouble. He ultimately understood, the frog was taken out, calm descended and I was glad I was given a truckload of armed police.

Finally, we spent one night at Adabar tea garden, in the magical Wild Mahaseer Guest House. It is a residence full of old colonial charm. One could only imagine the hacienda style excesses of the heydays of the early British tea gardens. The manager takes great pride in the colonial links and tells me that even recently there was a 'lord' from England who had come and stayed there. He rushed and brought out a picture of the lord at the Mahaseer Guest House. By a great coincidence it turned out to be Lord Nicholas Stern, or Nick Stern—senior economist and a dear friend and mentor to me.

During this stay, I also visit many rural works sites—NREGS, Anganwadi, and Rajiv Gandhi water mission. Somehow Assam raises my hopes for India. I have always been partial to Assam. My first encounter with it was in Rabindranath Tagore's fiction—*Shesher Kobita*, which made it out to be a painfully romantic place. I have not been to Assam too many times but I love it every time I go. It is a state that represents a confluence of cultures, with tribal societies, old Hindu relics and pockets of Christianity and Islam. And through it all winds that magnificent River Brahmaputra. Over and above that, this time I felt positive vibes about its economy. I am convinced that if law and order comes to Assam, it can be a frontrunner state in India.

7 November 2010, Sunday

I was invited to the prime minister's residence for a dinner with Barack and Michelle Obama. There is always a lot of jockeying for invitation for high-powered events like these. I did not do any jockeying because I find that so unsavory, but I was really hoping I would be invited and so was delighted when the invitation came a few days ago. There were approximately sixty Indian guests and ten Americans. Bollywood and corporate India were well represented. Azim Premji, Narayana Murthy, Shabana Azmi, Aamir Khan, Ratan Tata, were among the guests.

There was a slight mismanagement at the entrance to 7RCR, which is quite rare at the PM's residence. One road to the residence was cordoned off, I believe for special security reasons because of Obama. When I arrived at that road and explained to the police that I was going to the PM's residence for the dinner, they directed me to another road which was a one-way road, also cordoned off. Half-way there, my car could not move forward or backward. Sharad Pawar was in the car in front of me. We both got down and started walking, with Pawar complaining that this should not happen to a senior minister.

The prime minister's lawns were beautifully decorated, in a non-flamboyant style and there was live Indian music. As we stood sipping soft drinks in a large cavernous room, at 7:45 pm all guests were told to form a crescent and Obama, the prime minister and their spouses would go around meeting the guests. I happened to be with Narayana Murthy and Tim Geithner. Geithner's easy-going manner is impressive. We chatted about economic problems of our mutual countries. Obama came in and moved along the crescent from person to person, uttering a sentence or two to each. When they reached our cluster of three, Manmohan Singh introduced me saying that he had brought me from Cornell, to advise his government. Like Manmohan Singh, there is something very gracious about Obama. He exudes decency. He also has a certain ease with words. On hearing that I was India's chief economic adviser, he pointed to Geithner on my right and said to me, 'You should give this guy some tips.'

At dinner, I was seated at the Borlaug table with Montek, Prannoy, the U.S. Ambassador to India, Tim Roemer, Srikumar Banerjee, Prithviraj Chauhan and Harsimrat Kaur Badal, member of Parliament from Bhathinda, Punjab. Prannoy and I gossiped a lot and all of us chit-chatted pleasantly about nothing in particular.

13 November 2010, Saturday

I travel to Goa today to address the Indian Academy of Science at its annual conference held at the National Institute of Oceanography at Dona Paula, just off Panjim. It is a Jet Airways flight and it reaches nearly three hours late. The flight is packed—about 25 per cent with light skin and Slavic features. These are, I presume, the famed Russians of Goa. As soon as the flight takes off an overweight woman of the group is taken unwell, and there is a flurry of activity of flight attendants running up and down. I am impressed by the thirst for knowledge that Indians have and law-abidingness, which is something new. None of the passengers take their seat belts off but they simply loosen them and turn around to see what is happening. The plane takes off with all the front rows of Indians facing the rear of the plane.

As luck would have it, one Dirsh Kaushik and his wife Labt Kaushik occupy the seats next to mine. The flight attendant reads off our names and says, 'So lunch for the full family of Kaushiks?' While there is no reason to distance myself from the 'family', I awkwardly mutter, 'That is a coincidence.' Dirsh Kaushik clearly belongs to that school that believes coincidences come in shades, and he hastens to add: 'Pure coincidence.'

I am put up at the International Center at Dona Paula and the conference is held at the nearby National Institute of Oceanography. I speak on higher education and development. It is one of my fluent days. Uncharacteristically, I speak without pause for forty-five minutes. There is the usual share of mad questions. This disappoints me a little coming from India's premier science academy. But I later comfort myself that the ones who are aggressive enough to ask questions in a big auditorium are probably the reason-free ones. The next morning at breakfast, I have a wonderful, intelligent conversation with a bunch of scientists—Ram, Dipankar Chatterjee and his wife, Professor Bose (related to Sugata Bose), and several others.

After my lecture we are taken on a cruise and dinner. The cruise is a bit disappointing with an oppressive entertainment show. But the conversation is pleasant, with Professor Sood (president of the academy), Kalyan Sinha and others.

The following morning, I go, accompanied by Ronnie Das Gupta, to see the new apartment we have bought in Salegaon. It is a beautifully designed small apartment in a lovely building with seemingly nice people. Goa is such a civilized place.

Later, accompanied by a team from the Goa government, I am taken to see some NREGS sites. A pleasing young local girl is the main guide. She has a natural confidence, nicely ordering my driver around. The running of NREGS continues to disappoint me. I should clarify that I am (unlike other critics) in favor of spending the amount of money we are spending, and maybe even more, on direct anti-poverty programs. It is just that NREGS, I feel, has design flaws. This visit confirms my misgiving. There are one or two nice jobs done using this labor, such as the badminton court at Chicolna Bogmalo. But the rest is pedantic. My guide (who is a program officer from District Rural Development office) tells me the main work going on here is the 'cutting of bushes'. She keeps showing me road edges with no bushes ('cutted bushes' in her words). We drive some distance in one direction for me to see a whole yard where the 'cutting of bushes' had occurred. But when we arrive there, alas, we find an overgrowth. She is a bit flustered and disappointed and says, 'Because of rains the bushes have grown again.' She explains to me how a carefully maintained log of employment is being created for the 'cutting of bushes'.

I assure her that this is all very efficient but ask her why these bushes needed to be cut. Her reply is immediate, 'In order to create jobs.' Keynes would be happy.

I am glad NREGS is there, because in its absence the money would be used up on wasteful government consumption or profligate subsides to the rich. I just wish it were designed differently, and given more as handouts without holding up the labor, which could be used elsewhere and generate more income for the poor.

My guide is a sweet person. She asks me if I am in the IAS. When I say no, she is visibly sad for me and asks me if my job in government is a permanent one. I tell her: 'No, I am on a contract job with limited tenure.' She looks happy and says, 'Just like me.' And she commiserates about our predicament.

19 November 2010, Friday

I am invited to Teen Murti to hear the prime minister give the 'Inaugural address' for the 10th Indira Gandhi Conference. Sonia Gandhi also speaks eloquently; her affection for Indira Gandhi is obvious. I get a message saying that the prime minister wants to see me at 5:15 pm. So I rush from his talk to his residence. We chat for forty minutes on various topics. He is in a warm and friendly mood. Actually, I believe he is always warm, but today there is outward manifestation of the warmth. At the same time, he is clearly depressed about the state of the nation—its economy and politics. He wishes things could be straightened out but India is a complex organism. We brainstorm for a while. I always get impressed by how little time he has for party politics. In all his conversations there is an urgency about what we need to do for India. There is little on politics and political competition which is such a preoccupation with most career politicians. I do not know other politicians at the helm of their nation closely. But Manmohan Singh must be unusual. Nehru was probably like this. I suppose so was John F. Kennedy and Jimmy Carter. In our times, Angela Merkel may be similar. But my hunch is that this is a small minority.

After that I head home, but return to his residence later for the conference dinner.

20 November 2010, Saturday

The Indira Gandhi Conference, organized by Sonia Gandhi, begins at 9:30 am. Mrs Gandhi is there bang on time. I am there, two minutes late, which is bang on time for me. It is a remarkable group she has assembled—Joe Stiglitz, Montek Singh Ahluwalia, Aruna Roy, Sri Mulyani Indrawati, Rob Riemen from the Netherlands, Nandan Nilekani, Nemat Shafiq from the IMF and others. I am impressed by Mrs Gandhi's easy-going, modest style. There is none of the jostling for 'respect' that so many politicians indulge in. She comes and goes with no fanfare; and sits through the entire proceeding, speaking little but listening with great attention.

In the evening she hosts a dinner at 10 Akbar Road, which both Alaka and I attend. We get to meet the sarod maestro Amjad Ali Khan. It is a marvelous evening, with some dancing from Northeast India and excellent food from different parts of India.

21 November 2010, Sunday

The conference continues. I speak in the morning, trying to convey some important conceptual arguments, keeping in mind that it is a mixed audience and I have to leave out technicalities. There is a bit of a sharp exchange with Jean Dreze. He is such a brilliant person and leads a remarkable life of personal sacrifice. But there seems to be a righteous anger in him. This is a common problem with many sincere people. They think everybody else is insincere. I hope he does not view me that way, both because he will then be wrong and because I am so fond of him.

Alaka and I host a dinner at home. 'Conversation and dinner with Joe Stiglitz' we call it. There are around twenty people. Joe is as usual funny and brilliant. It is a thoroughly enjoyable evening for everybody.

27 November 2010, Saturday

If you are well-known but not well-known enough and want to be treated as if you are, then Lucknow is the place to go to. With its old-world customs, it really lays it out. Alaka and I came to Lucknow yesterday. The university is to confer an honorary D.Litt. degree on me. We were received at the airport with flowers and a car with flashing red light, siren and an irascible driver with total disregard for the proletariat pedestrian.

I gave an informal lecture at the university, had tea with the ever-gracious and scholarly governor of Uttar Pradesh, B. L. Joshi, at his manor, and dinner with B. V. Chaubal, chief general manager of the State Bank of India in Lucknow, Manoj Mishra, the vice chancellor of Lucknow University, who made the sensible choice concerning who to confer the degree on, and a few others, at the Taj Residency.

We are staying at Clarks Awadh, our window overlooking a beautiful bend of the Gomti. The first time I peer out I am taken in by the beauty of the river navigating this ancient city. Scrambled lines from Premchand's classic short story and Satyajit Ray's film *Shatranj ke Khiladi*, flit through my head—in the time of Wajid Ali Shah. Lucknow was a city steeped in luxury and indulgence, in opium and art… I suddenly realize that what was routine in me, pausing to admire beauty, I have not done in ages. I fear that life on the frontlines of national policymaking may be robbing me of my sensitivities. There has been so little time to pause these last several months.

This morning, Lucknow University conferred the D.Litt. (Honoris Causa) on me at a very well-organized convocation event. The timings were perfect and the pageant gracious without ostentation. The only flaw I could spot was in the typed program. There was a ten-minute item, just before the convocation ceremony, which said, 'Rabbing for convocation.' I was wondering what kind of wild venture that would be when someone walked in with a robe to deck me up for the dais.

We return to Delhi and head straight to the home of the Nilekanis—Nandan and Rohini—for dinner.

29 November 2010, Wednesday

Some time ago, I can't quite recall exactly which day, I sent a note to the prime minister saying that Oxford University Press would be publishing a collection of my popular writings, entitled *An Economist's Miscellany*. The collection is supposed to include one essay on the prime minister, describing one of my first meetings with him, much before he became a prominent politician. It was a spontaneously written piece, published in my BBC column, way before I had anything to do with governments and policymaking. It had some praise for his modesty and fastidious personal integrity. I wrote to him saying that as an ordinary citizen I would not have asked the prime minister for his permission to publish something I had written about the PM. But since I now worked for his government, I wanted to check if he had any objection to my publishing the piece. I was sure, given the content of the piece, all praise for him, he would have no objection. But a few days later his personal secretary, Indu, called to say the PM would prefer if I did not publish it. I don't think any other politician in India would miss such an opportunity for free advertisement. Of course, I did not include the essay.

2 December 2010, Thursday

Today the Indian bureaucracy took the cake in demonstrating its aversion to change. The 'Mid-Year Review of the Indian Economy', which my division had prepared, was sent out for approval. A senior bureaucrat (let me withhold the name) put in an objection asking me to explain why I was breaking tradition, by doing the review in four chapters, given that it normally has three.

3

Shingles and Musings

8 December 2010, Wednesday

Done it. One year since I joined the government. I have pulled it off without being thrown out, without giving in to the occasional urge to say goodbye to this crazy world and returning to the shores of Lake Cayuga.

29 December 2010, Wednesday

I went to Kolkata on 9 December for the day for the HLCCFM meeting. My mother's passing has taken away the reason to extend these visits. She would be overjoyed by my spending extra time with her. On the flight back I kept feeling a strange tingling around my left ribs. I dismissed it as caused by exhaustion. But I was wrong. I learned on Sunday 12 December, when I went and saw my long-time favorite physician, Dr Anjan De, that I had contracted shingles (herpes zoster, I think he called it). The past two weeks or so have been very difficult for me. I missed work only for one day, but I had to cope with low-grade pain and exhaustion throughout.

Some forms of herpes are contracted through sexual transmission, but herpes zoster, unfortunately, does not come that way. It is a flare up of latent chicken pox, that can be triggered by exhaustion and stress. My colleagues in office, when they learn about the kind of herpes I had, will respect or disrespect me depending on their attitude to sexual promiscuity. More than a year in the government, I can guess pretty accurately who the ones are in whose esteem I will go down by virtue of the word zoster.

I wonder what triggered it because I am overworked but not stressed. I am lucky I do not get stressed and am generally a happy human being. I don't know where I get that from. Maybe from the one 'psychological episode' suffered in life, which (I feel in retrospect) has given me a certain robustness. It happened when I was an undergraduate student in St Stephen's College. I don't even quite know what it was—depression, anxiety? For many years I mentioned this to nobody because, apart from anything else, I was embarrassed. In later years also, I could not have told more than three or four persons about this.

Having lived a fairly sheltered childhood, with my parents and sisters—all older—in Calcutta, I was excited but also nervous when I prepared to leave home for the first time in July 1969 at the age of seventeen for Delhi's St Stephen's College for my undergraduate studies. The fact that there would be one or two months of intense ragging by the college seniors did not help. My first months, despite all those tensions, passed fine. I made new friends, some that would last a lifetime. I took the ragging in my stride. Maybe because it was all so busy, I had no time to think or be homesick.

In October, I went home for the usual autumn break. It was after I returned, by when the ragging was over, that the 'depression' and 'anxiety' struck me. I did not sleep well, had some nightmares, but on the surface life carried on as usual. I had friends, went to class, went to the movies, made friends with the girls in the neighboring college, Miranda House. But the inner sadness and anxiety steadily got worse and it came to have a strange but clear pattern.

I woke up everyday reasonably normal. As the day wore on, the anxiety would set in gradually and by afternoon would weigh down on me heavily till evening and then it would lift off totally, to return again the next day. Gradually, it started happening earlier and earlier. As it came on, I would actually feel a sight palpitation and the racing of my pulse. When it lifted at night, which also got later and later, I would feel calmer. I remember some nights looking up at Delhi's clear night sky, with stars twinkling, and wondering about the mystery of life and the mystery of what was happening to me.

The overall feeling however was one of despondency and darkness and what was most striking was that I had lost interest in everything. My interest in philosophy, which was always a part of my life, was gone. My interest in art was gone. I also did not feel sadness for all the objective things for which people feel sadness. I lived life for no reason or purpose and just saw darkness ahead of me. It was reminiscent of the crisis John Stuart Mill had had where he suddenly felt he did not care for all the things he had deeply cared for thus far. But I do not recall if Mill had the clear daily cycle which I had and which I feel must be some kind of a known phenomenon to psychologists.

I remember going home for the winter vacation in December. I was too embarrassed to talk about my state to my parents or anybody else. And in any case, I saw no hope. I did not believe psychological counselling or medicine could help me, and in any case counselling was so rare in India in those days, I would not know how to go about getting help.

I recall one of my worst days was the day of Holi, the Indian festival of colors, in March (I think) 1970. With a bunch of good friends, we decided to escape the crazy color throwing and go to Connaught Place early in the morning, to gallivant around, eat in restaurants, to celebrate the festival. I went through the motions with my friends, laughing, joking and teasing one another, but felt weighed down. At its peak, during the first seven or eight months of 1970, I became certain that this would never lift. I would lead life listlessly and with no joy, no ambition, nothing but darkness. I never had suicidal thoughts, so I would just go on like that endlessly, just learn to bear up with this weight on my shoulders.

I was so certain about this predicament that I was surprised when after another year or so I suddenly realized that the depression had lifted and I was more or less back to my normal self. But for many years I lived in fear that it would come back and I was so nervous about it that that was one reason I did not talk to anybody about it. I did not want to stir the demon.

After I went to London, met my to-be wife, Alaka, I told her in bits and pieces about this experience. And many years after that I told the wife of a dear friend of mine, Subbu. Prabha, I knew was a psychologist and I was, and still am, close to both Subbu and Prabha. I wanted to know why I now have such a stable disposition, after such a dreadful episode, and described the whole episode to her. Prabha told me that people who go through such an experience and manage to come out of it actually have a sturdier psychological disposition than most other people. Well, in that case all I can say is that I am grateful for that year or so of suffering.

1 January 2011, Saturday

A glorious start to a new year. I awoke at 8 o'clock feeling better than I have felt in weeks. The shingles is wearing off at last, if wearing off is what shingles do. The fog over Delhi has lifted and a strong sun greets us, reminding me of Delhi of the early '70s when I was still a student. Winter then meant clear blue skies and endless sun. I had decided not to have any work or social agenda this weekend and that soothes the soul. Adding to the pleasure is the fact that I wrote a little this morning with the first Mont Blanc pen I have ever owned. ITC gifted it to me recently after a lecture I gave in Kolkata.

Tulu, Jawhar, Bulbul and Partha dropped in for a late morning coffee. Since I do not get to see my relatives often these days, we caught up on a lot of accumulated family gossip—almost as interesting as political gossip. After they left, Alaka and I lunched in the sun on our porch and later I went for a walk to Khan Market and even managed to sneak in a much-needed haircut at Looks. In the evening, Sandy Darity and his wife, Kirsten, dropped in for tea. It felt wonderful seeing them after such a long time. I like Sandy's economics and also his obvious love of human beings.

And now, at day's end, I sit writing, with romantic O. P. Nayyar songs playing in the background. The only dark spot marring this otherwise blissful day is the discovery that the Mont Blanc pen does not seem to live up to its reputation.

7 January 2011, Friday

I woke up early and saw the daylight break while taking a morning walk outside our home. Shahjahan Road is such a mixture of elegance and history that I did not mind the bitter cold. At 9 am, I head to Mrs Kaur's café in Khan Market for breakfast with Aruna Roy and Nikhil De. Excellent eggs and salmon and a wonderful conversation. We discuss the shameful sedition charge against Binayak Sen, the problem of inequality and poverty in India and many other things. Both Aruna and Nikhil are charming people and, more importantly, totally genuine as social activists. In addition, Aruna has a sense of humour and can take light-hearted banter, which is refreshing. Yet I cannot help feeling that they let their emotions get the better of their reason. As a result, they will not manage to create the ideal world they want to usher in. This is a shame because I share many of their ideals.

I instinctively like such people, their total commitment and selflessness. If they trusted me, I could deliver on their own targets better than they could. It is entirely possible that they treat my fastidiousness with reason and logic as a ploy to maintain the status quo.

From breakfast, I ran to the first pre-budget meeting of this year. This was with the agriculture sector specialists—for them to give new ideas to the finance minister and senior policymakers. Ashok Gulati stood out, speaking clearly and well.

16 January 2011, Sunday

I took the Air France flight late at night from Delhi, technically on the morning of January 15th, to Paris, for the G-20 meeting. I was heading the Indian delegation. I arrived in Paris early in the morning, and was whisked off to the Hilton, not too far from the Arc de Triomphe, took a short nap and headed to Café Le Procope for a brunch and talk to a group in Paris that has a special interest in India and meets regularly. The audience was a mishmash of industrialists, journalists and, mainly, intellectuals and scholars, along with the Indian ambassador, Ranjan Mathai. Mr. Mathai is a bit of an intellectual himself and fits in well in this relatively academic gathering. Le Procope is one of the world's oldest cafés, having been founded in 1686, eight years before the Bank of England was founded, my host reminds me, I don't quite know why. It was a captivating place, of fashion and intellectual discourse, once frequented by Voltaire, Rousseau, Jefferson and Benjamin Franklin. It is also close to where Sartre and Simone de Beauvior lived and worked. It must be the history of the place that inspired me because I excelled in my talk, combining anecdotes, tales and arguments with reasonably serious intellectual content.

The G-20 meeting of deputies had me occupied all of last evening and all of today. I made up for the good lecture at Le Procope with a rather uninspiring talk at the G-20.

22 January 2011, Saturday

Today is one of those days when one feels despondent and questions oneself. Is what one is doing of any worth? Will all the sweat and tussle to improve policy and push for a better world have any effect? Is it not folly to think governments can be budged? A good letter can make all the difference on such days. That is exactly what Joseph Zeira's email did for me this morning. Here is what he wrote.

Dear Kaushik,

I am sure you are working very hard now, but I am also sure you are doing something very important. India is around a billion people and if you can contribute even a bit to the well-being of some of them, you earned your day. Good luck and I hope to meet you soon. Maybe in India...

Joseph

Those few words had a therapeutic affect, because I have been feeling almost existentially low the last few days and it peaked this morning. I don't want to exaggerate the despondency because in this job I am so busy I don't have time to wallow but I have been in a low-grade questioning mode about the value of what I was doing.

Two other letters which I got after I started this job which I treasure in a similar way were from Robert Solow—this was an actual letter—and an email from Ariel Rubinstein. I must dig these letters out some time. Both of them assured me that it was worth trying to do what I was doing or trying to do. Ariel also told me that on days when national politics get me down I should just remind myself of departmental politics in universities and the pettiness of those would surely comfort me. There is indeed some truth to this.

I do not want to give an exaggerated sense of frustration that comes with trying to change policy and not succeeding. I am not foolish the way some academics, who complain that you give all this good advice and the political leaders do not listen, are. I am aware that political leaders have reams of advice coming their way, much of them contradictory. It is pure arithmetic that the bulk of the advice will fall by the wayside. And I am lucky I am working with a government that is reasonably open to ideas.

My occasional frustration comes from elsewhere. I meet many economists who say they became an economist because of the desire to help the world. I cannot claim the same. I became an economist because the puzzles of our social, economic and political life fascinates me.

Bertrand Russell said that he owed his interest in logic and geometry to his brother: 'I began Euclid, with my brother as my tutor. This was one of the great events of my life, as dazzling as first love. I had not imagined that there was anything so delicious in the world.' I can fully appreciate this. In my case the inspiration for logic and geometry came from my father. In my school, St Xavier's Kolkata, geometry started in Class 7. It was taught poorly and in the first geometry exam at the end of the first term, I failed. My father, who usually took little interest in my studies, was disappointed. He said geometry was nothing but logic and he would show me how easy it was. He was going through a busy period in his life. He had just finished his term as mayor of the city of Calcutta, won the state election, and become speaker of the West Bengal Assembly. But in the midst of this, for about one month, he spent a little time every evening teaching me school geometry. He would quickly leaf through a couple of pages of my school textbook and then teach me with the fluency of someone who has been teaching geometry all his life. His obvious pleasure in this kind of reasoning rubbed off on me. That you could discover patterns and regularities in nature by pure reason and by staring at the world and contemplating was fascinating, and this love has been a constant in my life.

I was always a socially concerned person and I want to see

the world a better place, but my ten hours of work each day had nothing to do with that. I treated my work akin to that of a mathematician or a music composer. I did it not for money, not to create a better world, but purely because of the innate joy of this kind of work—the search for regularity and patterns in nature. I hoped this would in the long run help the world but I would do this work even if it did not. I did not feel guilty about this but was aware of the solipsism of my work.

As mentioned earlier, in 2009 when I got the invitation to be chief economic adviser, I told myself I would do it to make up for my life of self-indulgence. I resolved to be single minded in my new job—I would strive to make economic policies for a better India, a better world. The occasional despondency I have felt over the last year has been predominantly because I felt I was not doing enough to fulfil the vow to myself. Today was one such day and I was so glad to get the letter from Joseph. It buoyed my spirits.

In the evening, I went to the KHOJ Marathon, in which Hans Ulrich Obrist, the Swiss art curator, interviewed me for twenty minutes. What he was doing was a marathon interview, of a string of eminent artists and art critics. I was the exception—the only economist in his roster but he knew of my interest in art and I suppose that was the reason I was invited. We went there in a group, Alaka, me and our friends, Pilar and Max Pfeffer, who were visiting India from Cornell. It was a beautiful, artsy event, held under open skies, on the edge of the Lodhi Gardens. It was the sort of evening that knits up the raveled sleeve of care; the sort of evening that is sore labor's bath and balm of tired minds. It was the perfect evening to put the day to rest.

28 January 2011, Friday

Wherever I go, I find a raging debate and discussion on India's inflation. There is palpable anger that this is all deliberately caused by the government. This is completely wrong. Once inflation gets started (and there is no doubt that government has some responsibility for that), it is difficult to control. It has to be a slow process bringing inflation down because otherwise you can crash the economy. Of all the economic ills, inflation is one that governments do not want because people do not need official data to realize this is happening. Each person knows this almost every morning or evening when they buy the day's supply of food or go shopping. Inflation causes the popularity of governments to fall more than any other economic ill, from growth slowdown and recession, to rising unemployment.

I have now understood why people assume inflation is deliberately caused by the government. Human beings have a propensity to believe that someone or some well-defined agency is willfully responsible for whatever happens. It is this propensity that has led humans to many false beliefs through the ages, ranging from God having created the universe to governments causing inflation to persist.

29 January 2011, Saturday

We organized a lunch party on our lawn for over fifty people. The weather was glorious, bright sun and blue skies, which are increasingly rare in Delhi. The food by The Fat Chef was very good. Anjolie Ela Menon came, as did Vikram Seth, Sanjay Bhattacharya, Kumari Selja, Narendra Jadhav, Isher Ahluwalia, Puran and Nandita. My mannequin in a dhoti on the balcony of our home was a great attraction. Vikram was especially taken in by it. He even carried some single malt up to the balcony to do some 'whiskanjali' to the mannequin.

4 February 2011, Friday

I travelled to Kolkata early this morning for the 6th K. C. Basu Memorial Lecture on Law and Economics, named after my late father, to be delivered by Montek Singh Ahluwalia. The organization by WBNUJS that hosts the event was pretty dismal. Asim Dasgupta, the finance minister of the communist government in Bengal, Mahendra Singh, director of WBNUJS, Montek and I were on the dais. The relatively small audience was disappointing, given that Montek usually draws big crowds, but the lecture was advertised poorly. Because of the disappointment and maybe also the state of my stomach, I gave a pretty desultory introductory talk. Montek, more seasoned in handling awkward situations, gave his usual sparkling lecture.

After that we had dinner at Mainland China, with my sisters and their husbands. In the middle of it, the prime minister's office called to tell me the PM is inviting me for lunch at 7 Race Course Road, his residence, on 8 February.

5 February 2011, Saturday

The prime minister's office calls when I am bathing. On the way to the airport to catch the Mumbai flight, I call back. I am told the prime minister is coming on the line to speak to me. The roar of traffic outside is deafening. I tell my driver, Manbir, to roll up the window. The prime minister quickly gets to the point. He says while India's black money problem is serious, most people, including politicians, misunderstand what creates black money and the hazards and challenges of controlling black money. It needs to be curbed but done wrong can backfire and hurt ordinary people. He rightly anticipated that I would agree with this and so decided to call me. He asked me (casually, I think) if I could write up something that he can use in parliament should the opportunity arise. He thanked me for my letter to him from the previous week—the letter that I sent him with some inputs for the president's speech to the parliament at the start of the budget session later this month.

After having joined the Indian government and given that corruption scandals have erupted every now and then, I had been giving it a lot of thought. People get angry about corruption, as they indeed should, but what they often fail to realize is that corruption control needs both passion and determination, on the one hand, and intellect and analysis, on the other. In an economy, corruption flourishes side by side with legitimate activity. To use too blunt an instrument to control corruption can end up damaging legitimate business and exchange. This can damage the economy and exacerbate human suffering. So the existence of corruption is not a sign that the political leaders do not want to banish corruption. Many may not, but many may. The fact that corruption exists does not give you an answer.

There are three kinds of politicians. Those who take money for themselves, those who take money as karma, for the sake of their political party, and those who do not take. While I have never seen an incidence of bribery in my presence in the government I am of course aware that it happens; and for the politicians with whom I interact, I feel I can guess which of the three categories each of them belongs to. I have utter disrespect and disdain for the first group: those who are corrupt and take bribes to enrich themselves, their family and friends. I have huge respect for the last group. And though I have distaste for the ones who take money for their party and to compete in elections, there is a problem in morally categorizing them. If they want their party to win with genuine good intentions for the welfare of the masses and money is essential to run election campaigns, what choice do they have? It is a systemic problem instead of a problem of individual moral failing. How one views such persons depends on whether one is a moral consequentialist or a believer in deontological ethics.

I usually consider myself to be a consequentialist but in recent times have had some dilemma.

There is another genuine problem with corruption control, especially in countries where corruption is pervasive. Many a political leader comes to power genuinely wanting to curb corruption. On getting elected they soon realize that corruption being widespread, they have an embarrassment of choices. Who should they arrest, since they cannot arrest all? Political instinct tells a leader that it is better to pick up those who oppose him instead of his friends. Soon corruption control becomes an instrument of political oppression, to harass opponents and media personalities who criticize him. This has happened time and again in the world. We have to put our minds to thinking about how to change this.

Sitting in the airport lounge I mull over these matters and what I may write up for the PM, when some people recognize me and come up to talk to me. As I reluctantly put aside my papers and turn to them, I get a lucky break. Mithun Chakraborty walks into the lounge, all bluster and style, probably to catch the same flight to Mumbai, and I am summarily abandoned by all.

8 February 2011, Tuesday

I went for lunch at the prime minister's residence. It was in honour of Cambridge University's vice chancellor, Sir Leszek Borysiewicz. At lunch I got to sit on the prime minister's right. The vice chancellor, whose name I failed to master through the entire afternoon, was directly across from us. There were about twenty of us at the table, which included Sheila Dixit's son, an MP from East Delhi, and Chandrasekhar Dasgupta, IFS, and former ambassador.

The prime minister was polite but quieter than usual. Managing a country the size of India must have days of highs and lows. I did a lot of the talking. The vice chancellor, a medical researcher, spoke with passion about education and research. It struck a chord in me when he said that he loved his work as VC but 'acutely' missed the life of research and the regular interaction with patients that he had had as a practicing doctor.

At the end, when I got to speak one-on-one with the prime minister, he expressed concern about inflation, and the need to think through new combinations of fiscal and monetary policy mix that we may have to use. There was growing political disquiet in the country. He wanted me to do something and, not quite knowing how to respond, I said, sounding rather stupid, that I would.

13 February 2011, Sunday

Bleary-eyed we sat for one more day of pre-budget meeting—the finance minister and five of us advisers. The usual snacks arrived despondently on our table. The only cheer was brought by the fact that the cutlets had been carefully carved into heart-shapes, in anticipation of Valentine's Day, I think. I don't think the finance minister noticed it.

While I was working in the office late, the prime minister phoned to talk about some fiscal policy related matters.

25 February 2011, Friday

The *Economic Survey* was tabled in Parliament. My advisees and I did a 'Meet the press', organized by PIB. These are always grand affairs and, I cannot deny, I enjoy these. After that (since the press embargo was still on at the Finance Ministry and so media people could not enter the premises), I told some of the TV channels reaching out to me that I would speak to them at home from 4:30 pm to 5:30 pm. When I reached home at 4:45, there were TV crews and trucks lined up outside our home. It felt like one of those Latin American coup scenes. The Indian media's appetite for information is gluttonous and they love to dissect and question government data. This, of course, puts a strain on us, that is, those of us who are a part of the government. But I don't mind it because this is the strength of India's democracy and makes the country stronger in the long run. If there was not this kind of scrutiny by a critical and questioning media, India could well be captured by a few big businesses and a handful of politicians, as has happened in so many developing nations. We are fortunate to have escaped such a predicament.

I did fairly elaborate interviews with NDTV's Anjana Menon and CNBC's Shireen Bhan. Their quality of questions and, admittedly, also grace, inspired me. Thereafter, I got tired and did rather mediocre, boring interviews.

20 March 2011, Sunday

It is Holi today—a day of contemplation. If people spoke only sense, there would be much more silence in the world than there is. This has nothing to do with Holi, just a realization on my part after fifteen months in the government and fifty-nine years in the world.

25 March 2011, Friday

Alaka and I spent three days in Washington. We left Delhi early morning on 23 March, for a non-stop Air India flight to New York and then to Washington. These long-haul flights are really a blessing. Listening to Ameen Sayani and old Hindi songs without having to look at my watch is a pleasure, as is the ability to watch and listen to old Hindi film songs. And there is the joy of sleeping, seemingly endlessly. We reached New York feeling fresh, and changed planes for Washington, still feeling energetic. So much so that I had a brief luncheon meeting hosted by Mr Senthil of the

Indian embassy and then a pre-dinner meeting with Paul Rochon, my Canadian counterpart concerning G-20 matters. Paul is such a balanced person and with such a good a sense of humour that it is always a pleasure to meet him.

24 March was a day of endless G-20 deliberations. A lot of this seems pointless to me. Or am I excessively cynical? So much of the world is nothing but conversation. Maybe conversations, even without content, contribute to amity and cooperation and, via that, to progress, and so I should not complain about the G-20 meetings. And therein lies another problem of mine. I can see both sides of everything, which is an ideal recipe for doing nothing.

The day ends with a family dinner—Alaka, me, my niece, Buiya, and her husband, Rohit.

This morning I have meetings at the IMF and then a lunch with Arvind Virmani in the World Bank's basement restaurant. The evening dinner is again with family, Alaka's sister Anjali, her husband Ramakrishna and the two of us, at Saigon Restaurant in Georgetown's M Street.

26 March 2011, Saturday

Amidst the rough and tumble of my new life, I occasionally miss the quiet of academe and university campuses. So I had decided to fit in a short Cornell break during this trip. Alaka and I traveled this morning from Washington to Ithaca, via Newark. It is cold but sunny. The Finger Lakes shimmer at a distance and the winter sun blazes over Cornell's sprawling campus. We are staying at Statler Hotel and visit 131 Cayuga Park Road, our home. The house is in good shape, very different from what happens in the tropics when you leave a house abandoned for a year. The two zebras that I had painted on our garage door stare at us like strangers. The old pictures hang from the walls and the familiar books on the shelves create a feeling of warmth and welcome. A strange sense of sadness envelopes me. Returns are always painful, probably because deep down they create a feeling of remorse. The books, the shelves, the pictures, seem to say: you abandoned us for so many months.

Thinking about myself I get a strange feeling of being adrift in life. Should I continue in the hustle and chaos of India, where one is not sad simply because one has no time to think, or return to brooding Ithaca? The person who needed me most in India, my mother, is no longer there. But there are others to worry about. And perhaps my work in India contributes a little to building a civilized society and a better economy.

27 March 2011, Sunday

Honest individuals seldom do well economically but honest societies generally do. This is the great free rider problem that societies need to overcome in order to prosper. What I mean is, for a variety of activities if we can trust one another, we can do better. If there is a society that is known to consist of trustworthy people that society will do well. In other words, such societies have evolutionary strength. They will prosper. However, individuals who are not trustworthy but part of an overall trustworthy society are likely to do even better. People will trust such a person by virtue of her group identity and then she can cheat and do even better. The success of societies depends on their ability to solve this free rider problem.

29 March 2011, Tuesday

The three days in Ithaca pass quickly. Old friends, students, coffee and conversations. We try to do a thousand things from filing tax returns to finding a tenant for our home.

We take the Cornell bus to New York in the evening.

30 March 2011, Wednesday

Today I participated in the Columbia University Roundtable on the Indian economy with Amartya Sen, Prabhat Patnaik and Joe Stiglitz. It went off extremely well; I talked freely and fluently on the big challenges confronting the Indian economy and how we were dealing with them. When you are the official 'establishment' person, as I was at this meeting, everybody is supposed to take pot shots at you and that makes it hard. But the audience and co-panelists took kindly to me. All in all, we conducted a fascinating policy discussion, exactly as great universities are supposed to do.

This was happening in USA but this is one respect in which India matches up fully to America. Prabhat is a strident critique of the Indian government's policies but there is no effort to muzzle his speech. He is openly critical of the prime minister's policy but he can argue his case in large public forum, at the Delhi School of Economics, JNU or on any campus. I disagree with Prabhat on many policy matters but we are close friends and not once has any politician tried to tell me to keep a distance from him. I think this is a great asset of our nation and has contributed to strengthening our institutions and even helped promote economic growth.

In talking about my differences with Prabhat, I should clarify that in terms of the kind of society we, ideally, want to establish, we probably share similar views. Karl Marx's dream of a society in which we work and give according to our ability and get according to our needs is ideal. It has such moral resonance. But many of the policy interventions that Prabhat and other communists would recommend would not, I believe, take us to that ideal. They may even make matters worse as happened in the USSR. So my disagreement with Prabhat and many communists is not so much in terms of the society they aspire to build, but the means that they recommend. Some of those means are much more likely to end up creating a crony-capitalist society than any kind of socialist utopia.

After the seminar Joe, Prabhat, Akeel Bilgrami, his wife Carole, Alaka and I have an informal lunch in Columbia University's Uris Hall cafeteria.

In the evening Karna, Shabnam, Alaka and I have a Korean meal. It is tastier than the lunch.

1 April 2011, Friday

Yesterday morning, I spoke at Waldorf Astoria in New York to potential investors for India. It was a meeting organized by ICICI securities. Most people abroad are impressed by how quickly India's economy pulled out after being hit by the global slump in 2008–09. It is a tribute to India's policy professionalism that we have managed this.

After the talk I had a quick lunch with my former student Vidya Atal, her husband, Sauptik, and Alaka, and then I headed to the airport to catch the flight to Delhi.

I am back in Delhi now, Alaka will return after three days. I feel an inexplicable ennui—I think the Turks call it 'huzun'—mixed with jetlag. Actually it may not be that inexplicable. It must be a manifestation of my childhood anxiety of being alone. This is no longer a serious problem and has morphed more into huzun than anxiety, but it was a problem through my childhood and even youth. My ideal was and still is to be left alone but be able to hear voices in the adjacent room. Luckily, thanks to India's over-population, most of the time you can hear voices in the adjacent room.

This aloneness may be genetically hard-wired in me. I suspect my father had it. My mother used to say that on those rare quiet days in his life, my father used to insist that my mother did whatever she was doing in the room where he was.

In addition, my father, like Mary Warnock's mother, was totally dependent on other human beings for the commonest of activities. He could never crane his neck to read the time off the clock on the wall. He would call me or one of my sisters or one of the servants and ask what the time was. In terms of lack of exercise, I have seen few people that could match my father. He was lean, tall and had almost no health problems, apart from migraine.

7 April 2011, Thursday

Last evening, Alaka and I took the Air India flight to arrive in Kolkata. Today, from 5 to 7 pm was my book release (*An Economist's Miscellany*) at Taj Bengal. Nigel Portwood, Chief Executive of Oxford University Press, Manzar Khan, Rudrangshu Mukherjee, Amitava Bose, Amit Chaudhuri and I were on the dais. It is a light, easy-to-read book and, I think, funny. The event went off splendidly.

Then Alaka and I went with Khokan Mookherji to the Bengal Chamber of Commerce, where I, yes, again spoke.

8 April 2011, Friday

I woke up bleary-eyed at 4:30 am to take the morning flight to Delhi. I was to appear as part of the Parliamentary Standing Committee on Finance in Parliament at 11 am. It was one of those high-powered meetings. Sushama Nath, Gopalan, Sumit Bose, Shashikanta Sharma and I were in the docks. We would be grilled by Yashwant Sinha (who was in the chair), Gurudas Dasgupta, Bhartruhari Mahtab, S. S. Ahluwalia and a host of opposition members of Parliament and maybe some Rajya Sabha members.

It turned out to be one of the most enjoyable days for me in the government. Since much of the discussion was on government policy to do with economics and finance, I was the focus of most of the grilling. All these people were aiming their guns at me. I took it all with aplomb. I find that a little irreverence can go a long way. Just as they grilled me, I too pointed to some of their contradictions. At one point when I was giving out some numbers, Gurudas Dasgupta said that he does not believe in statistics. Then half an hour later when I made a stray comment he asked me to substantiate my claim with statistics. I pointed out that a short while ago he said he did not believe in statistics. I could see Gurudas's friends and other opposition politicians holding back their smiles.

23 April 2011, Saturday

My life continued as usual, measured out not in coffee spoons but in meetings, committee work, and Empowered Group of Ministers (EGoMs). In recent times I have created a lot of controversy by proposing an idea for amending India's Prevention of Corruption Act, 1988. The idea is simple. By the Indian law, the giver and taker of bribes are both considered liable. I suggested that for certain kinds of bribes, where one has to give a bribe for something that is legitimate, the bribe giver should not be punished. Only the government servant taking the bribe should be treated as liable. My argument was simple. In the present situation, the bribe taker knows that after giving the bribe the bribe giver will collude with the taker to hide the fact of bribery, since otherwise both will go to jail. By making bribe giving legal, this post-bribery collusion will be disrupted. And knowing this, the bribe taker will be more hesitant to take the bribe in the first place. So corruption will decline. Much turmoil had been created with the posting of my paper with this proposal on the Ministry of Finance's website, and this continued to simmer, with occasional calls for me to be asked to resign from the government.

As part of this continuing interest in the topic, I had Barkha Dutt's office calling me repeatedly today, asking me to appear on her television show, 'We the People', the next morning, where I could explain my corruption idea and have it debated. When I finally took the call, Barkha insisted and said mine was an important idea that deserves to be discussed. I was in a dilemma. I like Barkha and I do not mind being attacked in debates. However, I was acutely aware that I had caused the government a lot of grief with the posting of my idea. Recently, newspapers reported that Communist Party member of Parliament, D. Raja, had written to the prime minister, complaining about me and my 'immoral' idea. A copy of the letter dated 23 April 2011 addressed to the prime minister, with a cc to the finance minister, not only described my suggestion for the amendment as morally flawed but also faulty as 'economic reasoning', though he gave no reason to explain why my reasoning was faulty. The letter ended asking for my paper to be taken down from the ministry's website. There was also a letter, dated 21 April, written by S. Sudhakar Reddy, former MP and deputy general secretary of the Communist Party of India, addressed to the finance minister. He also asked for the paper to be removed from the Finance Ministry's portal and went further and asked for a 'detailed probe into the real motives' for my posting the article.

Others also had written to the finance minister that my paper should be taken down from the ministry's website. I was disappointed by the members of the Communist Party getting so upset by my idea. In India, the communists are generally the more cerebral politicians. It was sad to see that instead of engaging with my interesting idea they were giving in to knee-jerk politics.

I decided that if the FM or the PM asked me to take it down, I would of course do so. They had the right to order me to do so and as a civil servant I was obliged to obey the order. However, I had the right to resign from my job, and I would do so too. To the great credit of Pranab Mukherjee and Manmohan Singh, they made no such request. They had been good to me and so, hesitating whether I would stir the debate by appearing on television on this, I thought I would do what I hated to do: ask their advice on whether I should appear and try to clarify my thoughts on corruption control.

I told Barkha I would call her back soon and hung up. I learned that the finance minister was away in Vietnam. So I called the prime minister's residence and said that I wanted to talk to Dr Singh. Within ten minutes the prime minister called back. I asked him if he had advice for me about whether I should appear on Barkha's program on corruption control and risk stirring the pot. This was the first time I was talking to him directly about my corruption paper, though we had been going back and forth through intermediaries as the controversy brewed. Manmohan Singh began by saying that he had of course received the complaints about my idea from members of Parliament and read some of the newspaper reports, though he had not read my paper on the Finance Ministry website. He went on to add that on the basis of what he had read, he did not agree with the amendment to India's corruption control law that I had proposed. I tried to gently defend my proposal but he sounded adamant that he disagreed with me. Beyond a point, how much can you argue with the prime minister and so I kept quiet, expecting him to say that I should stay off the debate and let the idea die a natural death.

But what he said next caught me by surprise. He comforted me by saying controversy was a part of political life, so I should not be perturbed. Then he added that though he disagreed with my idea and it was causing him political difficulty, that did not mean that I should not speak about it. The role of an adviser is to bring ideas to the table, even if they are controversial. So I should feel free to appear on Barkha Dutt's program. The decision, he said, was mine.

On putting down the phone, I called Barkha's office and declined.

This was a remarkable experience for me. It showed up a side of the prime minister which was quite extraordinary. It takes a quiet courage (not the school yard bully's behavior, which many voters mistakenly equate with courage) to give others the space that he gave me.

27 April 2011, Wednesday

On the 24th I took the night flight to Mumbai for an Exim Bank Board Meeting, catching glimpses on television of Barkha Dutt devoting her 'We the People' to my idea of bribery control. Like always on Indian television, it was a shouting match.

25 April was devoted to the Exim Bank meeting. We went through lots of details of projects and investments in various countries. I like the meticulousness of this kind of work, even though I am no good at it myself. What disappoints me is that there is so little scope for big ideas. I had once or twice raised an interesting, if somewhat Machiavellian idea, of whether India should consider lending money to countries in rupees. Since the Indian rupee is not a properly convertible currency in the international financial markets, the countries that get Indian rupees will be forced to buy from Indian companies, government or individuals. This would give a boost to Indian sales. This would effectively be a tied credit policy. I would be open to discuss the pros and cons of this policy, including its ethical implications, but unfortunately, we never get to that. I was simply told this is not the way we lend.

This is what convinces me that the obstruction to change and dynamic policy comes much more from the rusty thinking habits of bureaucrats than vested interests of groups.

I met Diksha at Salt Water in Bandra, one of my favorite restaurants and took the red eye to Singapore. 26 April and, today the 27th, passed in a string of meetings in Singapore, with plenty of discussion on the pros and cons of starting a sovereign wealth fund in India, Singapore being a success story of sovereign wealth fund (SWF). The standard response to this is that SWFs should be set up if you have a windfall gain, like Norway did with the discovery of North Sea oil, or you are an exporter of some critical commodity. I don't buy this argument. A small segment of our foreign exchange reserve, say 5 per cent of it, tucked away as a SWF can be put to some critical use for stabilization. It is true that India is an oil importer. But if oil prices suddenly fall, instead of treating this as a boost to immediate consumption, some of this can be tucked away in the SWF, to be used when oil prices begin to rise again and put a strain on the economy.

I also get to spend some time with India's very gracious high commissioner, T. C. A. Raghavan, and have dinner at his stunning residence. Among other things, we discussed which individual politicians are corrupt.

Amidst all this, the Tanglin Club of Singapore organized a discussion of my book *Beyond the Invisible Hand*. This is a non-technical book, true, but full of nuanced economic and philosophical arguments. It is a testimony to Singapore's excellent education system that the discussion turned out to be of uniform high quality.

28 April 2011, Thursday

I got to see the prime minister for a one-on-one meeting at 7 RCR this evening, from 7:15 pm to 7:40 pm. We had *lassi* and brainstormed about the Indian economy. I can see how he will go down as a major figure in India's economic take off. Unlike other politicians, he wastes no time on political trivia, and quickly gets down to policy imperatives. This must have played a role in India's remarkable growth take off after he became the PM in 2005.

For me too this is a great relief from the hurly burly of Indian politics. In some sense, both for him and for me these periodic discussions are a form of escapism but ultimately they are useful in designing and implementing policy. Today we touched on monetary policy as an instrument of inflation control. I feel with globalization each country's monetary policy has become less effective, because what central banks do elsewhere has a huge impact on your economy. The US Fed injecting liquidity in olden days would boost US growth and prices. Now that impact goes all over the world, making monetary policy and liquidity flows less effective in USA and creates upward price pressure elsewhere— India, China, Vietnam.

We also talked about multi-product retail operations in India. In India, the gap between what farmers get and what consumers pay is one of the highest in the world—I had the data collected some time ago. The Indian middlemen are the cause of this. The way to break this is to let some big retail corporations like Walmart into India. As soon as you do so, critics will scream that we are enabling big corporations to exploit India. It is difficult to explain, that often the choice is between two evils. And once you are at the helm of policymaking you do not have the luxury of the critic, who can be against all the available choices.

We also talked about corruption control. I can see that corruption troubles him greatly since he is so fastidious in his personal behavior. There are people who tell me that if Manmohan Singh is so strongly against corruption, he should resign from the government, given that there is corruption in the government. What these people miss out on is, by this argument, every honest person should immediately resign from the government since there is always some corruption. The fact of the matter is, when you join any government, you have to be prepared to tolerate some bad behavior on the part of others. Otherwise you will not last a day. At the same time, I think there has to be a line. There are certain kinds of behavior you do not want to be associated with and, if you see such behavior in a senior leader in the government, you have to make it clear: either you have that person or you have me. I can think of individuals such that, if I had to work with them, I would refuse to serve in such a government, no matter how coveted the job.

8 May 2011, Sunday

There is a write-up on me in the *Indian Express* Sunday magazine, 'Eye', today. Some days ago my office set up an interview for me to be done at my home by an *Express* journalist. I was all set for the usual round of boring questions: Will inflation come down? ('Yes', though in reality 'Don't know' would be the correct answer). Will there be a slowdown in India's growth? ('No', though in reality 'Don't know'). Are we going to hold on to our fiscal deficit limits? ('Likely yes', which could also be reworded to 'Likely no').

I call these questions boring but of course I understand. These are all-India concerns and if a journalist does not ask the chief economic adviser, whom will they ask. So I was ready, they would do their job and I would do mine.

The interview turned out to be refreshingly different. A young woman called Shruti Ravindran showed up at home. She had the irreverent style of the troublemaker student in class and her interests were off the beaten track.

I can see those qualities in the rather unusual and well-written interview. She has titled it 'The Man with the 23-Page CV'. If I knew this would be the title I would have used a larger fontsize for my CV.

18 May 2011, Wednesday

This evening, I delivered the First Gautam Mathur Memorial Lecture at the India Habitat Centre. When invited I was keen to do it because of my regard for Gautam Mathur.

My lecture was titled 'Inflation: The Emperor of Economic Maladies'. So much of my first year-and-a-half has been spent on inflation management that I thought it was time to do some stock-taking. I wanted to persuade people that once inflation gets sparked, bringing it down without bringing the entire economy to its knees is not easy. Moreover, in today's age of globalization, when goods, services and liquidity flow across national borders with alacrity, inflation has a lot to do with policies being formed beyond your borders. The US Fed is injecting liquidity into the American economy to jump start it. Unlike in the olden days when this would be an effective tool because a lot of the liquidity would remain within the USA, today a lot of the money is ending up all over the world. We thus see inflationary pressures in India, Vietnam, China and Turkey. And for the same reason, the Fed's policy is not having as much success in getting the USA to grow and create jobs as would happen in earlier times.

Montek Singh Ahluwalia was the commentator for my lecture. He was in high spirits, which showed in his comments and the whole event went off well. This pleased me immensely since I really liked Gautam Mathur. He was an old-fashioned left-wing economist, with a heart of gold and totally obsessed with research. I believe he was from one of the wealthy Hindu families from Lahore, who rejected his own class status, though he could never quite get rid of bourgeois charm.

From the lecture, Alaka and I went for dinner to the residence of Nirupama Rao and Sudhakar. It is a beautiful home, decorated with artefacts from around the world, reflecting Nirupama's career in the foreign service, as Indian ambassador to several countries and now as foreign secretary, and also her good aesthetic sense.

The dinner guests included the Afghan and Sri Lankan ambassadors, the Odissi dancer, Ranjana Gauhar, the television magnate Preetham Parigi, and several other interesting people. At dinner's end there was a surprise. Nirupama and some others sang

English classical songs and light '70s stuff, with a gifted Sri Lankan lady playing the piano.

7 June 2011, Tuesday

Two days ago, Dipak Dasgupta, Gyan Bhushan and I came to Guwahati. We stayed at Ashok Brahmaputra. I love this city and the state. Assam is like Bengal of yesteryear, with old-fashioned homes and music spilling out of windows, with people who are friendly and welcoming, and the vast Brahmaputra River, immortalized in Bhupen Hazarika's song, quietly flowing in the background.

I had dinner at a restaurant with Nilay Dutta and Mridu Kagti, my old St Stephen's friends. It brought back memories of my Stephen's days—leaving home for the first time for me, new friendships being struck and then watching the rise of the Naxalite movement. Nilay was among the eighteen or nineteen students who abandoned college to join the Maoist-Naxalite revolution. We had dinner while talking about our college days, contemporary politics and economics.

Yesterday morning, Dipak, Gyan and I flew to Dimapur, had breakfast at Hotel Saramati and set out by car for Kohima. In Guwahati I asked some people how long the drive would take from Dimapur to Kohima. One of them said, 'If you have a Naga driver, you will reach Kohima very quick.' And someone else added, 'If you reach Kohima.' As it turned out, we did have a Naga driver and reached fast. I discovered the technique the driver was using. He drove in as much of a straight line as possible on a curving road. It is like placing a rope from Dimapur to Kohima along the road. Then pulling the rope from the two ends to make it taut and then using the rope as the path to drive on.

It is a one-day visit to this enchanting place. I am here to present the *Economic Survey 2010–11* and to discuss regional

economic problems. Immediately on arrival we were taken to a
lunch hosted by Professor Kannan, vice chancellor of Nagaland
University, and headed out after that to Khonoma Village, with
a brief halt at the War Memorial. Khonoma is about an hour's
drive from Kohima. With a population of barely 3,000, the village
is quite remarkable. With high literacy and progressive mindsets,
the villagers have created a virtual 'village republic'—reminds me
of Robert Wade's book with the same title. In 1993, the villagers
had started a green movement, and it was declared a green zone
in 2005. There are dustbins at regular intervals along the village
paths, with signs saying 'Maintained by KSO (Khonoma Students
Organization)'. Inhabitants of Khonoma have been instructed not
to put detergents in the local tanks. Restrictions are placed on
hunting to make sure that animal life flourishes. I have a meeting
with Mr Phizo. Though that does not quite distinguish him since
everyone here seems to have that name, he is the village leader. He
is an impressive person.

It is a working dinner in the evening with Alem Temshi Jamir,
from the IAS, A. K. Das of the State Bank of India, T. Kire
from the Nagaland Government, and some others including
representatives from the EXIM Bank. We talked about the local
economy, and what is closely related to that, namely, the problems
of insurgency, which though limited now, is not non-existent.

Yesterday was the formal meeting. I gave a short talk on the
'Economic Survey', and went on to discuss the great potential
for North-East India. This does not need too much effort on my
part because I keep feeling India's North-East has the potential
to be the growth leader for the full country. We have to get a few
key policies and institutions in place and we can trigger a take-
off for Nagaland and the entire region. We have discussions with
David Sinate of the EXIM Bank, Lal Thara, chief secretary of the
Nagaland Government, and some local officials.

I utilize the few moments when I am not in meetings, to
walk around the streets. This is a land of fairytale beauty. The

hilly terrain, the homes, and the people are beautiful and both men and women have a natural elegance. It is difficult to believe that this was once a region of serious insurgency. Nowhere do I feel uncomfortable as an obvious outsider. In recent times, the village has been receiving a trickle of tourists from around India. Chatting with people on the roadside, I gather they also had some tourists from South Korea. The people here seem to love Korea. Some of them believe they are descendants of Koreans.

8 June 2011, Wednesday

I am back in Delhi. Bureaucrats must learn to use three words more often: 'I don't know.' And they must not thereafter get into long arguments on whether these are three words or four.

I met Gopal Gandhi in the afternoon to discuss the appointment of a new vice chancellor for Visva-Bharati, in Santiniketan. He is chairing the search committee, and U. R. Ananthamurthy, one of India's most celebrated (and controversial) writers, and I are members of the search committee. I have a soft spot for Visva-Bharati, for Santiniketan, for Gopal Gandhi and for Ananthamurthy, and so when I was asked to serve on this committee I agreed promptly, and it is turning out to be work that I enjoy. I could not have asked for a better group to work with. Both Gopal Gandhi and Ananthamurthy are intellectually strong and amply endowed with a sense of fairness and moral courage. These are important in doing selection-committee work in India because, inevitably, there is effort to influence the decision by people with self-interest. It is evident that none of us is the kind who would give in to this kind of pressure. I may add that one of my proudest moments was when I used to handle admissions at the Delhi School of Economics and refused to admit the vice chancellor's daughter, who did not have adequate grades, but nevertheless wanted to join the Delhi School as a student.

I have got to appreciate Gopal Gandhi greatly from the interactions I have already had with him. He has held high office, having been governor of West Bengal, but is a person of humility with a sense of right and wrong. The one gentle disagreement we may have had was during a conversation we were having about Rudrangshu Mukherjee's book, *Great Speeches of Modern India*. We were both praising the book, when I said that I was particularly appreciative of the fact that the collection included the last speech of the man who killed Gandhi, Nathuram Godse. I told him this was a good editorial decision because people should be exposed to all sides and also that it makes one proud of India's freedom of speech and publication that we can publish a book that contains a speech by the man who killed the Father of the Nation. From his brief response, I felt he disagreed with me. In retrospect, that is so understandable—it was probably insensitive of me to bring this topic up—because for him Gandhiji was not just the founder of modern India but a grandfather who was assassinated when he was barely three years old.

9 June 2011, Friday

I met Pranab Mukherjee today. We are all troubled about the relentless inflation that India is having to cope with and for him as finance minister, it is particularly distressing. I explained to him that there is no way to halt this suddenly through government diktat as used to be tried in the olden days, with prices and income policies and announcements of price caps. These are almost impossible to implement and if implemented successfully will give rise to shortages and queues like seen in the USSR and other communist countries. We have to persist with a combination of fiscal and monetary tightening and this will have an effect with a lag. What was also complicating matters was that the injection of money in rich countries, in particular the USA, was cascading through the world and causing upward pressure on prices everywhere. India's inflation rate in recent times has hovered between 8 and 10 per cent per annum. By global standards this is not high inflation. People in many Latin American countries would laugh at anyone complaining about this level of inflation. But India has historically been a low inflation country and people are upset and this does not augur well for the political party in power.

After that we went on to talk about Bengal politics. He clearly has a soft spot for Mamata Banerjee and said how she has some remarkable qualities and added that, if she could develop a few other complementary qualities, she would go great guns.

Pranab Mukherjee was in a friendly mood and told me that he wants me to stay on beyond the two years that we initially agreed upon. In fact, he said I should stay on for 'some more years'. I told him that that is unlikely, given that I am on leave from another job and that, all said and done, I am a researcher and want to get back to that.

17 June 2011, Friday

The Sydney mission comes to an end tomorrow morning when I head back to Delhi. It began on June 15th with me giving the first Australia-India Institute lecture at the University of New South Wales on 'The Arrival of the Indian Economy'. Kevin Fox hosts dinner for Alaka and me at Icebergs on Bondi Beach, with Alan Woodland, Alan's wife, and a few other people.

Yesterday was spent on several one-on-one meetings and dinner at the home of Gautam Bose and his wife Lakshmi. It turned out to be a good old academic style evening—with good Bengali-Australian food, meeting up with researchers I had heard of earlier but not met, and more than anything else, adda.

Today turned out to be a most interesting day. I gave a regular departmental seminar on 'A Model of Financial Crises'. This is a theoretical model I had constructed in the nooks and crannies of my policy life to explain the suddenness of the Great Recession of 2008. I was glad to have an opportunity to give a research seminar. So I worked hard for it and gave a decent lecture. It was the retreat into my old life that made it so interesting. The talk was followed by an excellent dinner at Seviche's, with Gautam Bose, Alberto Motta, his Romanian wife, Isabella, and a Dutch-Greek French-speaking economist whose name I did not catch.

In the morning today, I had a most interesting meeting with the famed governor of the Reserve Bank of Australia, Glenn Stevens, in his office. Amit Dasgupta, India's senior-most envoy in Sydney, and two of his advisers, sat in as observers. We had an excellent conversation, discussing Indo-Australian economic relations, the challenge of inflation management, the nature of autonomy of the RBA and some of our shared concerns about global liquidity. Amit had told me that Glenn Stevens was a quiet, thinking person and it turned out to be a slow brooding conversation. There seemed to be a sadness to him. He spoke softly but clearly, enunciating both his ideas and words clearly. The top job of the central bank everywhere is almost a mystical job and there is a sense of loneliness involved in being at the helm of managing a nation's money. The central bank governor's job is part science and part guesswork, intuition and commonsense—mysticism?—and I sensed this more with Glenn Stevens than other central bank governors I have interacted with.

One of economics' great caveats is the link between the world of money and the general equilibrium system of goods and services developed by Leon Walras, Kenneth Arrow, Gerard Debreu and Lionel McKenzie. When I was a PhD student at LSE in the mid-1970s and for some years then on, there were a host of top mathematical researchers trying to integrate money into a general equilibrium system. Names like Yves Younes, Frank Hahn, Yves Balasko and Jean-Michel Grandmont easily come to mind.

But the problem turned out to be mathematically too difficult and was never fully resolved, which meant that a touch of mysticism was unavoidable in the central banker's top job.

Meeting Amit Dasgupta after so long was also wonderful and at the same time a source of melancholy because it brought back so much nostalgia. Amit and I were classmates in Kolkata, at St Xavier's School. Amit was one of the more anglicized students in our class. He spoke better English than most of us and lived in an anglicized part of Kolkata, on Park Street. We would occasionally go to each other's homes. He joined the Indian civil service and we lost contact. I would hear about him, mainly about his bravado in trying to control corruption. He had some run-ins with some prominent politicians, whose behavior was truly shameful. Amit was always upright and had a child-like enthusiasm for detective stories, and tried to live some of that in his work life.

22 June 2011, Wednesday

I am back in Delhi, and feeling tired, with a slight cold. But Government of India is not a place for leisure. After a short rest I am back at work. In the evening, at 7:30 pm, there is the important EGoM meeting to discuss a turnaround plan for Air India. It is attended by Finance Minister Mukherjee, Jaipal Reddy, Montek, Union Minister of Overseas Affairs Vayalar Ravi and a bunch of senior bureaucrats. It is quite evident that Air India is a real dismal story, guzzling money and delivering poorly. But I don't think there is any hope of being able to privatize it, not because of vested interest as for force of habit. I personally think it should be privatized and suggested that to senior ministers, including Pranab Mukherjee in private conversations, but decided that trying to push this would be a waste of time.

Montek spoke eloquently at the meeting. He is really a cut above most of our politicians. Like Manmohan Singh, his primary interest is to implement good policy. It is this commitment of his that makes it a pleasure to work with him. Ideologically he is to my right for sure, but that is not so important in day-to-day policy decision making. The ideological breadth of the feasible set of what can be implemented is usually small; and so in everyday policymaking these differences do not matter much. On the other hand, the scope for making plain, simple policy mistakes is so large that clarity of thought and the intention to be effective and not be guided purely by political gain is more important than anything else.

If I were writing a manifesto for where I want India to be over the next twenty-five years, I would not want to do it with Montek as co-author. But in terms of crafting effective, short-term policies it is a pleasure to work with him. India is lucky to have a professional like him at the helm. It is a pity he is not politically powerful enough to push his ideas through.

Speaking of ideology, I am instinctively left-wing. I would love to see the kind of world Karl Marx envisaged—fair, equitable and free of exploitation. But I also know that it is not easy to get to such an ideal world (and maybe it will forever be beyond our reach). It is utterly foolish to do what many left ideologues have done, which is to delude oneself into believing that it is easy to get there. Many of these left ideologues, I am sure, would consider me no friend of theirs, but that is only because of their own confusion. One can see their lack of clarity in major global experiments. By the late 1980s, the USSR was basically a crony capitalist society, captured by a few money hawks and power hawks. That was not the intention of the revolutionaries of 1917 and the early communists of Russia, but it was the outcome of their foolishness. Big government must not be the mantra of the left.

Looking at Air India, I am convinced 'big government' is folly, at least at this stage of world history. Governments are generally wasteful and unnecessarily intrusive. My ideological view is that a government ought to be a lean body that taxes the rich and transfers the money to the poor. The government must not hold on to the tax revenue and grow big. Sooner or later it will get captured. But the marginal tax rate for the super-rich should be super-high, including possibly a cap, which means a marginal tax rate of 100 per cent, beyond a certain level. It is utterly wrong to have the level of inequality that we currently do. And this I say with no anger about the super-rich. They have got what the rules of the current game allow. There are a few evil ones but, in general, the fault is not theirs, but of the rules of the game. Indeed I like to believe that there are some super rich who agree with me and believe that though they will not unilaterally give up any of their wealth, ideally, all of them should give up a huge amount of their wealth and see it transferred to the poor.

27 June 2011, Monday

I left early morning, yesterday for the USA. It was a long flight, one of the longest in the world, nonstop from Delhi to Chicago. I love these long flights. Sleep for eight hours, listen to music, read. And Air India has the best collection of old Hindi film songs, dripping with romance, culturally diverse with strains of the Islamic and Persian, influenced by the music and poetry of Rabindranath Tagore, with touches of jazz and rock. It is quite a staggering achievement for India to have created such a diverse and inclusive society.

I reached Washington—the eternal Willard Straight Hotel— in time for a late room-service lunch. I pretty much stayed in my room all day preparing for the numerous meetings over the next two days and for the USA–India bilateral gala, organized by CII and Brookings where I was to give the opening keynote.

The US–India conference at Willard began this morning with a brief inaugural session, with Strobe Talbott, Lael Brainard and others. Then in the first main session, chaired by Kemal Dervis, I gave a keynote address on India's growth prospects. In these public lectures on policy, I have now learnt, the topic is unimportant. No matter what the topic, one gives roughly the same lecture—growth, inflation and globalization, interspersed with light-hearted tales. It's the tales that I enjoy most.

In the evening, Surendra Bagde and I went to Kramers and then had a bite at Teaism. Among my junior colleagues in the government, Surendra is one of the most intellectually gifted. We chat about policy and also research, even though that world seems so far away.

28 June 2011, Tuesday

The day begins with a high-powered meeting in the US Treasury to iron out a variety of Indo–US matters. The USA side has Tim Geithner, Ben Bernanke, Gene Sperling, Mary Schapiro, Lael Brainard and a few others; our side has Pranab Mukherjee, Subba Rao, the governor of the Reserve Bank of India, Secretary Gopalan and a few others. It is a nice session where, off camera, we have the more serious discussion of Indo–US economic relations.

In the evening, the Indian ambassador, Meera Shankar, hosts a dinner. I am at the high table with the ambassador, the finance minister, Acting Director of the IMF John Lipsky, William Cohen, former defense secretary of USA, Sandy Berger, Purnendu Chatterjee, Aneesh Chopra and another Cohen—I never caught the name. It is a pleasant evening in a home of great splendor.

30 June 2011, Thursday

On the Washington–Chicago flight yesterday, I am seated next to an US Airforce pilot, Col. Robert ('Stix') Martin. He says he rarely travels first-class and so laps up the little luxuries. He turns out to be an extremely pleasant and well-informed person. He used to fly F-15s. We chat about his experience in Iraq and Saudi Arabia, and briefly about India.

On the long Chicago–Delhi flight, I watch *Pakeezah*. Maybe it is the ambience of the cabin and the absence of other preoccupations that makes the film magically beautiful. The dialogue is like Urdu poetry, the film drips with old-style romance, Meena Kumari and all the other women are stunningly beautiful, and it has music to die for.

I arrive in Delhi this morning and plunge into activity. To work for the Indian government is the best way to deal with jet-lag. There is just no time for it.

11 July 2011, Thursday

On the 6th, Alaka and I took off for Geneva and from there we took the train to Lausanne. We are here to lecture at EPFL—this has become an annual affair. This time we have accommodation on the edge of the campus. It is not as grand as our usual Chatteau d'Ouchy on the lake, but it is beautiful in an austere way. A maize field stretches endlessly outside our window like a Van Gogh painting. There is light, casting long shadows, till late evening. After the hurly burly of Delhi this is sheer heaven. Ghalib must have meant Lausanne.

The following day I gave my marathon six-hour lecture on the Indian economy. Before I began working as adviser to the Indian government this kind of a lecture would mean several days of preparation. It always took me more time to prepare for a policy lecture than for economic theory. No longer.

Yesterday we came for a day to Berne to stay at the beautiful home of Hans-Peter and Beatrix, who are not around.

Today morning, I had a meeting with State Secretary for Foreign Affairs Michael Ambuhl, in Geneva. I was taking advantage of being in Switzerland and had this informal meeting set up. Much of the discussion was on exchange rate management, in which the Swiss have had a lot of experience in recent years. I have some novel ideas on how to use 'market methods' to control the exchange rate. I do not want to tell him what my ideas are—I would keep them for India; but I want to know what the Swiss are doing.

From the meeting I went directly to the airport to catch a flight to London and from there to Delhi.

17 July 2011, Sunday

I flew yesterday to Kolkata with Alaka and Karna. Our home feels desolate. Bijoy, who looked after my mother in her last days and now maintains the Kolkata home for us, is not around—he has had surgery and gone home for a break. My mother's bedroom is perfectly set up as though she has just stepped out. There is the beautiful wooden almirah with a large mirror. I remember it from as far back as my memory stretches. There is the small steel cupboard with small idols of gods and goddesses on it, and some burnt out incense sticks, exactly as they must have been when mother died last year. Because of her long life she was a part and parcel of my life. But no more. Life is strange. Why do we show up and why do we disappear? And why do we have minds that ask such questions?

We had lunch today at didi's (my eldest sister's) house. This is a ritual in Kolkata. Didi is my half-sister. Her mother died on giving birth to her. But we are very close. In fact, I did not know my mother was not her mother until I was eight or nine years old, when a sly man who used to visit my father told me while waiting to see my father outside his chamber. I ran in, distressed, to tell my mother of the utter nonsense of what he was saying. My mother confirmed that he was a wicked person telling the truth.

20 July 2011, Wednesday

The shuttling between cities is getting exhausting. On 18 July, I gave a lecture at IMI, Kolkata, with Harsh Goenka, Amitava Bose, and of course, students and faculty in the audience. On 19th morning I flew to Delhi, worked all day in office and caught the evening flight to Bangalore. And all morning today I have been locked in a meeting with U. R. Ananthamurthy in connection with the search for the new vice chancellor for Visva-Bharati.

Gopal Gandhi could not come. He sent me a nice, funny letter. He said he had been unwell but was hoping that he would be well in time for this meeting. He said he even tried prayer but it did not work because, unlike me, he has prayed too often (referring to my Hakone experience in Japan, which I had written about), and God does not seem to respond to him.

In the evening there was a book release event for my *An Economist's Miscellany* at the Bangalore International Center. Dasgupta and Ravichander were on stage with me. It was a whopping success. I was in good form. And it also helped to have an intelligent audience.

The PM phoned me late evening, saying that we need to take stock of a range of policy matters and need more coordination across different branches of government. I told him I would see him in Delhi tomorrow.

21 July 2011, Thursday

I met with the prime minister at his residence at 11.40 am. It was an intense one-on-one meeting for about thirty minutes. We talked about the fact that India's growth was stalling. He is clearly despondent about something, which reflects on his views about the state of the economy. He lamented that he has become a 'reactive' leader. I suppose what he meant was that he is perennially in fire-fighting mode, having to react to the problem immediately on hand. He no longer has the time to build up policy plans from inception to execution that he had done so effectively when he was finance minister in the early 1990s. If that was what he meant, that is indeed true. Prime ministers and presidents rarely have the luxury to be able to build ideas and plans from scratch. Most prime ministers and presidents relish politics so much that they don't mind this. Manmohan Singh's difference is, he does.

Our conversation drifts to the Indian Economic Service and we talk at length about this. As chief economic adviser I am the boss of the Indian Economic Service. There are over 400 IES officers, mostly based in Delhi. It is an immensely talented group and I have found them to be an asset. I had been thinking for a while that the IES should be a service with state-based cadres, akin to the Indian Administrative Service (IAS) or Indian Police Service (IPS). I told him that one problem with economic policymaking in India is that, while there was a lot of talent in Delhi, every time I phoned some state capital to discuss some local matter it was obvious that there was a dearth of skills there. I told him that I hoped that, before my term was over, I would make the IES a larger state-based service.[9]

23 July 2011 Saturday

It is a busy day in office but the morning is devoted to something unusual and altogether pleasurable—designing a calendar to celebrate fifty years of the IES. The budget I have is small but I have been able to persuade one of the greatest living Indian artists, Sanjay Bhattacharya, who is a friend of mine, to do twelve quick sketches for the twelve months. To minimize controversy, I have decided that the sketches will be of Nobel laureates, with

---

9. This did not happen.

two exceptions. There will be one page devoted to Kautilya and one to Keynes. I spent much of the morning working with Sanjay Bhattacharya and a few others in my office on the design of the 'Nobel laureates' calendar. It is a learning process to see how fussy an artist is about art. I suppose the way I am about writing a paper. It does dismay me about how little thought bureaucrats give when they write papers. They do fuss about some details, but the wrong ones. I suppose it is the same in reverse between Sanjay and me. He must have been getting impatient about what I was fussing over and what I was happy to gloss over.

After they leave, I write a letter to the prime minister (he has asked for this) about the new Food Security Bill and what its weaknesses were. I believe a right to food law is a good idea but its current design needs lots of correction. Well-meaning activists push for too many needs to be enshrined as rights—the Right to X, Y and Z, unmindful of the critical principle, commonly attributed to Immanuel Kant: 'ought implies can'. When you say someone has a right to something (or someone ought to get something), it must be the case that there is some way to fulfil that right. An ought or a right that is not feasible is a meaningless normative injunction.

It is for this reason that I have opposed giving everyone the right to work that some activists have pushed for. I have clashed with activists on this, on the simple ground that I do not think in a large and complex economy such as India, this right is feasible. There is no way we can guarantee everyone gets a job. To write down every basic need as a right recognized by the government is a travesty of the 'ought implies can' principle. It is actually worse. By declaring too many such rights which by definition will not be satisfied, we debase the nation's law and the meaning of rights itself. Then when we declare a right that can be guaranteed, no one pays heed to it. The law languishes on paper, as happens for so many laws in India.

The right to food, I think, is feasible. Government can guarantee this because it can take steps to ensure it is fulfilled. But even with such rights, we have to keep in mind that there may arise times when there is an aggregate shortfall in food. In those times, everyone cannot be guaranteed a basic minimum food. We should spell out explicitly how we would handle those special occasions, when the 'can' of the Kantian injunction may not be fulfilled.

Economics today is such a vast subject that it is virtually impossible to command expertise over its range. Yet—and I feel this especially now, being the CEA—people often expect that of you. I recall talking to Amartya Sen about this. Amartyada told me that he became acutely aware of this after he got the Nobel Prize. People called on him to speak and comment on subjects far and wide, unmindful of his expertise or assuming that being a Nobel laureate he knew it all. He said he used to accept a lot of this immediately after he won the prize, mainly not to disappoint people. But he decided he would have to put his foot down after he got an invitation to give a keynote address to a conference on lower back pain.

He told me another funny story, leaving it a bit ambiguous if it was about himself or someone else. It went somewhat along these lines. A Nobel laureate of economics was asked by the central bank governor of a small African nation what his views were about the fact that the nation's repo rate was 8 per cent at that time. Now Sen (or whoever the Nobel laureate was) had no clue what a repo rate was. But, being a laureate, he felt he could not disappoint his interlocutor by telling him the truth.

So he decided on the only other available strategy in such situations, which was to deduce what the repo rate was through some deft questioning, and then join in the discussion. So he asked the governor, 'Are you sure you need to keep the repo rate at that level? What is your reasoning behind that?' Reverential as ever, the governor said, 'Really? You think it is too low? If *you* feel that way, I can raise it by 25 basis points.' That, of course, did not help him understand what it was. So he persisted: 'Tell me, do you really think that 25 basis points would make a difference? What would it do, according to you?' To his dismay, the governor looked worried and responded, 'You think 25 basis points increase will not have any effect. I should, in that case, raise it by 50 points.'

The conversation went on for a while and the Nobel laureate said that, while he was no wiser at the end of it, what he knew was that he had ended up raising whatever it was from 8 to 9 per cent in that nation. He took the early morning flight out of the country the following day.

4

Home and the World

24 July 2011, Sunday

I take the Air India flight to London. The first four seats abreast are taken up by me, Gopalan, Gopalan's daughter and the finance minister. Over these last few months Gopalan has become a very good friend. He also, despite being a career bureaucrat, has a research streak in him. His daughter is a student of economics. We get to chat a lot. The two flight attendants in service in our section are Bengalis. So the main language in our cabin, as we head to England, is Bengali.

I chat briefly with Pranab Mukherjee. He is relaxed and, after we discuss FDI flows from India to UK, and how this has been outstripping flows from UK to India in some recent years, we start talking about Bengali literature. He tells me the story of Rajsekhar Basu's *Ulta-Puran* (including the bits about 'Jochhonadi' and 'pora mukh'). We both laugh loudly.

Pranab Mukherjee has gone up in my esteem after one recent incident. During my search committee work for the vice chancellor of Visva-Bharati, Santiniketan, Pranab Mukherjee one day called me to the finance minister's office and asked me for a briefing of how the search was going. After a little bit of discussion, it seemed clear that he was pushing for a particular candidate, whom he praised a lot. I later thought about it and felt that that was not a good enough candidate for this. I told Gopal Gandhi about my feelings and told him that if he agreed with me, I would resist the pressure. I then told the finance minister that we did not agree with his suggestion and that we as members of the search committee had therefore decided not to choose the person he was recommending.

I never had any second thoughts about the line I took. I was on the search committee and not the finance minister. He certainly had the right to suggest names and even push them, but I had the right to turn his recommendations down. I was nevertheless worried that I would have to face his wrath. Most politicians cannot stand their 'suggestions' not being treated as order. But much to my surprise, he never raised the matter again and did not show the slightest displeasure. Whether he was always like this or he showed some special respect for me I do not know but I greatly appreciated the way he conducted himself on this.

25 July 2011, Monday

The reason we are in London is the UK–India Economic and Financial Dialogue. There are several meetings and in one of them I had an important address to make to a small but distinguished audience, which included the Indian finance minister, of course, but also the UK Chancellor of Exchequer George Osborne, Lord Adair Turner, Creon Butler, Nick Joicey, Spencer Dale and several others, including some Indian government secretaries. It is a sign of how flat the world has become compared to colonial times that I feel completely comfortable giving my address to this group. It is also a sign of British decency that they have taken the descent from their colonial heights with grace and maybe even a bit of embarrassment about their own behavior in the past. I gave a summary of the recent challenges faced by the Indian economy and how we were handling it. I discussed the scope for greater economic collaboration and interaction between India and the United Kingdom. Using some excellent analysis done by my team from the IES, I commented on growth, inflation and the course of monetary policy we could expect to see in the near future in UK, Sweden, Switzerland and Norway, adding that, 'It is a sign of India's changing status that we nowadays track industrialized economies the way the industrialized economies used to track emerging economies.' I thought I saw George Osborne smile. I gently admonished the Bank of England for not raising interest rates. After my talk, Spencer Dale, from the Bank of England, explained why the economists in the central bank felt that inflation would peter out on its own.

I went on to discuss the challenge of regulating the financial sector that we faced in India and how we had our own 'Too Big to Fail' problem and we felt the need for our own version of the Dodd Frank legislation, adding that, 'I have to confess that my repeat attempt to read the Dodd-Frank law ended in failure, with sleep intercepting.' I thought I saw George Osborne smile again. I then went on to make quite an important point I think. I argued that by putting up extra capital to shore up big corporations against future risk we were of course enabling ourselves to deal better with the failure of big corporation. But at the same time by providing these buffers we were creating a moral hazard problem by encouraging decision-makers within corporations to take more risk. What we need to do instead is device systems where, when big corporations fail, we shore up the corporations but make the decision-makers within the corporations pay a price, including the possibility of foreclosure on some of their personal wealth. In a later discussion Adair Turner expressed some sympathy for this.

The final segment of my lecture was on Tony Blair's favorite topic—Public Private Partnerships (PPPs). I told them of various PPP projects in India but went on to warn that we have to be wary of some of the risks of PPPs as well. The first two Ps of the PPPs are such different creatures that having them together is like having a tiger and a sheep in the same cage. There is a risk of one P, the private, eating up P, the public. While speaking, I remembered a wonderful cartoon, I think from the *Daily Telegraph*, which was meant to be a critique of Tony Blair going on and on about the virtues of PPPs. The cartoon showed a man about to be operated in a hospital, and the anesthesiologist telling him that he would not give him any anesthetic and instead giving him a lecture on the benefits of PPP. It would have the same effect. I held myself back from telling this joke for fear that if I made George Osborne smile a third time it could hurt Indo–UK relations.

My talk on the dangers of bringing two very different Ps together stuck a chord with the chancellor. He went on to point out that in several British public–private partnership deals the government has come out bruised. He gave an example from Leeds, where the private player walked away leaving government to bear the loss. These PPP contracts have to be very carefully crafted and the private sector usually brings in so much specialized talent to the drafting table that the multi-tasking career bureaucrat cannot match up to it.

28 July 2011, Thursday

I arrived in Mumbai last evening, checked in to my hotel, and went over next door to the Oberoi Trident for a formal dinner with T. C. A. Ranganathan (host), Yu Yongding (chief guest), Y. V. Reddy, Subir Gokarn and a few others. Yu Yongding is from the Chinese Academy of Social Sciences (CASS) and is here to give the Exim Bank Commencement Day Annual lecture this year.

This morning was taken up with the Exim Bank Board meeting. I put forward my interesting, Machiavellian idea for promoting Indian exports that I noted earlier. This entails India lending money to other countries in Indian rupees. The rupee not being an internationally convertible currency, the recipient will be forced to spend the money on Indian goods, thereby boosting Indian exports. There are no takers for this idea. This is not central to any of my other concerns that I want to bring up today, and so I let it go.

I am staying at the Taj Mahal Palace Hotel. This is my favorite hotel in the world. I always insist on staying in the old wing. The musty monsoon climate in the corridors, as soon as you step out of your room, adds to the charm. After the Exim Bank meeting I headed to the hotel gym for some quick exercise.

In the evening, I delivered the 8th D. R. Gadgil Memorial Lecture organized by the Maharashtra Economic Development Council on 'Two Decade of India's Economic Reforms: Reflections and the Road Ahead'. The audience took in the lecture with full concentration and thereafter there was a lot of bonhomie and camaraderie with the listeners.

9 August 2011, Tuesday

I sat in on an Empowered Group of Ministers Meeting (EGOM) on urban transport. EGoMs are India's most powerful decision-making bodies. I have a rather dormant role. Just as sitting in on EGOM meetings on Air India and its mounting losses leaves me in a mood of despondency about whether we can get anything right, hearing Mr Sreedharan describe the Delhi metro, its achievements, and future plans made me feel excited about what is possible in India.

13 August 2011, Saturday

India's battle to improve punctuality is obvious from the folders or files that the Department of Economic Affairs, Ministry of

Finance, distributes to its officers for them to keep their papers and documents in. Ever mindful not to miss out on an opportunity to educate people, the two inside pages of each folder have a list headed: 'Commonly used phrases on the files by the Heads of Departments/Senior Offices'. These phrases are then listed in Hindi and English, also to make sure that officers learn both the English and Hindi of these important phrases.

The list begins with, 'I agree/Main sahmat hoon' and then has forty-four commonly used phrases. What is fascinating to see is how many of these pertain to avoiding delays and being punctual. I reproduce here a few of these instructions verbatim:

- Expedite action
- Delay cannot be waived
- Delay should be avoided
- Delay must be explained
- On return from tour pending cases may be disposed of early
- Reply today/early/immediately/without delay
- Issue reminder urgently
- Enquiry may be completed and its repost submitted at any early date
- Issue today

If despite such urging, India continues to be unpunctual; we deserve appreciation for tenacity.

Punctuality is actually a fascinating topic. We grew up in India, notorious for its tardiness, especially in matters pertaining to the government. But what I have discovered after joining the government is that this is changing rapidly. India has become a much more punctual country than it was even ten or fifteen years ago. I have written with Jorgen Weibull on how punctuality or its absence is not a hard-wired trait in society but an equilibrium response to other people's behavior. In other words, each society has multiple equilibria. It can be unpunctual, in which case it is rational for individuals to be unpunctual and that is what bolsters the equilibrium. Equally, the same society could be in a punctual equilibrium.

My paper with Jorgen was a simple game-theoretic sketch. What bolstered my belief that the theory was talking to reality was when a Japanese sociologist directed me to some writings by European visitors to Japan on how unpunctual the Japanese were some 100 years ago. Clearly, Japan has moved from one equilibrium to another.

I think India is in the midst of such a transition. I objectively know this is good but I also feel some nostalgia for the old, easy-going, non-materialistic, and yes, unpunctual ways. What is time after all?

14 August 2011, Sunday

In government meetings, a lot depends on stature. For the most part you can do precious little about stature—either you have it or you don't. But a little fillip can be had from the height of your chair. If you are on a relatively higher chair, peering down on others, it gives you an advantage in meetings. To achieve this, the technique is easy. Most Indian office chairs have a little lever under the chair, on the right-hand side. Without drawing attention to yourself, reach out for the lever and gently pull on it. Be careful not to pull too hard for you will be abruptly thrown up, creating a comical scene. Done gently, you will rise slowly and come to occupy a commanding position. The only risk is, if others at your meeting do the same, you will have no relative advantage. All participants will simply be at a higher altitude, legs adangle. Occasionally, seeing the heights of chairs in government meetings I suspect that many Indian bureaucrats have discovered this technique.

15 August 2011, Monday

It is India's Independence Day. I am up early in the morning, since I have to go for flag hoisting and the prime minister's Independence Day speech from the ramparts of Red Fort. As last year, I am in the VIP arena, around the PM's bulletproof cabin from where he gives his address. Being able to sit here once a year is reason enough to join the government. One gets a magnificent view of old Delhi. Along the horizon you see temples, church spires, Jama Masjid, the bird hospital, an outline of Chandni Chowk, basically an outline of seven or eight hundred years of history. This year we are drenched in rain as the prime minister speaks but that does not take an iota away from the joy of witnessing history.

Beneath all this there is a sense of foreboding, from the awareness that Anna Hazare will go on a fast from tomorrow to protest against various government policies. Hazare does not seem to have any cogent agenda but I instinctively take to protestors and so, even though I disagree with his views, I find him quite a fascinating character.

It is a leisurely day today. I use it to do some stocktaking of work, life and happiness. Though I have little patience for everyday management, I have been a fairly good manager. The reason, I think, is I enjoy interaction with people, even the wicked ones. And, probably for that reason, people who work for me are very loyal and I, in turn, find them totally dependable. I rarely get angry. This comes not so much from an emotional temperament as from a philosophical predilection. I am a determinist. I believe that all creatures are fully determined by their genetic make-up and environmental influence. In other words, human beings live scripted lives. That being so, it is difficult to get angry with anyone. That is my attitude towards human beings.

I am a person of cheerful disposition, and this seems to be monotonically improving—each year feels better than the previous. The reason for this is not that I have had a better deal in life. I may have, but more importantly, I have an inner resilience which comes from reason and my realization that ultimately life is beyond our control. It is a scripted theater that we are mechanically a part of. When tragedy strikes, you have to reconcile to the fact that tragedy would strike. I am not denying that there are situations where, if you had done something differently, tragedy would not have struck. I am claiming that that you would not do something differently was scripted. This reconciliation creates a resilience against tragedies and disappointments.

Moreover, I believe that there is a possibility that, apart from my mind, nothing exists in the world. In bad times, such as when I am pained by the sadness of someone else, I switch on this awareness that the other person who I think is in pain may not exist and, even if he or she (I don't know what pronoun to use for non-existent creatures) does exist, the person may be in a very different state from what I perceive.

27 August 2011, Saturday

I arrived in Kolkata to speak to the Indian Chamber of Commerce. The officer who picks me up is visibly upset about the recent price increases. Aware that I am the government's chief economic adviser, he asks me why the government is not lowering inflation. I tell him prices are not centrally orchestrated and arise from the decentralized decisions of millions of people, and that being so, it is not so obvious how it can be controlled. I can see from his countenance that he thinks I am hiding something, that there is a conspiracy to let prices rise. I don't know why but I persist in trying to make him understand. I explain to him about trade-offs, basically trying to make him understand the Phillips curve. When I finish and look into the rear-view mirror, he is fast asleep with an expression of utter confusion.

19 September 2011, Monday

The social kiss has arrived in India. This leads to awkward situations. When you meet someone with whom you were very friendly in the pre-social kiss age, a big question arises about whether to kiss or not to kiss.

This must be like the dilemmas that arose in Sweden on 3 September 1967 when the nation switched over from driving on the left-hand side to driving on the right. In the early days after that, when you saw an oncoming car in Sweden, you would have to make a quick guess as to whether the driver headed your way belonged to the old school or had transitioned to the new custom.

26 September 2011, Monday

Early morning on 20 September, soon after midnight, Alaka and I left for Washington. I was headed for another round of the IMF–World Bank annual meetings and, as always, these were used by the Indian government to set up several other meeting on the sidelines. The day after my arrival in Washington, a large part of the day was swallowed up by G-20 deliberations. The G-20 had played a major role in 2008 and thereafter in tackling the Great Recession but it is a somewhat jaded body now. This is a pity because I think the need for global policy coordination is even greater now. With economic globalization, it is imperative that the world's major economies should coordinate policies—tax and other kinds of fiscal policy, monetary policy. But to do this effectively the G-20 needs to be restructured and empowered. There has to be more representation of developing countries and emerging economies, at least the larger ones. The group can then be renamed G-Major countries. And they have to be given powers to help coordinate monetary policies to prevent countries from working at cross purposes, as they do currently. But, for now, this is a pipe dream, way beyond my reach.

Three days ago it was the BRICS Washington meeting. The
Indian finance minister was in the chair. A communique by all five
countries was being attempted. Pranab Mukherjee called upon
each country, one by one, to give suggestions. When it came to
China, an unusual problem arose. The governor of People's Bank
of China went on, seemingly interminably. I was sitting next to
Pranab Mukherjee, who suddenly turned to me, and said, 'Can you
ask him to conclude?' I have no idea why he thought I was right
for this task. We were all sitting at a large round table. I was one
of the non-speaking members at this event. For me to suddenly
speak up and ask him to stop talking would sound absurd.

Not quite knowing what to do, I walked around the table and
spoke to the Chinese finance minister, who was seated next to
the People's Bank governor, who was holding forth passionately.
I softly requested him to ask his governor to conclude. He was
blunt and said he could not do that to his central bank governor.
If I wanted, he added, I should ask him myself. I realized I had no
choice. Having instructed me, Pranab Mukherjee was reading a
paper and I could not make eye contact with him. So I mustered
up courage and tapped the governor of the People's Bank of China
on the shoulder. He looked at me, mid-sentence, baffled. I told
him to conclude. He was so taken aback by this mysterious person
from India asking him to stop, that in two minutes, he stopped.

So much for central bank autonomy.

Yesterday I travelled to New York, where Alaka, Karna, Diksha
and Shabnam and I had dinner at a lovely Japanese restaurant.

Today was my last engagement in America. I had to attend
a meeting at New York University's Stern School, organized by
Mike Spence. I got to meet Wes Clark, Robert Rubin and others,
who were also at the meeting. I spoke about the potential for
greater economic collaboration between USA and India.

Then Air India once again, to New Delhi, non-stop.

I met Rahul Gandhi at his Aurangzeb Lane residence. At the last meeting of the steering committee of the Rajiv Gandhi Institute of Contemporary Studies he had mentioned, as I was leaving, that he would like to have a chat with me some time. I phoned one of his assistants two days ago, saying that I was back from Washington and ready to meet him. She promptly called back, politely asking about my convenience, and we agreed on 4 pm today. She gave me the impression that there would be others at the meeting.

After I got through layers of security, I was taken to a room where, because I was facing an open window with a glare, I did not see the one person standing there. Rahul Gandhi stretched out his hand and said, 'Hello.' I blinked, recognized him, and said, 'Rahul, hello. So nice to see you.' He showed me to a seat and we began to chat. We did so incessantly—about politics, caste in India, how I came to join the government, how he liked or disliked being in politics. It was just the two of us and we talked for forty-five minutes. I am impressed by his unassuming style and the fact that it was a conversation without his trying to get something out of me. This is so rare in politics that it is a relief.

In the conversation, he referred to 'CP'. I wondered what that could be. Was he suddenly talking about Connaught Place? Soon it was evident that CP was a person. When CP came up for the third time, I was compelled to ask him, 'Who is CP?' He said, 'Congress president.' Thereafter, I also referred to Mrs Gandhi as CP, even though I did not have much to say about CP.

It is impossible not to be impressed by the civility and sensitivity of Rahul and Sonia (I barely know Priyanka). To me they seem to be an embodiment of good values, an instinctive inclusiveness and an instinctive sympathy for the poor and the marginalized. The Gandhis are routinely criticized as a dynasty. But a dynasty is when the descendant of the nation's leader has a *conferred* right to be the leader. If a descendant is *chosen* or elected to lead, that is not a dynastic system. No one should lose the right to lead because his or her parent or grandparent was a leader too.

Moreover, I get the impression that Rahul is not keen to be a leader at all cost. I like that quality. The most important requirement of a democracy is to have leaders who have limits to how far they are prepared to go to get the top job, and also to what they are willing to do to hold on to that job.

3 October 2011, Monday

The prime minister wanted to see me to have a one-on-one meeting on the economy. We met at his residence. He seemed more relaxed than at my last one-on-one meeting with him. He is concerned about the economy and in particular growth, but in a dispassionate way. Inflation has slowed down but not as much as we would want. As a political leader, he realizes that from a political point of view tackling inflation is more important than any other economic ill. When the stock market does badly, the rich are hurt immediately, with the effect on the masses coming in, if at all, later, and in indirect ways. When unemployment goes up, you have a cousin who does not get a job, a friend who complains that her son is not finding work, and so on. When corruption increases you read about it in the newspapers and may have an occasional encounter. But when prices rise, each and every adult gets the data directly from the market place every day. This makes this the politically most sensitive parameter. People scream about other things more—corruption, unemployment— when the real trigger is inflation. As an economist/prime minister he gets a lion's share of the blame, since most people presume inflation can be switched off at will. We talked about measures to be taken, especially concerning food prices. We discussed the pros and cons of India joining the OECD, and also the new food security or right to food bill.

We also discussed steps being taken to curb corruption. He is aware that, as steps are taken to curb corruption, there is a concomitant slowdown in bureaucratic decision-making, since bureaucrats realize that the safest course for them to be above suspicion is to take no decision. They have not done anything corrupt because they have not done anything. Unlike many other politicians who are either corrupt themselves or been in politics long enough to have become inured to the problem, corruption is something that troubles Manmohan Singh deeply.

5 October 2011, Wednesday

There was an unexpected call from Rahul Gandhi's office. He wanted some urgent advice on the Food Security Bill that was being debated.[10] I believe, though I am not sure, that the idea for such a law has come from the National Advisory Committee (NAC), which is headed by Sonia Gandhi, and was now being considered for being enshrined as an act of parliament.

So I went to 12 Tughlak Lane at 5:30 pm. Kirit Parikh, Harsh Mander and I explained to him the pros and cons of a food security law. It was not a very coherent explanation because we had disagreements among us. This bill and in fact NAC itself has been a source of controversy within the government—a kind of battle between hard-headed economists and soft-hearted social activists. A whole lot of people in the government have told me that the NAC, with left-wing social activists, like Aruna Roy, on it, has compromised the Planning Commission's domain of influence. They assume that being an economist, I will sympathize with them. My problem is my instinctive sympathy is with these activists. Most of them are genuinely well-intentioned, and have little interest in money. I like that. I am aware that they often make

---

10. This would later become the National Food Security Act, 2013.

mistakes. I have had lots of arguments with these activists wanting to enshrine everything as a 'right'. I keep reminding them that to enshrine something as a right, when you have no way to ensure that the right can be fulfilled is to diminish the value of a right. Thus, I have opposed the idea of the right to work.

I, however, believe in the right to food, because it is a basic need, and because I think the government can ensure it. I have had disagreements on this with economists, especially right-wing ones. At this meeting I find myself in agreement with Rahul and Harsh. Kirit argues that the rich should be excluded from such a right. I see the spirit of this point but I do not think we need to specify this, since the rich will, on their own, be able to satisfy their food needs.

I am not sure on one technical matter whether Rahul Gandhi, Harsh Mander and I are on the same page. I believe that in most cases it is best to satisfy this right by making sure people have enough money to buy food, instead of buying food and handing that over to them. In brief, I think something like the American food stamp program is the better way to go.

I have one more academic point, involving nitpicking moral philosophy. Even though the government can, in most situations, guarantee food for all, there may be special situations, such as climatic disasters and famines, when it is impossible to guarantee food to all. I felt that the Food Security Bill should be explicit in how to handle such situations. My own view is that in such situations food should be rationed for rich and poor alike. There must be no advantage in terms of basic needs such as food by virtue of being rich. I muttered this point feeling self-conscious about it being too academic.

Rahul Gandhi's interest in all this seems genuine. He asks lots of questions and gets into the weeds in discussing the details.

14 October 2011, Friday

I arrived in Rome on 11 October. I am staying at the beautiful Bernini Bristol Hotel and the following morning I had meetings at the Italian Treasury, including a discussion with Lorenzo Codogno, chief economist at the Treasury, effectively my counterpart in Italy. Italy is an important trading partner for India, and the European slowdown has been a concern for us.

After that I gave a lecture on the emergence of the Indian economy to the Treasury staff. There was a strange experience before that. As I settled down on the dais for my lecture and was being introduced by the chairperson to the audience, a man rushed up to the dais and whispered something to the chair. The chair stopped abruptly, turned to me and said that that Mr Giulio Tremonti, Italy's minister of the economy and finance, would love to talk me. I asked, 'When?' He said, 'Now,' and asked me if I was agreeable. This was very awkward, with my audience ready for my lecture. This would be unacceptable in some countries but not so in others. I said, it depends on the audience and asked him to ask them. The audience on hearing this, cheered me to go upstairs, and said they would wait.

So I was taken up to the office of the minister. The Italian Treasury is one of the most magnificent government buildings I have seen anywhere in the world. Tremonti's office was ornate and spectacular. I could sense the magnificent history of Italy and Rome as I walked to his office. He was waiting to see me, came to the door, shook my hands and ushered me in (this would not happen in India).

I was a bit apprehensive. Why was he so keen to see me that he had my lecture interrupted? Would he want me to carry some missive to the Indian prime minister? Did he want to complain about some Indian trade policy? I wondered as I stepped into the room.

We sat beneath a framed photograph of Silvio Berlusconi. Since I think of Berlusconi as an awful person, I felt uncomfortable at the thought of him peering down at us. There was something about the body language of Tremonti that made me feel he shared the same feeling towards Berlusconi. This made us comfortable with each other.

He began by asking me how India's economy was doing. I gave a quick summary account. Turning to Italy, he talked about the big regional difference between north and south and how this complicated policymaking. He asked me about India's regional differences and we talked a bit about that. We talked about the fiscal policy challenges of the two countries. He said he was hopeful that the Italian budget would be balanced by 2013. There was a lull in the conversation. I had long been a believer in Eurobonds which was originally Tremonti's and Junker's idea. To break the silence I told him that I think that some minimal joint liability, as is implied by the idea of Eurobonds, is unavoidable if the Eurozone is to survive. He got interested and held forth on this for a while. He then said he should not hold me up from my talk much longer. We shook hands and I went downstairs and gave a lecture.

In retrospect, I think Tremonti met me not with any purpose but to relieve himself of some loneliness at the top. By then he was having a lot of problems with Silvio Berlusconi. He knew I was an outsider in the government, an academic in the world of policy, and wanted the pleasure of some idle conversation.

From Rome I flew to Barcelona, and, almost directly went to have dinner with Andreu Mas-Colell and his wife Esther. Because of my interest in art, Andreu chose Els Quatre Gats or 4Gats, a well-known restaurant at the crossing of Portal de L'Angel and Montsio, made even more famous by frequent visits by Picasso and Gaudi. It is indeed an artsy place which was inaugurated in 1897.

I have known Andreu, not well, but a little, from his academic days at Harvard. I have occasionally taught his famed microeconomics book to my graduate students. Andrew is one of the most accomplished mathematical economists in the world. It seems safe to deduce from this that he is the most gifted mathematician among all politicians in the world. Because of our common backgrounds, it felt relaxing being with them. We gossiped about academics, chatted about Picasso, politics and economics.

The following morning, that is, yesterday, I gave a public lecture at the Barcelona Graduate School of Economics. This was quite a grand occasion. Artur Mas, the president of the Government of Catalonia, was there on the dais with me and gave a closing speech. Javier de Agustin, CEO of AXA-Spain, gave the welcome address. There were also short speeches by Ramon Marimon, Ana Ripoli and Josep Joan Moreso. There has been a lot of discussion in Spain in recent times on the rise of India and so I chose to give a talk on the 'Emergence of the Indian Economy'. Trust the Spaniards—the event ended with a glass of Cava.

Today I am back in Rome to speak at Roma 3 to the Italian Economic Association. It is a serious academic paper, which is to be published in their journal. Then I head back to Delhi.

15 October 2011, Saturday

The prime minister called a small group—five of us—for a meeting at his residence to discuss growth and inflation. There was Subbarao (RBI governor), Saumitra Chaudhuri (from the Planning Commission), C. Rangarajan (chairman of the PM's Economic Advisory Council), Montek Singh Ahluwalia (deputy chairman of the Planning Commission) and me. The meeting also included some of the finest people in the prime minister's staff: Pulok Chatterjee, Jaideep Sarkar, Harish Khare, Vini Mahajan and Pallavi Jain. The prime minister opened by saying that he was concerned about growth, the persistence of inflation, and the risk of 'stagflation' and wanted to do some brainstorming. He asked Rangarajan to open.

Rangarajan said that he was worried about the growth slowdown but did not foresee stagflation because he felt that the back of the inflation had been broken. He endorsed the monetary policy being used and suggested without saying so that interest rate tightening should continue.

Then Manmohan Singh turned to me and asked me to speak. To keep my intervention brief and taking advantage of the fact that this was a small and serious group, I quickly got to the point and expressed my views as honestly and clearly as I could. I said that my analysis of the data prompted me to believe that the interest rate tightening by the RBI was not having its desired effect. It was holding back growth without having any effect on inflation. I felt that India's monetary policy is too imitative of what is done in the West. We need more research and the development of our own rules of intervention. As an example of unusual policy, I gave the example of Turkey which had in the middle of high inflation last year lowered its interest rates. Turkey did this to counter carry trade but some people were worried that this would fuel inflation. In reality, the opposite happened. Turkey's inflation went down. I went on to give a theoretical explanation why this happened in Turkey. I did this a bit self-consciously because, while theory always interests me, I am aware that others do not share my interest. Rangarajan gently countered my argument by pointing out that Turkey had actually used an unusual combination of policies. It lowered interest rates, while raising CRR.

This went on with comments and analysis from Saumitra and Montek. Finally, Subbarao spoke. He felt that we should be wary of drawing lessons from Turkey. There were too many differences between India and Turkey for Turkey to be relevant to us. From the prime minister's staff, only Pulok spoke. He talked about the need for a more efficient food reserve policy to dampen food inflation. India's food grain reserve storage was poor and led to a lot of unnecessary leakage.

The quality of the discussion was first rate. It is not difficult to see why through all the ups and downs, India's economy has, overall, done so well in recent times.

19 October 2011, Wednesday

The Rajiv Gandhi Institute for Contemporary Studies invited Thomas Pogge to give a special lecture. It was a distinguished audience of cabinet ministers, professors and senior journalists. Rahul Gandhi, Mohan Gopal and I made brief remarks and shared the dais with the speaker. Professor Pogge gave an excellent, academic lecture—no concessions for the ministers and politicians who had to listen.

Before the lecture, Priyanka Gandhi, Rahul, Gopal, Thomas and I gathered in (I think) Rahul's office at RGICS, under a wonderful portrait of Rajiv Gandhi, done by Sanjay Bhattacharya. We chatted informally, briefed Thomas a little about Indian audiences and then headed to the auditorium. The large audience had already taken its seat and our entry through the door on the dais would inevitably be somewhat dramatic. There was a bit of a hesitation about who would appear first. I told Priyanka Gandhi, 'Why don't you lead the way?' She said she felt uncomfortable with too much attention and pushed Rahul to go in first. The way she spoke I think she meant what she said.

24 October 2011, Monday

Early morning on 22 October, I left for Boston, via Munich. Nandita Das, her husband, and son, Vihaan, happened to be on the same flight. It was nice, as usual, chatting with them. Diksha came to Boston for one day. She stayed with me at Sheraton Commander. I have come for the jury meeting for the Infosys Prize. The Infosys Prize is arguably the most important prize given out of India, in recognition of pure creative contribution to various fields, from mathematics, computer science, economics and humanities to other fields. It involves months of reading papers and books and this is the final jury meeting for which we have assembled in Boston; Amartya Sen being the jury chair. Dinner on the 22nd was an informal one—nothing to do with jury work. We met at the Rialto with Amartya Sen, Emma Rothschild, Sunil Khilnani and Diksha.

Yesterday was a blissful, free morning. The autumn wore beautifully on Cambridge. I walked around Harvard Square and some other familiar places, feeling nostalgic for the year when I lived and taught here. From 6:30 pm to 11 pm we had a long Infosys Prize meeting at Rialto, comparing notes of our readings and assessment of the past several months.

The jury meeting continued this morning, in Sen's office, at Harvard. We finally selected Raghuram Rajan for the prize. It is a unanimous decision though there were plenty of debates and a few other prominent names actively considered, before we, ultimately, all converged.

After the meeting, much of the day is free. I had lunch with Sunil Khilnani at Harvard and caught the evening Lufthansa flight for Delhi, via Frankfurt.

13 November 2011, Sunday

Professor Pami Dua invited me and a few professors from the Delhi School of Economics to speak to devotees of the Radha Soami sect at a conference being held at the Dayalbagh Education Institute, in Agra. I rarely get to lecture to religious sects. I was curious about them. That, plus the fact that Pulin Nayak and K. L. Krishna, friends and former colleagues from the Delhi School, would be there was reason enough to accept. It would also be a nice break from my usual work.

So, day before yesterday, Alaka and I drove to Agra, Manbir in the driver's seat, as usual. We checked in at the Hotel Marina. Yesterday was spent entirely at the conference, lecturing to the Radha Soami devotees, and chatting with them. I knew nothing about the Radha Soamis beyond the fact that there is an area in Delhi called the Radha Soami Colony. So it was fun and informative talking to them and getting a sense of their beliefs and devotion. They seem to be very disciplined and regimented. I gave my lecture to a motionless audience. No way of knowing what kind of impact I had since there was no behavioral manifestation of the impact one way or the other. But as always happens in these kind of gatherings, there is a great sense of community.

We drove back to Delhi today, with a halt at Vrindavan and a visit to the Banke Bihari temple.

19 November 2011, Saturday

I came to Chennai yesterday evening and am staying at the Madras Club on Boat Club Road. It is a wonderful, old, colonial place. Colonialism is dreadful but some of the markers it leaves behind are so nice. If we could get them without the colonialism that would be ideal. It is like the architectural excesses of maharajas and autocrats. They are cruel and appalling when they happen, running holes in the nation's budget, but they leave behind treasures for future generations. I am never quite sure how to morally evaluate these excesses of history.

In the morning I have a meeting with the Federation of Indian Export Organizations (FIEO). India has so much potential for exports but continues to under-perform. Luckily, there have been clear signs of a pick-up since 2005. The idea is to power this trend.

This afternoon I spoke to *The Hindu* and *Business Line* journalists at their office on Anna Salai. In the evening N. Ram and Venu organized a dinner-cum-talk for Chennai businessmen at the Sheraton Hotel. All the big businesses are here. They seem to be a fairly erudite lot and the conversation goes very well. India is clearly on the verge of a major economic take-off, unless political stupidity derails us.

Tomorrow morning, I head back to Delhi.

22 November 2011, Wednesday

This is the first day of Parliament for the winter session—never mind that it was adjourned soon after starting.

As for me, I was asked to give a lecture to some Congress members of Parliament on inflation to help improve literacy in these kinds of important topics and to enable them to make better interventions in Parliament so as to elevate the level of parliamentary debates. This was Rahul Gandhi's idea—good idea, I think.

I went to Jawahar Bhavan at 9:30 am for my 'lecture'. It turned out to be the wildest classroom lecture I have given. Among those present were Manish Tiwari, Sandeep Dixit, Anu Tandon (MP from UP), a Rajya Sabha member from Andhra Pradesh, another five semi-familiar members of Parliament, and three or four junior Congress Party workers. For about ten minutes, while I explained the base effect on inflation numbers, they listened. After that it turned into a roller coaster debate, like a mini-Parliament. They learnt little but loved it. At the end, they flocked around my chair saying they wanted more such classes. I felt like the popular teacher aunty in school.

It is bewildering how policies get made through this thicket of chaotic understanding. This is nothing special to India. The same must happen in USA, Japan, Korea, everywhere. Human knowledge is limited and this is more so among politicians. In rich countries there is more superficial polish but in terms of fundamentals there isn't much difference. Is it then mere luck that some countries make the right policy decisions and take off?

After the lecture, I returned home. I have been feeling flueey from last night. So I took leave of absence for tomorrow. I think this is the second day I have taken sick leave in the nearly two years in the government.

29 November 2011, Tuesday

I had got an invitation a few days ago from Rahul Gandhi, conveyed to me by Mohan Gopal, to address a large gathering of Youth Congress members at the Japanese Garden in Rohini. I was told the audience would include some 300 local Congress leaders and I should speak to them on globalization and inclusive growth. I know these large gatherings are not the best fora for serious lectures but Rahul Gandhi wanting to inflict important ideas on young Congress folks smacks of an idealism that I like. So I had agreed. I landed up for this unusual lecture event in Rohini. We had to take off our shoes as we walked up to the dais (never done that before) and on the dais we sat on a *gaddi*. As I began to speak and said something mildly interesting, the audience broke out in thunderous applause. Excessive, I thought, but I was pleased. So I kept going—on the meaning of globalization, how we may like or not like it but it is an inevitable part of life and so we have to learn to live with it and make the most of it. But it was evident that people had come to cheer and celebrate and were not really interested in the content. I kept the lecture short. When I turned around, I saw that Rahul Gandhi had come to the dais, along with Pranab Mukherjee and they were listening to me with full attention.

This was not one of my great performances but I have never

spoken in a forum like this. I feel confident that if I do this a few times, I can master the art of political speech. The only catch is my vocabulary in both Bangla and Hindi is rather limited and these speeches have to ideally be given in one of the vernaculars.

30 November 2011, Wednesday

It was an evening at the Sabyasachi Fashion Show in The Leela, Chanakyapuri. It is a more glitzy crowd than any I have ever been in. I am in the first row in front of the ramp and watch the models come gliding out, as I have seen only on TV before. Shubha Mudgal sings. Among models I recognize are Indrani Dasgupta and Noyonika Chatterjee. Sabyasachi's fashion design is pure art. It is on par with the works of some of the world's great artists.

2 December 2011, Friday

I worked most of the day on the 'Mid-Year Analysis'. India's IES is quite a remarkable body of cadres. I keep calling on them for facts and data and they run in and out with them. Also, there are still so many tricky aspects of Indian policymaking that I still do not fully understand. I have to keep calling them to explain things to me. It is a pleasure to see how good they are.

Later in the day I had a meeting with the remarkably talented Shiv Shankar Menon and four others to plan the next BRICS summit. I find foreign policy interesting but vacuous. I don't say this in a pejorative sense and am aware that everything cannot be statistics, algebra, and logic, which I enjoy and which constitute the body of economics. A lot of foreign policy is words, carefully chosen, and history, clipped and selectively used. I admire some people's talent for this and am aware of my own deficiency.

Dinner today was at Nandita Das' house. She had organized it to celebrate Jatin Das' 70th birthday. Nandita gave a short but lovely speech, saying half-jokingly how one had to be a daughter to love Jatin Das.

9 December 2011, Friday

I went to Kolkata yesterday for the Financial Stability and Development Council (FSDC) sub-committee meeting. The idea of a regulatory body like the FSDC was first proposed by the Raghuram Rajan Committee in 2008 and later set up by Pranab Mukherjee. The Great Recession that started in 2008 has meant that the FSDC has become quite an important entity.

This was the first time in Kolkata that I stayed in a hotel. It was a strange feeling. I had dinner at my eldest sister's home. Didi, my half sister, is a naturally gifted chef, and one of the most loving human beings. She had a very difficult childhood when her mother, my father's first wife, died.

I took the early morning flight today to Delhi.

12 December 2011, Monday

Kamal Ahmed hosts a dinner on behalf of Asian University for Women, Chittagong, at Le Meridien. Established in 2008, AUW is a remarkable experiment in providing higher education to women in traditional societies. It attracts students from several countries. The idea is not just to provide basic education but cutting-edge knowledge, and also to instill in the students a desire to take up leadership roles in life. Kamal has played a major role in AUW's success and, though I have never visited the university, I tried to extend as much support from India as possible. This dinner is to celebrate the initial years of AUW. Cherie Blair, who was appointed chancellor of AUW is here for the occasion.

I am lucky to be seated at the same table as her and so get to chat a lot with her. I am charmed by her nicely left-wing, irreverential style. She lacks self-consciousness, and is unmindful of social hierarchy (or clever enough to appear so). These are all qualities I like; we get along well. She clearly does not mind when I quiz her about her background, and toss in a few questions about Tony Blair; she holds forth comfortably.

14 December 2011, Wednesday

We had been planning the Delhi Economics Conclave for a while. This was my idea—to bring some of the world's finest policy-oriented economists to Delhi to speak and to interact with our policymakers. Manmohan Singh was enthusiastic and so it has taken off. I hosted a dinner at Ashoka Hotel last night for the speakers who were already here. It turned out to be a rather dreary event and I was worried how the actual conclave would work out. But today, the main day of the Conclave, was a whopping success. Participants have come from around the world—Amartya Sen, Justin Yifu Lin, Maurice Obstfeld, Richard Freeman, Yuval Steinitz, the finance minister of Israel, Winston Dookeran, the finance minister of Trinidad & Tobago and Craig Emerson, the minister of trade from Australia.

Steinitz is an unusual finance minister. His background is in philosophy in which he has several published works. I discover common interests with him. Dookeran, a gracious and genial person, is also an accomplished academic, who used to teach at the University of West Indies.

It is a daylong seminar at Ashoka Hotel; and there is standing room-only crowd. Mallika Sarabhai and her troupe perform in the evening. Mallika is a rare combination of intelligence and charm. The event ends with a grand dinner. The event ends but not the day. I have to rush from there to a small closed-room meeting with our finance minister and Israel's finance minister, Yuval Steinitz, in the finance minister's office in North Block. I am not key to the meeting but I get along well with Yuval Steinitz after discovering that, before joining the government, he taught philosophy in Israel. We discover a lot of common interest. I also get along well at a personal level with the Israeli ambassador and so it is a nice chitchat before the formal meeting begins. While we wait for Pranab Mukherjee to call us in, the ambassador asks me which other country's finance minister would be kept waiting by the Indian FM. I don't know the answer but decide to give the least offensive and at the same time credible answer. I tell him apart from USA, every nation's finance minister maybe kept waiting a little.

It turns out to be an intense meeting on not quite intense matters. Israel is interested in setting up intellectual and cultural collaboration with India and is willing to put up money. The Indian side is clearly cautious about getting into formal arrangements and tries to keep it all fluid. The meeting ends without any concrete decision but with bonhomie between the two sides.

15 December 2011, Thursday

It is a crazy day of seminars and conferences. The morning begins with me inaugurating the Indian Statistical Institute (ISI) winter conference, which was started by my Cornell student, Tridip Ray, and has become quite a celebrated serious research event, with young scholars coming from all over the world. From there I go to the CII conference at Le Meridien where I have to participate in a panel. And from there, I head to the Taj (Mansingh Road) for lunch with Noyleen Heyzer, head of ESCAP, and then I go to speak in an ESCAP panel. In the evening, at the India International Centre I speak at Oxford University Press's book release for the *New Oxford Companion*.

The day ends with a dinner hosted by CII in honor of Yuval Steinitz. I am seated next to him and make the opening toast.

It had to happen someday and, juggling so many conferences, today turned out to be that day. After beginning to speak at the ESCAP seminar, I forgot which organization's seminar it was. UNDP? UNCTAD? I frantically tried to recall, as I mouthed away meaningless niceties. I kept referring to inanities like the 'great work being done by *your* organization', emphasizing the 'your' because of my guilt. I assured them that '*your* organization taking an interest in the globe and in grassroots matters is very important for human welfare'. Later I was told my lecture was very apt for the organization.

18 December 2011, Sunday

The day before yesterday, I spoke at the ISI conference. I thought it is a good occasion to give a serious talk on corruption control. The audience being non-political and without media presence I could do a stocktaking of my ideas that had caused controversy. It is a testimony to the high standard of the listeners that the lecture went down well and the discussion and also the criticisms were high quality.

From there I headed to an event being organized by CII at Le Meridien Hotel. The main speaker was Amartya Sen. He seemed to be in great shape and gave an excellent lecture.

Yesterday I took the morning flight to Mumbai for the Financial Sector Legislative Reforms Commission (FSLRC) meeting. Justice Sri Krishna was in the chair. He is an impressive person and it was a meeting with a long agenda. I stayed all day at the Sahara Airport Hotel, where the meeting was held and took the evening flight to Udaipur, where I stayed at the Shilpi Gram resort. Udaipur is magnificent and soothes the nerves.

This morning I delivered the V. V. Giri lecture at the annual conference of the Indian Society of Labor Economists in Udaipur. From there I went to see Ajay Mehta in his lovely, sprawling home.

Ajay was one year my junior in St Stephen's. He now runs one of the most amazing NGOs in India, Seva Mandir. Always polite, warm and soft-spoken, Ajay is a wonderful person to chat with. We talked about college days and grassroots activism (on which my interest is entirely academic, whereas his is based on actual work). I took the evening flight back to Delhi.

21 December 2011, Wednesday

I sent Rahul Gandhi an email today giving some of my own ideas on to how to make political campaigns more effective. The gist was to take more direct personal responsibility. He emailed back saying that while he understood that, the problem with that strategy was that it would feed into the speculation about whether he is proposing to be the chief minister himself. The more I interact with Rahul, the more I feel that he has no great interest in power, which is a rare, good quality in a politician. He is also a person of ample basic goodness.

Diksha has a Cosmopolitan photoshoot. Alaka, Diksha, Mikey and I go to Olive, in Mehrauli, for this. From there it is off to the opening of Blue Frog—a music bar, where NOJAZZ from Paris performs. I am always slightly uncomfortable in these kinds of settings, even though I enjoy such occasions. I hide my discomfort and fit in well, chatting with a bunch of very fashionable people.

24 December 2011, Saturday

I feel I need to go for anger management counselling for an unusual reason—I have too little of it. When I see the advantage some bureaucrats and politicians get from their anger tantrums, I feel I am losing out. I do not have enough anger because of a philosophical pre-disposition, namely, that the world is pre-determined. The future, including the lives of people are as precisely scripted as the past, moving on a causally determined path, even though we may not be privy to the causal laws. Thus, a bad person and a good person are what they are because of the laws of nature, which they did not choose. For that reason, I believe that the anger people feel directed at other people is a flawed emotion. We do not get angry with tigers on the ground that they bite. We know that is the way tigers are. They do not choose to be biters; they are biters. On the other hand, we get angry that someone speaks rudely, not realizing that the rude speech, including the choice of rude speech, by the person who speaks rudely, is like the bite of a tiger. Of course, we may need to take action against the rude speaker the same way that we take action against a tiger. We do not get angry with a tiger but we just take steps, often harsh ones, to prevent the tiger from biting. We should deal with people the same way. Take the necessary measures without getting angry. I have persuaded myself so well with this reasoning that I really have very little anger.

The only problem that this has given rise to, which I have realized, watching other senior people in the government, is that, even if anger is wrong, the display of anger has its uses. It often helps you to manage others better. So the right policy is to have no anger but have the ability to fake it. The anger management class I need is one that will train me to display anger without being angry. Maybe what I need is to go to theater school instead of anger management counselling.

29 December 2011, Thursday

It needed some work to create space but I am determined to take a break and so today, on a wing and a prayer, Alaka and I left for a four-day vacation to Sri Lanka. I had taken leave three days ago. Supriyo and Somanathan worked hard to pull off the planning and organization of the trip. Finally, Alaka and I flew out last evening to Chennai, spent a short night at Madras Club, and took the morning flight today, on Air Lanka, to Colombo.

Though it is a personal trip, word has got out, since I was in contact with the Sri Lanka embassy in Delhi, and we are received in Colombo in style, whisked out through the VIP exit to our car and ferried to Taj Samudra. Finally, we are on our own. I tell the external affairs officer who received me that I would prefer not to have any hospitality while in Sri Lanka.

We have booked a nice room, overlooking the sea. Looking out of the window one feels an immediate sense of calm and serenity. We grew up in India with tales of Sri Lanka. It is widely believed that the Sinhala people are descendants of Bengalis who had migrated from Eastern India to the little island in the Indian Ocean.

We do the usual tourist spots. Alaka and I walk on the beach in the evening and call it a day fairly early.

30 December 2011, Friday

We hire a taxi for the day and see temples, parks and lots of Sri Lankan art which I have long admired. It is a treat to see originals of George Keyt paintings. We buy roadside art. One piece in particular has become a precious part of my street art collection. It is a line drawing of a dejected man and a woman—a couple that has given up. It reminds me of some of the sketch art of the Swiss artist Ferdinand Hodler, who was a master at capturing disappointment and dejection. We lunch at the beautiful Raja Bojun restaurant in the, if I am not mistaken, Kollupitiya area.

In the evening, I decide to take some regular city buses, which I enjoy but have not been able to do over the last two years given the nature of my job. So Alaka and I hop on to a commuter bus with regular office-going Sri Lankans. A young woman, realizing we are not locals, is very helpful, telling us how to buy tickets and giving tips on navigating the city. This would be so unusual in a Delhi bus that I feel good and start chatting with her. Then she asks where we are from and is excited to hear we are from India because, she tells us, she works in the Indian High Commission. She asks me what I do. I hesitate and tell her. She is visibly excited and offers to get me to meet people in the Commission, which I politely decline.

1 January 2012, Sunday

One more year draws to a close. To celebrate, though it is not clear what is there to celebrate, we had planned to go to Kandy. We rented a car and a driver and set out from Colombo yesterday morning. We had a nice, polite driver. He spoke English fluently so it was easy to communicate. We decided to stop at a well-known elephant nursery. Pinnawala Elephant Orphanage is a place where abandoned elephants are cared for, nurtured and also bred. Apart from seeing the lovely baby and adult elephants we had an unusual experience for Sri Lanka. As we were entering the orphanage, a man came with packets of elephant food, each packet was for Rs 100 (nearly US $2). He told us elephants love it and so I bought one packet. As we reached the entrance, the guard asked me what I had in my hand. On hearing my answer, he said feeding elephants is strictly banned. I protested that this was sold to me literally twenty yards from the entrance by a liveried man. He said he knew nothing about that, and that I would have to throw the packet away. I had no choice and just tossed it on the roadside dump. As soon as I did that the man who sold it to me ran, picked it up and went off to sell it to the next gullible tourist. What was clear was that the guard clearly knew about this. It was obviously a racket that was carefully choreographed, and coming to think of it, a phenomenally profitable scheme for recycling food.

I am glad this happened because during the two days in Sri

Lanka I was beginning to wonder how Sri Lanka was so different from other countries in South Asia in terms of no cheating. It was reassuring to know that there is no scientific puzzle to be solved.

We stopped briefly at the university—serene and physically well-maintained, and eventually reached our previously booked hotel, Hotel Suisse. I took to the hotel at once, full of colonial, old-world charm. The charge for the room for 31 December included the fees for the New Year's eve dinner and dance. With no familiar faces in sight, Alaka and I decided to descend on the dance floor and dance away badly and wildly, ushering in 2012.

This morning we drove back to Colombo and took a late morning flight, Colombo to Chennai, and then on to Delhi.

5

Curtain

This was the day of a surprise birthday lunch for me—to celebrate my having turned 60 on 9 January. The surprise turned out to be a bit of an embarrassment. The idea had come from Alaka, Diksha, Karna and Shabnam. But after some time, as had to happen, I discovered this was happening and it was impossible not to participate at all in organizing the 'surprise'. I soon got involved in planning the event and selecting the lunch menu. It was a caterer from Chittaranjan Park that organized the meal, cooking some of it in one corner of our lawn. Alaka and the children had decided on a traditional Bengali lunch—from paturi and hilsa to luchi and chutney.

A large number of relatives, friends and colleagues from the government had been invited to the luncheon. They did not know that I knew about the surprise and that I also knew that they did not know. It was awkward for me when some of them came in saying, 'Surprise!' Writer Upamanyu Chatterjee was there with his wife. Anjolie Ela Menon was there with her husband. Vikram Seth, several ministers and politicians—none of the nasty ones but only the good ones—were there. There were several friends from our college days, some of whom had recently turned sixty and would no doubt have fights with their spouses and children for not having had an equal celebration for touching that magical number. We milled around on our home's lawn, with food being served in one corner and table and chairs scattered around for people to sit or stand as they wished. It also turned out to be an occasion to celebrate the fact that my stint in India and the time for curtain was coming to a close.

30 January 2012, Monday

From 2 pm to 3:30 pm today I attended a small meeting at Jawahar Bhavan with Priyanka Gandhi, Ashok Ganguly and Suman Dubey, Preeti Sahai and a few staff members of the Rajiv Gandhi Institute of Contemporary Studies. Priyanka speaks little but eminently sensibly and with grace and modesty.

From there I headed to the Habitat Center to deliver the Ambedkar Memorial Lecture on Economic Growth, Identity and Inclusion. I gave a reasonably good lecture—a bit too moralistic for my (retrospective) taste. There were several students in the audience. Many of them came up to me and were friendly. We chatted casually about the evils of caste and how India needs to get rid of it once and for all. They were clearly comfortable with me because a small group of men and women came to me to say that they belong to former untouchable castes and they were very happy about my speech. While chatting I asked them if they still sensed any discrimination at work and in class. They said they did and went on to argue that all Indians are casteists. I contested this vigorously. While I agree that many believe in and practice casteism, many, like me, do not. We got into an argument. I told them that I do not have the slightest sense of caste and in none of my decisions and actions does caste play any role, except occasionally as affirmative action. They remained friendly till the end, laughing and joking with me. I felt good about this but was also left with a lingering thought. Am I wrong about my having zero sense of caste or are they wrong in seeing everybody practice casteism?

4 February 2012, Saturday

Alaka and I took off from Delhi by car at 5:15 pm last evening, reaching Jaipur—Rajasthan University Guest House, at 10:30 pm. We are housed in the vice chancellor's guest suite—an artlessly done, large, two-room set. The hospitality, as always happens in smaller towns, is immense. Professor Vijay Vir Singh, head of the economics department and dean received me.

This morning, I delivered the 6th Raj Krishna Memorial Lecture at Rajasthan University. Thanks to a cold, I have lost my voice. I needed to make a huge effort to speak and then too it was a squeak. The auditorium was jam-packed with people squatting on the floor. The lecture was greatly appreciated, damaged vocal cord notwithstanding. I managed to combine content with humour. Since deep down I think life is a joke, this comes naturally. I am aware that I have a bit of a proneness to think I have done a better job than I may have done. But today I do feel as though I have taken Jaipur by storm.

At 2 pm, we set off for an NREGS site at Patan, Kishangarh, Ajmer District. It is impressive. A group of women in colourful saris, with a lot of red and pink, chatted cheerfully with Alaka. We visited the Dargah Sharif at Ajmer, the Circuit House, majestically perched atop Anandsagar Lake and the Brahma temple at Pushkar.

Back in Jaipur, we had dinner with friends from our student days in London—Ravi Tiwari and Rumi Goswami, and their two daughters.

24 February 2012, Friday

The *Indian Express* today rated me as the 40th most powerful person in India (and the most influential economist). This makes me feel good even while being aware that it is utter nonsense. It is nonsense because surely it is not possible to be so powerful without knowing it.

This reminds me, soon after I joined Cornell, the dean asked me in a public meeting, 'Have you ever been DGS?' I had no idea then that DGS is a commonly used acronym in American universities for director of graduate studies. I remember I responded by asking him, 'Is it possible to have been DGS without knowing it?' which had caused some merriment but it was a serious question.

27 February 2012, Monday

I phoned Alaka from office about something and asked her what she was doing. She said, 'I have been very busy trying to get my salary.' When we decided to move to India last year, Alaka took up a visiting professor's job at JNU. And that is what she was referring to. This happened each month. There aren't too many countries in the world where you need the expression 'trying to get my salary'. Hats off, India.

28 February 2012, Tuesday

I met with the prime minister at his residence at 10:50 am, bumping into Ratan Tata on the way in. We had a one-on-one conversation for forty minutes. The PM was in a candid mood. We discussed fiscal policy, the brewing Vodafone fiasco, India's Food Security Bill, the BRICS summit, G-20 related research, and—this was rare—the dependability of some individual politicians.

It was a usual busy day in office. At 5 pm Gopalan and I sat in on the finance minister's phone meeting with South Africa's

finance minister, Pravin Gordhan. I had earlier exchanged emails
with Pravin to set up the meeting regarding the BRICS bank
and also to discuss what position India and South Africa should
take on who should be the next president of the World Bank.
In the process I got to know Pravin a bit. I like the fact that
he seemed to stand for much less formality and pageantry than
Indian ministers. This is refreshing. I do not know if that is to do
with his personality or that is the South African culture. But he is
anyway quite a remarkable person, having struggled against South
Africa's apartheid, worked with Nelson Mandela, and served jail
time.

7 March 2012, Wednesday

It is a quiet morning in Silchar. The sun is streaming in through
the open window of my room in Cachar Club. It is a rare free
morning. I lazily read the morning newspapers. The sound of
honking cars and hawkers peddling their wares waft in through
my window. These sounds have almost vanished from large Indian
cities, where drivers have got westernized and learned not to start
beeping for no compelling reason. I feel as though I am back in
the Calcutta of my childhood. What adds to that nostalgia is that
during the two days here I have been speaking more Bangla than
I almost ever do nowadays. Silchar rose into some prominence
when British ships began docking here on river Barak in the
late 18th century. Given that Calcutta was then the heart of the
British Empire in India, Bengali traders and merchants would be
coming to Silchar all the time. When later Silchar, a part of Assam,
declared that Assamese would be the official language there,
major language riots broke out with shootings and deaths and in
1961 it was decided that in three districts of the Barak Valley the
main language would be Bengali. And nowadays people speak
the language with more abandon than almost anywhere else. The

people are thrilled to have me here and I, get the impression, speak even more in Bengali than they normally do.

I had left Delhi the day before yesterday, stopped in Kolkata for a night, slipping in a dinner at my eldest sister's home as I almost always do in Kolkata. I went to sleep at midnight and woke up at 3 am to catch the Kolkata to Silchar flight yesterday morning, at the unearthly hour of 5:15 am. But the effort is worth it for a selfish reason. I am here because Silchar University is to confer on me an honorary D. Litt. (Honoris Causa), during its graduate convocation ceremony.

As always in these matters, it is quite a grand ceremony. What makes it more charming is that there are the minor organizational slips of a small town ceremony and no one seems to get ruffled by them. I love this aspect of small-town India.

Last evening, driven by Vikram Singh, I visited the Chandighat tea estate, and had dinner at Cachar Club. And in keeping with all timing being turned topsy-turvy, a local journalist, Joydeep Goswami, came to interview me at 10:30 pm.

After my quiet morning today, I had something in-between a brunch and a lunch—I am not quite sure that there is a word for it—with Niranjan Roy, registrar of the university, and faculty members Amit and Debnath, and caught the afternoon flight to Delhi via Kolkata.

8 March 2012, Thursday

It is Holi today. I cherish these rare quiet days, with no office and no travel. Shahjahan Road has little traffic. There is the occasional car-load of Holi revelers and some fleeting vehicles carrying a few conscientious office-goers or lonely men and women who seek refuge in office. The sky is clear and blue with a hint of change of season, heralding Delhi's all-too-brief spring, before the fury of summer.

A few friends drop in with colors, and we gently rub them on one another's cheeks and foreheads and share *mithai*. We do not have any of the wild festivities of Holi, splashing fists full of colors and drenching one another with buckets of water. Holi was always more of a sensuous event than a religious or spiritual one. But today, sitting quietly in our Shahjahan Road home, I have a sense of peace and calm—a spiritual feeling. No, not enough for my atheism to be shaken, but a reminder of what I have always believed, namely, that there is more to life and the world than meets the eye. I don't think there is an all-powerful, all-merciful creature who created the universe. But at the same time there is no reason to believe that what we see, feel and hear is all there is to life.

It is also time to mull over longer-run policy problems which inevitably get overlooked in the government because we are always in fire-fighting mode. Economic reforms and initiatives have slowed down. We need to put our mind to navigating the difficult politics of coalition government to get the reforms going again. The key ministers should get together and declare some fundamental features of a reform package as non-negotiable. With a coalition government, making things non-negotiable may mean the government will fall. My advice in such a scenario is: Let the government fall. If it falls for taking bold steps, it will be voted back to power soon. And if it is not, then so be it. It is better to fall for a ethical cause than to win through a moral compromise.

As for corruption control, I feel convinced that the passion and anger against corruption has to be combined with intelligence and good design. There is corruption in the government but a majority of people—the bureaucrats and even politicians—that I work with are not corrupt. It is a pity that we are not able to crack the problem. Of course, we have to be realistic. We cannot start a drive to arrest all those who break the law. Indian rules and laws are so complex that there are walks of life where it is not possible to function without breaking the law. So virtually everybody breaks some law.

To go after all will mean bringing the system to a halt. If, on the other hand, the government decides to go after a small set, as it indeed has to, the natural tendency will be to go for those in the opposition and media channels that criticize the government. To do so will be the start of crony capitalism, with a handful of big businesses cozying up to the government and getting away with anything, with the media silenced. Fortunately, the prime minister is hyper-sensitive to cronyism. He told me once that all nations, and especially developing ones, have this risk and we need to be extra careful. Because of Manmohan Singh, we are safe for now, but there is always the risk that corruption control will morph into an instrument of crony capitalism.

India is indeed lucky that while there is cronyism, it is not out of hand, as happened in several Middle Eastern countries, in Pakistan, in some Latin American countries, the Philippines. Crony capitalism is the biggest risk and biggest curse for emerging economies. It ends invariably the same way, with the economy eventually collapsing. We saw that happen under Marcos in the Philippines in the early 1980s, we saw this happen under Ben Ali in Tunisia. The whole economy was captured by a few big businesses—his friends and relatives, till his fall in 2011.

15 March 2012, Thursday

The *Economic Survey 2011–12* is tabled in Parliament. The annual *Economic Survey* is entirely under the charge of the chief economic adviser. And I think I have been more hands-on in this than many of my predecessors. I end up writing most of the first two chapters. Of course, data and statistics pour in from all over government and the IES professionals who work with me are extraordinary individuals. More low-key than the IAS but unbelievably well-informed and trained. It is a testimony to India's professionalism that we have such a cadre of pure experts.

I end up doing an exhausting round of press interviews and TV appearances about the *Economic Survey*. I do a lot of this in the yard in my home on Shahjahan Road, where various TV crews come, record me and leave. As always with my *Economic Surveys* I spend a lot of time on the cover design. This year it is a usual Phillips curve, with a vertical long-run Phillips curve intersecting it. It is meant to be purely an exercise in aesthetics but invariably some people try to read some secret message the government is giving through this. It is not too bad this year, because most specialists know about the Phillips curve. Two years ago I did a geometric representation of a fixed-price, Dreze equilibrium. It had no significance but I liked the design and art aspect of it and it was a geometric depiction of equilibrium that I had developed and published in a paper. I had to do quite a bit of explaining to assure people that there was no secret message in it.

16 March 2012, Friday

Budget day is here again alas. My third round. I had joined the government for two years and two budgets. In the first months I feared I would leave with zero budget. But here I am for one more than originally planned; and I am feeling like quite a pro.

At 9:15 am sharp, the finance minister and five main advisers go to the grand Rashtrapati Bhavan to meet Her Excellency, President Pratibha Patil. I can't help feeling life is surreal. So much of what we do is pure ritual like the Stone Age people dancing around an arrangement of stones, chanting to the rain gods. Just in case any school kids read this, I should clarify that I have no idea what Stone Age folks did. What I am stressing on is the importance of ritual in human lives. In any case this is one of the most spectacular homes in the world—thanks to our British rulers—and the setting is majestic.

The president is more talkative this time than on the two previous occasions. Her attendants come with trays of good-looking small eats. Just as I warm up to the idea of those treats (I had a very quick and light breakfast today) as accompaniment to the ritual of presenting the Budget to the president, Her Excellency mysteriously waves off the attendants with, 'Woh nahi lete.' Well, *hum zaroor lete but kya kare.*

As usual Pranab Mukherjee explains the salient features of the Budget and she evinces little interest. I don't blame her. If one is not an economist, a financial journalist or a policymaker, the Union Budget is a rather boring document. We are quickly done.

Then we go through the usual drill of presenting it to the Cabinet. Some of them are really smart and with a deep understanding of fiscal matters. So it is a good discussion. Finally, there is the presentation in the Parliament by the finance minister. This is such a majestic occasion of pageantry and serious, intellectual engagement with policy that it creates a strange high.

After that there are the rounds of media engagement, debate, grilling, and explaining to the public what the Budget tries to do. I meet with NDTV at 1:30 pm, Press Information Bureau at 3 pm, ET Now at 7 pm, BBC News at 7:30 pm, Doordarshan at 8 pm and do an interview with Rajdeep Sardesai at 9 pm. In the middle of all this I spend an hour at the India Today Conclave, at Hotel Taj Palace. While waiting in the green room for our program, I meet Dinesh Trivedi. It is fascinating how different a person can appear on TV and in person.

It is an exhausting day but it feels good to see so much work, slog and research converted into actual policy. The only thing that leaves me with a feeling of discomfort is the retrospective judgement on Vodafone. This was one of those rare matters in the Finance Ministry where I had no prior knowledge. Was I kept out deliberately because my colleagues sensed I would object to it, or did it all happen on one of those days when I was away from Delhi and it escaped other secretaries to bring me in the loop? I do not know.

All morning, till 2 pm, I chaired the BRICS meeting to produce a statement on the new BRICS Bank being planned, for inclusion in the Summit Communique to be released on 29 March. To my pleasure I discovered a flair for diplomacy, using a combination of superciliousness and humoring to cajole cooperation among individuals who would otherwise be bickering. Miraculously, we managed to agree on a statement half an hour before the end of the meeting.

Today turned out to be special not for the BRICS meeting but because Naresh Chandra invited me to a dinner with Henry Kissinger and some thirty others to the Mountbatten Room at the Oberoi Hotel. I don't like Kissinger, but am fascinated by him as part of human history that one can in no way ignore. I could not give up on the opportunity to meet him.

At the start of the dinner, Kissinger was invited to say a few things. He staggered to stand up, said he had damaged a ligament, was not expecting to have to speak and then spoke, slowly, deliberately, in his baritone. It was evident that despite his protests, he was someone who enjoyed speaking. The only time he gave away his age was at the start when he began by saying he had been 'coming to China since 1961'. I am presuming that was a slip and he did not give the whole lecture presuming this was China. That would give a totally different meaning to his observation that the country he was visiting has developed amazingly since then, and especially over the last twenty years.

He ranged over India's prospects (very optimistic), dramatic changes in Indo-US relations (friendlier), Afghanistan, Iran, balance of power in Asia and the role India could play in the entire region in promoting peace. It was riveting, as though we were listening to a medieval Machiavellian philosopher, like listening to a latter day Metternich.

What was more exciting was, maybe because I was paying more attention than the others, he directed much of the lecture at me. At the end of his talk, Naresh Chandra said we were welcome to ask any question. There was a moment of awkward silence. To break that and also because I was genuinely curious, I asked him two questions.

The first: China has a totalitarian government and has done very well. But when such a government begins to falter because there is no easy way to dislodge it, it can destabilize the entire nation. Did he fear this?

He replied that he did fear this. There was a possibility, he added, that China would break up into multiple unstable nations. That would be bad news for India and USA.

The second question I had to pick up some courage to ask: Between him and Mao Zedong was there any feeling of 'warmth' or was it just two persons representing two nations and negotiating? I clarified that talking at that level is a lonely venture and despite each of them representing adversary nations there could be a warmth from the shared loneliness.

Kissinger replied at length to this. The gist was: There was always courtesy between him and Mao, but maybe not warmth. Mao was a person of great stature. 'He filled the room.' Those were Kissinger's words. Kissinger met Mao several times. At their first meeting, Mao told him (to help Kissinger understand Mao) that the Romanian president had just visited Mao and urged him to make peace with Russia, appealing to their common communism. But Mao told the Romanian president, 'Never.' He would wage 1,000 years of war against Russia. Then Mao added, 'Since you (the Romanian president) have come from such a great distance, I will give up 1,000 years and have a war of 900 years.' At the end of some back and forth, Mao settled on 700 years of war. Then he told Kissinger, 'See how easygoing I am, I can give up years of war at the slightest urging.'

23 March 2012, Friday

I have been leading a team from five nations to produce the 'BRICS Report'. We had two five-country meetings in Delhi and the report published by Oxford University Press is to be released at the BRICS Summit on 29 March. But the Chinese have objected to some phrases—such as references to Taiwan without adding 'Province of China', and references to China as a 'market socialist economy'. They wanted 'socialist' to be omitted. It was a day of frenetic activity with calls between Beijing and our office. For reasons of protocol I did not speak to Beijing directly but had my officer on special duty, Supriyo De, speak. Supriyo was rather effective in dousing emotions and enabling us to proceed with plans for the report's release on 29th March.

China, despite outward appearance to the contrary, is a nation lacking in self-confidence. That is what is at the root of their bureaucrats' aggressive behavior. Also, it is a nation with very poor delegation of power down to the government's junior actors. No one is able to take decisions because they are all nervous about what others and their seniors will think. The long-run prognosis of this is not good.

29 March 2020, Thursday

These were two busy days of the BRICS Summit. This is the 4th BRICS Summit and the first time India is hosting it. The heads of states of the BRICS nations—Dilma Rousseff, Dmitry Medvedev,

Hu Jintao and Jacob Zuma—are here. The preparations for these events are endless. My role in an event like this is peripheral. My team worked on the content of what the new BRICS bank can achieve. China's aim is rather different from all the other four nations. It hopes to be able to spend some of its large foreign exchange reserves and own currency via the BRICS Bank, which would help the renminbi to gradually become a globally acceptable money, which would give China a big seigniorage income, and also prestige. India's advantage, and I am sure the considerations are similar for South Africa and Brazil, would be to attract more investment and platforms to expand its manufacturing sector. Russia, I do not understand.

Last evening, the president of India hosted a dinner at her residence for eighty-four persons, based on my quick count while gorging on the excellent food. This morning was spent at the BRICS meeting of heads of states—I had no more than a spectator's role, sitting on the stage, in a row behind the prime ministers and presidents. I think Zuma gave the best speech.

The Indian PM then hosted lunch for all of us at the Taj Palace.

30 March 2020, Friday

Today we managed to get away on a long-planned escape from work. Alaka and I, accompanied by Sudipto Mundle and Preeta, Ruchira and Ajit Ghose, Bhaskar Dutta and Ashwini Deshpande, head off to Varanasi or Benaras for a three-day vacation.

We drive from the airport to Assi Ghat, from there take a boat to Shivala Ghat to reach Surya Udaya Villa, on the bank of the quietly flowing Ganga. The villa is an old, feudal home converted into a beautiful, hacienda-style hotel. It is really an oasis. Behind us is the bustle and utter chaos of this ancient city. And in front of us is the river. The waters are muddy but it is as beautiful as can be. It brings a rush of songs to my head—of rivers being quiet witnesses to history, of the rise and fall of civilizations, and of tales of love and longing. I remember Pussycats singing Mississippi, Bhupen Hazarika's ode to Brahmaputra and Ganga, and of course Paul Robeson's 'Old Man River'.

I am glad we found this place to stay. It is not like a boring 5-star hotel. At the same time, it is a perfect refuge at each hectic day's end. Benaras is as exciting as ever with history writ large at every turn, but the roads are filthy with litter and animal poop, or what I hope is animal poop. Varanasi goes back to over 500 years BC, and has been a major center of trade and traffic and continuously inhabited like no other Indian city. It is a mix of cultures reflecting its complex history, with traces of Buddhism, Hinduism, Islam brought in by the Moghuls, and Christianity that came with the East India Company and the British Empire. It is a mishmash that makes you feel proud of India. Like Rome, we can think of it as Varanasi Aeterna.

We go for a boat ride in the evening to watch the evening aarti at Dashashwamedha Ghat, from the river. As we set out on a somewhat ramshackle boat, drifting over the old river, the sky is a murky grey—*Shaam bhi thi dhuan dhuan, husn bhi tha udaas udaas*. Those were Firaq Gorakhpuri's perfect words. The sky gradually becomes a charcoal black night sky and the lights and candles come on in the old villas and temples.

The *aarti* from the river bank, with the chants reverberating through powerful microphones, is clearly choreographed for tourists but it is done well. With the loud chanting of ancient Hindu Sanskrit slokas by bearded priests standing on the bank, facing the river, with holy smoke rising from the ritual fires, it does feel like we have travelled back in time.

We have a dinner of chaats, at Keshri restaurant. It is a real ramshackle place, but is well known and atmospheric, and the chaats are excellent.

31 March 2012, Saturday

In the morning, we visited the famous Vishwanath Temple. It brought back memories of my previous visit there which was as a child with my mother and father. We then drove to Sarnath, where Gautama Buddha once taught and which is now a major pilgrimage for Buddhists.

No trip to Benaras is complete without a visit to a fortuneteller or *jyotishi*. Ruchira and Ajit know of a famous *jyotishi*, Kameshwar Prasad, and were keen to consult him to get a tip or two about their future, and I have an interest is all such people and am also curious to know what he thinks he knows about my future. So in the evening Ruchi, Alaka, Ajit and I set out for his home. When we arrived in the early hours of the evening, Kameshwar Prasad was in his prayer room. We stood outside the room for a while. The chiming of ancient bells, the smell of incense, and darkness descending outside, made for a heady brew. Shri Prasad is a handsome man with a benign smile and he looks magnificent in his flowing white dhoti. He took us to his consulting 'room', which is an enormous hall, with his desk with various religious texts heaped on it in one end. Alaka is terrified of fortunetellers just in case they blurt out something bad about the future. She came along strictly as an observer and, to make sure the *jyotishi* did not get a flash of insight into her, sat at a far corner. Ruchi, Ajit and I sat at his desk, rather like clients visiting a lawyer. He told us of various prominent politicians who consult him. Ruchi and Ajit had their fortunes checked in detail. I told Kameshwar Prasad that my interest was more casual, just in case he had something to advise me. He asked me some details of my past, date and time of birth, the city of my birth and so on.

He then looked absent-mindedly at the darkness outside the window and then whispered that I will have a very long life— likely to the age of ninety-five or ninety-six. For fortune-tellers this is always the safe forecast. If he gets it wrong and I die the following year, I will not be there to accost him about his failed prediction. If, on the other hand, he told me I would die the following year, he was taking the risk of my showing up in his home the year after that and having a confrontation. This show of cleverness made him go up in my esteem. He may know nothing about the future but he is an intelligent man. He rambled on a bit more about how I would be very successful and generally happy. It was a pleasant enough outing and Kameshwar Prasad was a charming enough person. But the visit did nothing to change my view of fortunetellers, namely, that they have no clue about the future.

2 April 2012, Monday

Yesterday in Benaras, we woke up while it was still dark, and took an early morning boat ride to see the sun rise over the Ganges. It was magnificent seeing the dawn break over this aeterna city, with the shimmering outlines of old dilapidated feudal homes, ancient temples and burning ghats gradually coming to light, as the sun rose over the horizon. It is the kind of sight that fills your mind and heart with the wonder of India, its distant and glorious history. I remembered Nehru's eloquent description of India as 'an ancient palimpsest on which layer upon layer of thought and reverie had been inscribed, and yet no succeeding layer had completely hidden or erased what had been written previously'.

Later in the day we had to catch a flight to Delhi, because today we had a long-planned bilateral India–UK meeting, concerning macroeconomic policy, trade and investment. George Osborne, the British chancellor, with his team of four or five advisers and Pranab Mukherjee with a similar number of us, advisers, sat face to face and went through a range of bilateral policy matters. It turned out to be a useful and pleasant meeting. Osborne is charming in a very British way. This is easy for me to relate to and makes me

nostalgic for my student days at the London School of Economics.
Pranab Mukherjee was in great form today. He has a phenomenal
memory. I can think of just two or three individuals in the world
with this kind of photographic memory. And it comes so easily
to him that he is not aware of it. During the meeting today he
kept effortlessly citing details of old British budgets, including
numbers and data, and chuckling to himself. I don't think George
Osborne had a clue about those details, and nodded benignly and
blushed a little.

11 April, Wednesday

I came to Pune two days ago. Alaka is travelling with me because
we plan to take advantage of my work in this part of Maharashtra to
check out how Karna is faring, doing field research in this region.
We are staying at the Le Meridien which was also the venue for
my lecture yesterday. From there we go over to see Mrinalda—
Mrinal Datta Chaudhuri or MDC, to generations of students
at the Delhi School of Economics. Mrinalda had a mysterious
illness, may be from a small head injury in Delhi or, some say,
tuberculosis of the brain. Whatever it was, he had strange dizzy
spells and had to stop teaching at the Delhi School and moved to
an apartment close to where his brother lives in Pune. Mrinalda,
once a dashing economist, educated at MIT, with multiple (serial)
wives was, by wide consensus, the heart and soul of the DSE. He
was the department chair who offered me the job after I finished
my PhD at LSE. A brilliant economist, who was also notoriously
lazy and hardly wrote anything in life. But he was a fixture in all
coffee house sessions and parties in Delhi. A genuine liberal, he
was like one of those French intellectuals, known more for their
conversation than their writing. It was sad to see him in this
vegetative state.

After this our plan was to go to Sajjan Garh to see Karna who is staying there and doing field work for a research project with some of his MIT classmates. We took advantage of this and first went to Satara, a two-and-a-half hour drive, stayed at the Maharaja Hotel and visited the Ajinkyatara Fort, which figures prominently in Maratha history. These forts in and around Pune fascinate me. It is wondrous seeing the twinkling lights of Satara from the fort in the evening.

This morning we visited Sajjan Garh. We met Karna and his research colleagues, saw some of the sites of his research and together with him headed to Pune, stopping enroute at a sugar cooperative—Kisan Veer, run by Madan Bhosle. We had lunch under a tree and talked to several members of the cooperative, who turned out to be unexpectedly articulate.

In Pune we visited the slums of Pimpri-Chinchwada to see JNNURM activity. It is one of the best-planned slum development projects I have seen anywhere in India. The aim was to increase the square footage area for each of the slum-dwellers by building multi-storey buildings. The slum dwellers were removed, buildings were built and the dwellers were brought back to live in homes which have more square footage than they had earlier. But despite that, land is saved for other purposes because by building up vertically more living space is created. From there we went to see a sewage purifying plant, finally returning to our hotel, drained and exhausted.

Tomorrow we head back to Delhi.

14 April 2012, Saturday

10:30 in the morning was our usual six-weekly meeting: RBI Governor Subbarao, Gopalan, Omita Paul, the finance minister and self, when the governor comes to brief the finance minister regarding the next monetary policy announcement. Pranab Mukherjee was in crisp, Bengali-style dhoti-kurta. The governor and I commiserated how we both are nursing a headache this morning.

There were some tense moments in the conversation as discussions on monetary policy invariably lead to. There was much back and forth, with the usual differences—the government preferring lower interest rates and the RBI resisting this. It is impressive to see that, in effect, India's central bank remains a powerful, autonomous, responsible body.

After the main policy conversation, Pranab Mukherjee drifted into talking about how worried he was about the larger idea of India—that is, beyond his current charge, the economy. He talked about India's long history. Given his awesome memory, he held forth effortlessly, going back a thousand years, about various regional and sectarian forces rearing their heads and threatening to splinter the nation. He hoped that he would not have to see any of that in his lifetime.

Rahul Gandhi came home for lunch today. I had invited him a few weeks ago, asking him to choose a date, half expecting him to decline. But we wrote back and we settled for today. The other guests whom we had invited were Ruchira Chatterjee and Ajit Ghose, Pulin Nayak, Isabel Huacuja (Alaka's Mexican student from Cornell; she also took my game theory class), and Mai, my mother-in-law. And Karna is, luckily, in Delhi with us. So there were nine of us at lunch. Rahul came at 1:20 pm and left just before 4 pm. I was impressed by him, with no affectation and easygoing, and most importantly, with a lot of basic decency. Unlike many other politicians, he had his truckload of security parked unobtrusively outside our home premises.

We shared laughter and ordinary conversation. He talked about politicians. Mayavati, Lalu Yadav, the prime minister and Mamata Banerjee figured prominently. He spoke naturally and without rancor. Another notable trait of his is his deep interest in the social world.

Our household staff—Rekha, her husband and son, and Sushma—wanted to be photographed with him and so we took lots of photographs in different permutations.

18 April 2012, Wednesday

I came to USA, with Karna, by the non-stop Air India flight from Delhi yesterday and am staying, as usual, at the Willard Inter-Continental Hotel, in the ridiculously large suite.

Since I was coming to Washington for the annual IMF-World Bank Spring meetings, I had agreed to give an address to the Carnegie Endowment, at 1750 Mass Ave, Washington, today. It turns out I have a large audience, with media presence. I spoke on the Indian economy and the looming 'Global Crisis of 2014'. It was pegged to the overall deterioration in the European sovereign debt situation and the repayment bunching of LTRO that would occur in December 2014 and February 2015. I made some remarks on India's reforms slowdown, as I have done on several occasions before. (A PTI report misreported, as I later learned, my remarks, by combining my reference to 2014 and the observation that there was a slowdown in Indian reforms, to assert that according to me no reforms would occur till the Indian elections of 2014. And this would turn out to be one of the stormy episodes in my policy career, showing how one sentence, rightly or wrongly reported, can blow up into a political storm. This is a fascinating feature of political life that I was unaware of before coming to this job.)

19 April 2012, Thursday

It was a daylong series of meetings with the IMF, the World Bank, G-20, G-24—the numbers after G were beginning to get addled in my head. I can never make up my mind how useful these meetings are. But with so many countries there, for any country to miss out would be a loss. So even if these meetings are overall not too useful, it is rational for each individual nation to be there. Prisoner's dilemmas do not happen in textbooks alone. In any case, I try to do as good a job as I can, representing India, keeping in mind what I deep down believe in, that our ultimate responsibility is to the world and not just the nation where one happens to be born. And I am also aware that G-something meetings, useful or not, constitute a form of global conversation and camaraderie and this is critical to have in our globalized world.

20 April 2012, Friday

Yesterday passed busy and well. I was blissfully unaware that my alleged comment at the Carnegie Endowment on India's reforms being put on hold till 2014 had appeared as front page news, giving rise to TV debates, with opposition MPs beginning to use this to criticize the government. It was as though I had spilled the beans on the government's plan to shelve all reforms till the election.

At 6:55 am this morning my phone rings. It is Rajneesh saying that Finance Minister Pranab Mukherjee, wants to 'see me' immediately. I am mystified. I have had lots of late night meetings with the finance minister but never been summoned so early. I am in the FM's suite by 7:05 (a record for me in getting ready in the morning). His suite is a flurry of activity, assistants running in and out. Pranab Mukherjee is in a hotel towel dressing-gown. He quickly gets to the point, showing me a news report that says I have started a storm in India. I sit there, read the report and tell him that it is total misreporting—my Europe 2014 comment is confounded with Indian election 2014. I did say that India's reforms had slowed down and am aware that many a real politico would not say that because they feel you are supposed to say everything is good about your government. I have never played that card. I think some self-criticism is worthwhile. Fortunately, the main political persons I interact with, such as the prime minister and the finance minister, never stopped me. But in this case, the reporting is completely wrong. It suggests the government is waiting for the next election to be over and then start the reform, and my saying this is a like an insider giving out a secret.

In any case, Pranab Mukherjee, being a political person, is quite calm about this. He helps me draft a clarification which is to be put out from the Ministry of Finance in Delhi. He tells me to fire up the PTI reporter for the misreporting, and give an interview to some independent television channel to clarify my position.

Alaka phones me from Delhi, sounding stressed which she seldom is on political or economic matters (she often is about other matters). She has been watching television and hearing opposition leaders say that I have given out the government's plans to delay reforms as part of election strategy.

It is again a day of marathon meetings. In the evening I call the PTI reporter, ready to give him a piece of my mind. He is extremely apologetic, saying that he was very sorry and did not realize that his trying to string up different parts of my speech would create the wrong impression. He had clearly already heard some harsh words from others in the government. He sounds so genuine that it is impossible for me to fire him up. In a complete turnaround I end up consoling him.

I give an interview to NDTV's Sarah Jacob and clarify my lecture at Carnegie Endowment, fully aware that in these kind of things once the damage is done, it is done. Nothing much can save the situation, but I am also aware that political tales generally don't last for too long.

22 April 2012, Sunday

Yesterday was the usual Spring Meeting day, packed with meetings, roundtables, and various negotiations. I have also been getting news that the controversy created by my remarks continues to be spun in newspapers, with one or two pieces of very good reportage, I have to admit.

The finance minister and I took the 11 am flight this morning from Washington to New York. I had to spend two hours with the FM in a special lounge at the JFK airport in New York. This can be quite boring but USA provides special security guards for Pranab Mukherjee, and one of them was friendly and looked like Angelina Jolie. The two hours passed quickly.

26 April 2012, Thursday

On my arrival in India, Alaka insisted that I had given the prime minister a lot of grief by my Carnegie lecture and that I needed to go and meet him and do a bit of explaining. I always find these things awkward but I still sought an appointment with the PM and got a prompt reply asking me to show up at his parliament office at 10 am today.

I don't like going to the prime minister's Parliament office because there invariably are journalists outside and they speculate about what one is going in to discuss. I love India's vibrant media— in many ways more vibrant than in many western countries but they can be exhausting. But I have no choice. I walked past a row of newspaper journalists and headed to Manmohan Singh's chamber. We talked from 10:05 am to 10:45 am, one-on-one. He was relaxed, smiling and joking. I began by saying I wanted to tell him directly about my Carnegie lecture and reporting. I told him it was just a case of remarks being picked out of context, and also some straight misquoting. I had spoken in this vein for barely two or three minutes, when he said, 'Now you know what we have to face routinely.' He then changed the topic by asking me if I was reading anything interesting on economics. As it happens, I am currently reading about the Great Depression and the first 100 days of Franklin Roosevelt's presidency. He clearly had a great interest in this and also seemed to know a lot. So we talked about this for a while, then went on to discuss a bit about the role of rating agencies and the constraints they place on policy actions. We also discussed some immediate Indian policy matters. He told me that P. N. Haksar had summed it all up when he wrote that in India, growth and reforms have to be delivered 'by stealth'.

As I left his office, some journalists rushed up to me asking what we talked about; one of them asked if the discussion was about my public lecture in Washington. I refused to comment because I did not want to rake up the Washington controversy and also because if I told them the truth, that we talked about Roosevelt's America, that would give rise to even more controversy.

Though I said nothing, my meeting with him was reported on TV and the next morning's newspaper with speculation about what we discussed—with no one guessing Roosevelt.

30 April 2012, Monday

The British High Commission invited Alaka and me to a reception to celebrate the Queen's Diamond Jubilee, with 'HRH The Duke of York KG' being the chief guest. I got confused and thought the chief guest was Prince William and was excited at the thought of meeting not him but Kate Middleton. On arrival, I asked the British lady welcoming us, 'I hope the chief guest's wife is here?' She said—the British have such a good sense of humor, 'Shhh, he's divorced.' The chief guest, I then realized with a jolt, was Andrew, ex-husband of Sarah Ferguson.

There was a large number of people gathered on the open

lawn of the High Commission. Within minutes of our reaching, an officer introduced herself and said we should move to a corner of special guests who would get to shake hands with the Duke. I had no interest in meeting the Duke but being singled out as special guest pleased me even as it left me bewildered. Why me? I wondered, since I had nothing to do with Indo-British relations.

Soon it was clear that it was a part of Andrew's plan to see me and put pressure on me on the matter of the Vodafone controversy and India's retroactive change in the law. After some jokes and bonhomie, he asked me about retrospective taxation and Vodafone, with the high commissioner joining in. Unfortunately, the Vodafone case was not something on which I knew much since it was not my charge. But it was soon evident to me that Andrew knew even less than me. In fact, he seemed to know nothing beyond the few lines that he had clearly been told just before the meeting. We argued gently. It was actually quite ridiculous discussing something on which I knew little and my interlocutor knew even less. One can see why the sun had to set on the British Empire.

5 May 2012, Saturday

I, along with Alaka, came for a quick trip to USA on 1 May, taking the morning Air India flight from Delhi. On landing, we headed for a family lunch in New York, with Karna and Diksha, and then I took the evening flight to Boston, for Esther Duflo's Tanner Lecture at Harvard.

2nd May was a pleasant morning in my hotel, The Inn at Harvard. I go to the gym and take a brief stroll around Harvard Square, and purchase some books.

Esther gave an excellent First Tanner Lecture. Amartya Sen and Angus Deaton responded. Then there was a superb dinner hosted by Harvard President, Drew Gilpin Faust, on 2 May. At the table we also have Dean Alan Gerber, Sen, Duflo, Deaton, Pasqualine Dupas and Homi Bhabha.

Esther delivered her Second Tanner Lecture on 3 May and I responded. I think I did a better job than Amartya or Angus. I am sure I worked much harder than them anyway. The dinner after the lecture was hosted by Homi Bhabha at Royal East.

Yesterday morning was once again devoted to a Tanner seminar. I had to then conduct the PhD examination for my student Shuang Zhang using Skype from my hotel. Shuang is special to me since I talent-spotted her some years ago when visiting China and then helped getting her over to Cornell for a PhD. Not surprisingly, she passes with flying colors.

After a hurried room service lunch, I head to Taj Boston to address a group organized by CII and USIBC. Rahul Ajmera of ICICI Prudential takes me to meet a group to discuss their concerns for India. I have a wonderful pre-dinner chat at Abhijit and Esther's beautiful Beacon Hill apartment and meet their daughter, Noemie, for the first time.

I have dinner at Tom and Peggy Simons' home. Tom was USA's ambassador to Pakistan. I got to meet him and Peggy some years ago through common academic friends and, such is their charm, that Alaka and I had become good friends with them.

I fly this morning from Boston to JFK, but the Air India flight to New Delhi has been cancelled. So I drive from JFK to Newark, quite fast, catch the non-stop Newark to Mumbai flight, spend five hours in Mumbai and then take the flight to Delhi, reaching around midnight. It must be the old Hindi songs on Air India that do it. I do not feel tired at all.

7 May 2012, Monday

While being driven home from my office at around 8 pm, I see Jairam Ramesh in kurta-pajama crossing the road. I stop and tell him this is impressive. I feel more politicians should walk and also use bicycles to shuttle between home and office, since most of them live in Lutyens' Delhi, close to their office. This will set an example for others and be environmentally good. I tell Jairam I don't think any other minister walks home. He assures me he does so almost every day, and adds with a smile, 'I hope this will make it to your diary.'

27 May 2012, Sunday

I just finished a packed two-day visit to Raebareli in Uttar Pradesh, with a small team from Delhi which includes Shweta, who is a talented member of the IES. Alaka was keen to see this part of the country and so she came along with me. This is a great help because a disproportionate number of meetings on this mission was with women's groups and having Alaka and also Shweta with me helps in getting the village women to open up and speak freely. There is a lot of women's self-help group activism in this region. I wanted to check how those were working out.

The trip began with a visit to Bramhauli village. We have surprisingly candid conversations with the villagers. When I asked them what was the one demand they would make if I gave them the choice, the answer was prompt. They wanted us to make sure that deserving people get their BPL (Below Poverty Line) cards, which are necessary to get subsidized food rations. The villagers complained that those who are close to the gram pradhans, unfairly get BPL cards.

At Usraina village of Raebareli District, we had many heartening discussions with village women. Time and again there were stories of how being freed from dependence on the village moneylender because of support from Self-Help Groups (SHGs) had given them hope and optimism. Sarla Devi told me how a loan from SHG allowed her to start up new activities and also enabled her husband to start a mobile shop that had transformed their lives. Rahinsunnisa told me how some SHG loans changed her life by freeing her from the clutches of moneylenders. Most importantly, she said, she got respect from family and peers and could get her daughter married without having to borrow from private moneylenders. Moneylenders typically charge 10 per cent per month, which compounded turns out to be more than 200 per cent per annum. Most villagers underestimate the power of compounding and get trapped by moneylenders.

These were two days of endless meetings. We visit the 150-bed Indira Gandhi Eye Hospital and Research Centre at Munshiganj in Amethi. It is an impressively managed hospital. I am taken to see a bulk milk-cooling center at Fursatganj, which is run by Mother Dairy. But what is most impressive are the meetings with various NGOs and conversations with village women. The women are articulate and self-confident. It reminded me of my visit several years ago as a researcher to Pathan District in Gujarat where, thanks to the activism of SEWA, the women were confident and enterprising, and that gave hope to the entire region. It was similar in Raebareli. The Rajiv Gandhi Mahila Vikas Pariyojana (RGMVP) seems to be doing here what Ela Bhatt's SEWA had done in Pathan District. It does not just help the disadvantaged but, importantly, empowers them.

One could see the green shoots of progressivity not just for matters of gender empowerment and gender equality, but also in matters of caste and religion. It was so heart-warming to see people of different identities, laughing and joking and rubbing shoulders with one another. A woman from Jhansi told me that, thanks to some support from NGOs, they had conducted a 'chappal rally', whereby lower caste women wore chappals (slippers or sandals) and walked past and even through the homes of upper caste people, something that would have been anathema till recently.

I returned to Delhi a more hopeful human being.

3 June 2012, Sunday

I have just completed a whirlwind tour of Australia and am headed back to Delhi. I came to Canberra on 30 May, via Singapore and Sydney. It is glorious weather and feels strange to hear Australians complain about the cold. The central purpose of the visit is to give the K. R. Narayanan Lecture at ANU. But I have managed to pack it in with many meetings to discuss Indo-Australian economic interests. It is a very well-organized visit because of the interest taken by the Australian high commissioner, the remarkably talented Peter Varghese.

I first met him with a very specific interest in mind. India has one of the most cumbersome bureaucracies, with sluggish decision-making, which slows down the entire economy. Since India's bureaucracy is inherited from the British, I wanted to study nations which had the same inheritance but had managed to reform themselves. Australia was one such nation and I wanted to understand how Australia had managed to do this. I met and quizzed Peter on this and we later become friends because of our common interest in art.

Thanks to Peter, the visit is crammed with meetings in Canberra. I meet David Bradbury, assistant treasurer and person in-charge of deregulation, Will Shorten, minister for financial services, John McCarthy, barrister and diplomat. I also do a lunch with the Indian High Commissioner Biren Nanda at the India House in Red Hill. India has a lot of mining interest in Australia and the Australians are somewhat worried about this. Strangely it seems like colonialism in reverse.

I do an interview with Jim Middleton for ABC Newsline, have a meeting on G-20 matters with David Crawford and Damien Dunn, and discussion on fiscal policy with Roger Brake from the Treasury.

I am given a friendly and super-efficient protocol officer, Arti Kumria, who works in Australia's Ministry of Foreign Affairs, to help me manage my meetings and visits. So apart from this procession of meetings I manage to spend an hour watching the Australian Parliament. I am totally impressed by Julia Gilliard— sharp, progressive and with no false pretension. I manage to slip in a visit to an art exhibition of Australian aboriginal art and Indian tribal art. It is stunning to see the similarities. This is something that fascinates me. Artists distort reality but in fundamentally same ways. It intrigues me that the bulls etched on walls in cave drawings of several thousand years ago have the same distortions that one sees in Picasso. Aesthetics clearly has a common code.

I deliver the K. R. Narayanan Lecture on 1 June evening. The vice chancellor, Ian Young, presides over the occasion, and my friend from Delhi who is now a professor here, Raghbendra Jha, delivers the Vote of Thanks.

Yesterday I flew to Melbourne, staying at the Grand Hyatt Hotel on Collin Street. I have an informal meeting at Monash University. It is lovely to meet up with former students and friends from Delhi—Ranjan Ray, Gaurav Dutt and Pushkar Maitra. I have dinner with Ranjan and Maitreyi and hit the sack early in preparation for the early flight today.

15 June 2012, Saturday

I was supposed to go to Hyderabad for the day for the FSDC sub-committee meeting. I have just come back from Bangalore and am feeling exhausted and so I did what I rarely do. I dropped out.

17 June 2020, Sunday

The big announcement has come that the finance minister, Pranab Mukherjee, is to become president of India. At 10 pm I go to his relatively modest residence to congratulate him. He is in high spirits. I sit for over an hour with him and with Omita Paul, laughing and chatting. There is a steady stream of visitors who are being let in one at a time by the security outside. They come in with garlands, congratulate him and leave. The last person to come (while I was there) was Kamal Nath. Being a prominent minister he settles down and begins to chat. In keeping with his reputation, he quickly gets to talking about some political intrigue. I can see that this is making Pranab Mukherjee visibly uncomfortable—not the content of what he is saying, since being a seasoned politician, he is used to it, but the fact that this is happening with me sitting there. Because I have come into the government from outside and, maybe more importantly, because I will soon be outside of the government, political intrigue and such matters are not discussed in my presence. I think it is also a bit of a sign of respect Pranab Mukherjee has for me that he has consistently shielded me from such subjects. I make things easier by saying that I have been sitting for long and should head home, and get up.

18 June 2012, Monday

A few days ago I wrote to Mrs Sonia Gandhi to say that I was on my way out from the government, back to academe, and would love to drop by and see her. With all the presidential turmoil, I had not expected a reply and, in fact, forgot about my letter. There were calls from her office in the morning today asking if I could come at 6 pm.

I was there punctually (working in the government has made me more punctual) and ushered in to her gracious drawing room in minutes. We had a twenty-minute conversation. She looked very good, with no visible signs of her rumored illness. She was warm and friendly. We talked about the very different personalities of Prime Minister Manmohan Singh and the now-to-be-president, the finance minister, Pranab Mukherjee. I am sure she was cautious about what she said (I prompted this topic) but it was good to see she spoke with ease. She must have sensed that I am reliable as a person, that I will not use this information. We also talked about Mamata Banerjee, Narendra Modi, Subramanian Swamy, of the communists, the RSS. I like her views and politics—they are close to mine. She also talked about the feistiness of Indira Gandhi, and how she responded to political slanderers. There was clearly a lot of natural bonding between daughter-in-law and mother-in-law.

26 June 2012, Sunday

Madeleine Albright came to see me in my office in North Block. I had heard so much about her and read so much on and by her that I was very excited about the visit. Once she sat down I told her that she is unlikely to remember this but she had met my wife and seen me. Some years ago, when Alaka and I were having dinner in a Chinese restaurant in Georgetown, Washington, D.C., Madeleine Albright came into the restaurant for a quiet dinner with her daughter. She was then a celebrity as secretary of state and we were impressed by the lack of fuss in the way she came in and seemed to have no security. Alaka insisted she wanted to talk to her and disregarding my advice that she must not disturb a private dinner, went up to her, said she was a fan and (all I could see was) comfortably sat down to chat. She returned ten minutes later and told me about their brief conversation. The only thing we were wrong about was the absence of security. When Madeleine Albright left, we noted that on her heels, two men in black suits, who were sitting at the bar and having a drink, marched out. I told her about this incident. She insisted she remembered the woman who came and spoke to her.

The conversation eased up with this start. This was a meeting without any serious agenda—almost a goodwill visit. We chatted about Indo-US relations, I talking more about economic relations, she about political. It was a cordial nothing-in-particular meeting (and a good prelude to the fact that I would meet her later in life, when I would live in Washington and have some friendly and non-diplomatic meetings).

29 June 2012, Friday

It is Statistics Day. T. C. A. Anant, chief statistician of India, and one-time student of mine (we also later taught game theory together at the Delhi School of Economics) had invited me to be on the dais with his minister, Shrikant Jena. The minister was to release three, progressively smaller-sized publications of the Ministry of Statistics. What no one realized is that the books were packed and sealed with what can only be described as industrial-strength sellotape. It became an unseemly sight as the minister wrestled to cut the tape. I, being next to him, had to join in to help him and soon the two of us were grappling and battling with the books to cut the tapes and release them. The audience had begun clapping as the minister started to cut the first tape and had to keep up a slow clap as the little wrestling match happened.

4 July 2012, Wednesday

I flew to Chennai on 1 July, and drove with Nadu (T. C. A. Srinivasa Raghavan) and Raghubir Srinivasan to Pondicherry, reaching there just before dinner and had an excellent dinner at La Terasse with Professor Ramachandran and R. Satish.

The next morning, I visited Aurobindo Ashram—always a balm for tired minds and souls; then lectured at Pondicherry University and left around 2 pm with Nadu and Raghubir for Chennai. On the way, we had a late lunch at the Radisson Blu Hotel in Mahabalipuram. Heading for Chennai we decided to stop at the North Shore temple. At the entrance, the guard pulled me out of the queue claiming I was not Indian and had to pay the higher fee meant for foreigners. This is presumably because I have a lighter skin than most South Indians. This became a joke among my friends who said they were looking at me with envy when I was pulled out of the queue. I argued and won, and paid the lower fee meant for Indians.

Dinner in Chennai was with Subbu and Prabha in their home in the foothills of St Thomas' Mount. I am staying at the elegant Chola Sheraton.

Yesterday I gave three lectures—at the South Indian Chamber of Commerce, at a function at Vaishnav College for Women organized by the Triplicane Cultural Academy, and, finally, to the Reserve Bank Staff College. Each lecture seems to go better than the previous one. At the third lecture, a young man was looking at me as if I were God. After my lecture he swooped down to touch my feet. I didn't know what to do. I decided that just because I did not believe in God was no reason to contest his belief.

I had dinner with M. Ramesh of *Business Line* at Ratna Café in Triplicane. He wanted to do a sort of conversational interview over a meal. Superb idli, endless sambar, the best rava masala dosa I have ever had, together with a wonderful conversation made it a memorable evening. The reason we chose Ratna Café is interesting. Several years ago, soon after I began my teaching career, I had gone as visiting professor to Madras University's Econometrics Department, at the invitation of Professor U. Sankar. Madras University has a separate Economics Department and an Econometrics Department. Someone whispered to me that only Brahmins are allowed in the Economics Department.

Professor Sankar organized for me to stay at the University Guest House on Marina. It was a place of very basic services but a magnificent view of the sea. One morning, bored of the daily lunch at the Guest House, I inquired about good Tamil food in the traditional city area of Triplicane. I was told by a hotel staff with a marked South Indian accent that the two best places are—what I heard as 'Ratna Cave' and 'Murali Cave'. These sounded like nightclubs. In any case, I picked at random, and headed to Ratna Cave, which turned out to be Ratna Café, a traditional non-fancy place, exactly the kind of interesting restaurant I was looking for. It had another advantage. There was little to choose from. When entering, you say, 'with yogurt' or 'without yogurt' and accordingly you pay Rs 6 or Rs 4, and the meal is brought to you. It was such a memorable experience that when M. Ramesh asked me where I wanted to have lunch, I said Ratna Café (and saved *Business Line* a lot of money).

11 July 2012, Wednesday

On 7 July, I spoke at the Bharat Chamber of Commerce in Kolkata, at the Park Hotel, and after lunch gave another talk at Taj Bengal, organized by Suman Mukherjee. Later, Mamata Banerji responded to my comments and I got drawn into an FDI controversy. The next morning's newspapers, especially the Kolkata ones, are full of this story.

I had a civil afternoon today at Sheesh Mahal at the Taj Palace Hotel in Delhi. It was a lunch with the Singapore prime minister, Lee Hsien Loong, hosted by the Singapore high commissioner. The conversation got quickly sailing since I had earlier met his father, Lee Kwan Yew, and sister, Lee Wei Ling, at a dinner hosted by Manmohan Singh. Lee Hsien Loong seems more polished than both his father and sister. They are clearly a talented family. The sister was eccentric but brilliant, as was obvious from my conversation with her. Prime Minister Lee Hsien Loong was a topper in mathematics (Senior Wrangler) at Trinity College Cambridge; so he must be brilliant too, but he does not seem to have any eccentricity, rather like the suave neighbor next door. It is meant to be an agenda-free lunch and we talked about academics, research and life in politics.

18 July 2012, Wednesday

It is time for my annual EPFL lecture in Lausanne. I came on the 12th. Diksha comes for a few days. Alaka and I give our lectures. We visited St Gallen, Berne, walked the beautiful bylanes of Lutry outside Lausanne, and it is time to leave for Delhi today.

23 July 2012, Monday

It was a very St Stephen's evening. I had dinner with Sid Khanna, Rakesh Chopra, Jyoti Sagar, Rahul Khullar and Shashank Raizada at the Oberoi. We laughed and joked, recounting pranks from our college days. I reminded them about how in college I once went to Chandigarh with one of our classmates. He had planned to meet a girl, whom he had a crush on even though they had never met. He invited her to a nearby city garden, saying that she should be able to recognize him easily, because he would be carrying flowers, while his friend (meaning me) would be in a yellow shirt. Just before this momentous meeting my friend's nerves failed him and he pleaded with me that I should just meet her myself and give her the flowers on his behalf. I must have appeared like a strange apparition to the poor girl—an amalgam of two persons walking up to her, wearing a yellow shirt and carrying flowers. Fearing that she would scream at this strange sight, I virtually threw the flowers at her and ran.

We laughed about the many wedding parties in Kamla Nagar, close to college, that we gate-crashed. Once we heard that there would be a big wedding with hundreds of guests, we would dress up well and wait in hiding outside the wedding venue. Once the groom arrived, we joined in, dancing with the groom's large entourage and go in, the groom's side thinking we are from the bride's side and the bride's side thinking we are from the groom's side. We would then gorge on the food, a welcome break from the college cafeteria, and leave. Some of our more courageous classmates would even hug the bride's parents and wish them good-bye when leaving.

24 July 2012, Tuesday

I met the prime minister at 11:05 am. It was an intense twenty-five-minute conversation. We discussed the Delhi Economics Conclave, the Indian drought, USA's corn prices, political corruption, who should be the next chief economic adviser, the choice of director for NIPFP, the scope for a South-South Bank, India–China dynamics, and the potential for India–Australia strategic relations. It is impressive that as PM, he can so comfortably get into matters of detail on so many topics. He also has an instinctive empathy for ordinary people. No surprise that one of the senior diplomats in the German embassy told me that Manmohan Singh is Angela Merkel's favourite political leader. He said her face lights up when she meets him. Despite all these discussions of policy, he nevertheless seemed despondent about the state of India's politics, and mused about the uncertainties of political life. On the way out, I stopped to talk to Pankaj Pachauri, Manmohan Singh's communications adviser. He was pleased about the *TIME* magazine story and the challenge of doing communications for a prime minister who is innately modest.

In the evening I did some work for the Infosys Prize jury, and had a phone conversation with Narayana Murthy. This Infosys work is a much needed refuge from the rough and tumble of my daily life on Raisina Hill.

27 July 2012, Friday

We, the secretaries of the Ministry of Finance, had to appear in front of a Standing Committee of Parliament chaired by Yashwant Sinha. I like Yashwant Sinha. He has an elder statesman's grace and a warm, avuncular way of expressing disagreement. And he seems to be a person of integrity. The meeting turned out to be a marathon one, from 12:30 pm to 3:15 pm, followed by lunch. BJP's Ravi Shankar Prasad opened, attacking me for the remark I had made about politicians 'at times being rabble rousers'. He omitted my qualifier 'at times', was upset by what he described as my blanket criticism, and left. Among others were Dr K. S. Rao (difficult to gauge), Gurudas Dasgupta (good man, confused), Piyush Goyal (man, confused) and Renuka Chaudhury (all charm but at the same time intelligent and sensible).

During lunch, Gurudas Dasgupta told me his views on Pranab Mukherjee, which were not particularly flattering. He clearly likes the prime minister, despite ideological differences.

31 July 2012, Tuesday

Curtain.

It is my last day as India's chief economic adviser. It is a day of farewell speeches, farewell gatherings and a sentimental dinner. There is gushing praise for me. In order to not get a swollen head, I remind myself of what Paul Samuelson advised someone who had to speak at some similar occasion. If I recall correctly, the person being celebrated was not particularly bright. Samuelson's advice to the speaker was: 'Remember you are not under oath.'

5 August 2012, Sunday

My time as CEA is formally over but I help out the office with some left-over work. The day before yesterday, I met Finance Minister P. Chidambaram and had a nice half-hour chat. To use a Delhi slang, he seemed PLU—people like us. He requested me to give some policy action points for his first statement to the media as finance minister. I worked hard yesterday to prepare eight action plans for Chidambaram to use, and handed it over to him.

Today Rahul Bose came for lunch. Rahul is famous as an actor and now more so because of the lovely film, *The Japanese Wife*, about a middle class Indian man, played by Rahul, who falls in love with a Japanese girl. Alaka and I decided to take him for lunch to Good Earth in Khan Market. A young Indian and his shy Japanese wife came up to us and said he would just have to interrupt us for a photograph of Rahul Bose, with him and his Japanese wife.

The last few weeks many people have asked me the same question: How do I feel returning to the quietude of academe and life in research, after the hurly burly of politics and managing large teams reporting to me? There is a hint of wistfulness in the question. But I do not feel sad at all. Research and a life of the mind has a special attraction, which, unless you have been a part of that life, you would not know. The excitement of a new argument or a new idea beginning to take shape in the mind can be riveting. My nearly three years in the policy world has given rise to many fledgling ideas that I want to pursue. I will miss the large team of administrative staff working for me and taking away all the drudge work from my desk, but overall I am ready to be back in the world of scientific inquiry, to ask new questions and try to answer them. I am ready for the quietude of academe.

PART TWO

The Washington Years

2012–2016

With Madeleine Albright in my North Block Office, 26 June 2012.

With former chief economists of the World Bank (L to R): Joseph Stiglitz,
Nicholas Stern, Francois Bourguignon, and Justin Yifu Lin.
Dead Sea, Jordan, June 2014.

Early days as chief economic adviser. Outside
my North Block office, New Delhi.

Mannequin, bought in Lajpat Nagar,
Delhi, attired by me, became notorio█
on my balcony in Delhi. Here in my
new home in Washington, D.C.

With Sheikh Hasina, prime minister of Bangladesh, 13 December 2015.
(L to R): Christine Kimes, Forhad Shilpi, Biru Paksha Paul, Atiur Rahman.

Meeting President Barrack Obama at the residence of the Indian prime minister on 7 November 2010. Along with Tim Geithner and N.R. Narayana Murthy.

With Manmohan Singh, Shabnam, Avaaz and Alaka on the occasion of Diksha's wedding ceremony in Delhi, 20 December 2015.

With Aung San Suu Kyi, in Nay Pyi Taw, 25 March 2015.

In Senegal, with Celestin Monga, meeting a group of students, March 2013.

A chess set, outside my World Bank office, for aesthetics.
With Laverne making an illegal move with the pawn.

George Akerlof, giving a lecture, preceding dinner, at our home in Washington D.C., 23 September 2016.

Lecture, organized by the Elliott School, George Washington University on Game theory in the real world.

Magic show for the children of the World Bank Staff, 28 April 2016.

After lunch, Rahul Gandhi at our home in Delhi.
Alaka on the right, 14 April 2012.

Meeting President Obama in the White House, 29 January 2015.

In our home on 9 January 2012, with Anne Vaugier-Chatterjee,
Diksha Basu, Upamanyu Chatterjee,
Vikram Seth and Himanjali Sankar.

In Addis Ababa, with contemporary Ethiopian artists, along with World Bank's
Nicole Klingen, Gelila Woodench, Albert Zeufack and Phillip Hay, July 2016.

With Michael D. Higgins, president of Ireland, at his home, 7 November 2014.

With the prime minister of Bhutan, Tshering Tobgay in Thimpu, Bhutan, 3 January 2015.

Introducing Joseph Stiglitz, at a World Bank Lecture, 29 September 2016.

With the World Bank president, Jim Yong Kim, at a meeting with the
World Bank's Board of Directors, 22 October 2015.

With the president of Mauritius, Ameenah Gurib-Fakim, 22 July 2016.

With Sir Anthony Atkinson, at his home in Oxford, 4 June 2016.

Discussing the World Development Report, 2017, at the World Bank with
Tharman Shanmugaratnam, Deputy Prime Minister of Singapore, 14 April 2016.

With Alaka, Jorgen Weibull and Florence Dalgard visiting Amartya Sen
at his home in Santiniketan, 15 January 2019.

6

Pennsylvania Avenue

8 August 2012, Wednesday

Some two weeks before 31st July, my last day as CEA, I got a call from the World Bank president's office. A man with a slight Indian accent, one of his assistants, a Sikh gentleman I later gathered, said that the president wanted to talk to me about various things. So much so that he wondered if I could do a brief trip to Washington.

I thought that since Jim Yong Kim had taken over as World Bank president recently (in June) and was quite a greenhorn in this kind of work, he must be calling up chief economists or treasury chiefs of various countries to get a briefing on their economies. That was a noble enough mission but it was too much to expect me to fly all the way to Washington to brief him. So I said I was happy to talk but that we could just as well have a long conversation on the phone. There were multiple calls related to this and I began to get a bit suspicious of Jim Kim's thirst for knowledge. So when his assistant called again a couple of days ago I asked him exactly what the World Bank president wanted to talk about. By then he must have received instruction that he could reveal it to me. Without any change of tone, he told me that the president was thinking of offering me the job of chief economist of the World Bank.

Hyperventilating is an over-used term these days but I think I hyperventilated, whatever that means. It was both exciting and unsettling. After nearly three years in the policy world, with seemingly not a moment to myself, I was looking forward to my first love, research and lecturing, and the joys of being able to close my door and read and write as and when I felt like. On the other hand, I knew what an exciting job this could be, and I had never thought it would come my way. For one, this job was typically reserved for economists from USA and Europe. The only exception was the last chief economist, Justin Yifu Lin, from China. Also, deep research questions are my obsession in economics and I did not think of myself as visible enough in the economic policy scene—though my previous years as CEA to the Indian government must have begun to change that.

In any case, so much of life is luck. My primary interest in economics was always economic theory; the policy interest is a by-product. I had one side diversion. I enjoyed writing for the popular media. This I think has helped me disproportionately, in getting these exciting policy jobs. One of my luckiest columns was the one I wrote for BBC. A few years before I got the offer of the chief economic adviser post, I had started writing a regular column for *BBC News Online*, at the invitation of BBC's Soutik Biswas. The column became wildly popular, with laypersons and politicians reading and commenting on it. I have a theory about why this happened. Soon after I began writing my column, BBC invited the celebrated (and stunning) Bollywood actor, Preity Zinta, to also write a column, and that used to appear next to mine. My hypothesis is a huge number of people came to see Preity Zinta's face and read my column, thereby giving me a major career break.

I had had one earlier experience with the World Bank and had a sense of what the job entailed. In 1998, Joe Stiglitz, then chief economist of the Bank, decided to invite some academic economists to the World Bank as visitors. Jean-Francois Bourguignon and I were the first ones he invited and I spent a full academic year, 1998 to 1999, at the Bank, on leave from Cornell. I had enjoyed the year and also fantasized once or twice how it would feel like being in the oversized office room that Joe had. But I never seriously thought of that as anywhere within the realm of possibilities. I should clarify, this was a surprise not because I thought I did not deserve it, but because I did not think anyone else thought I deserved it.

In fact, the only reason I think I fantasized on this was the World Bank had given me one of the smallest imaginable offices, and with no windows, for the year I spent there (even though the salary more than compensated for that). And to rub salt to injury, it got me visiting cards and letterheads made in which, below my name, it said: 'Office of the Senior Vice President, World Bank'. This did cause occasional awkwardness. To an innocent bystander, who else would be sitting in the 'Office of the Senior Vice President' but the senior vice president! That is what must have happened to Thea Sinclair. Thea was a colleague and dear friend during the first year of my working life, when I was finishing my PhD at LSE and began teaching at Reading University. I remember Thea, whom I had not met after 1978, phoning me from the World Bank reception and saying that she was visiting Washington and thought of dropping by to see me. I was immensely pleased and said I would come down to the reception. To that she firmly said no and added that she wanted to see the 'Office of the Senior Vice President'. There was no way of stopping her; she ran up the three flights and burst into my office. I think that was the first time I saw someone hyperventilate, caused by the shock of divergence between what she expected and what she saw.[11]

---

11. Sadly, that was the last time I saw Thea. Thea died in a horse-riding accident in 2006 at the age of fifty-six.

Anyway, to return to the phone calls, a compromise plan was hatched. The World Bank president had some work in London and it was decided that the Bank would fly me to London and we would stay and meet up at the Sofitel airport. That is what brought me to London yesterday. I had taken the 8:20 am British Airways flight from Delhi. So there was little sleep loss. On arrival, I worked for a while in my hotel room and then I phoned my friend, Gautam Sen, originally from Kolkata where we were virtual neighbors when we were of school-going age, and whom I met up again many years later when we were both students at LSE.

Since Heathrow airport is on the edge of Southall, which is an ethnic enclave of mainly Indians but also Pakistanis and Bangladeshis, I thought this was a great opportunity to explore Southall. I have always been convinced that deep down in me there is a closet anthropologist. Any place I visit I am much more fascinated by the ordinary people and their lives than the museums and palaces. Though I had lived in London for many years I did not know Southall, which sounded magical and romantic, as all ethnic enclaves do. Gautam and I walked around for a while and had dinner at Southall's favourite 'Brilliant Restaurant' that described itself as the 'only one of its kind'. The food was very good and I felt the use of the adjective was accurate.

From 8 am to 10 am today I had a breakfast meeting with Jim Yong Kim, World Bank president, in his grand hotel suite. My first impression was that of a terrific person. I liked him and for me that is always a critical step before I decide to work with someone. His political orientation seemed broad left, which I liked. We had common friends; we talked about Amartya Sen and Nick Stern. We talked about the policy challenges that the developing world faces today, the Indian economy and Africa; we gossiped a little about previous World Bank personalities and presidents—I liked the fact that he did so quite comfortably. At the end of it, he said he had of course already done his homework on me and based, in addition, to this conversation (he didn't call it an interview), he would want to offer me the job of chief economist and senior vice president, though this would have to be ratified by the World Bank's Board on 27 August.

I had lunch in a pub with my old friend Rupen Mallik and his partner, Mimi, and I caught the 5:40 pm British Airways flight back to Delhi.

10 August 2012, Friday

The prime minister hosted a farewell lunch at his residence, 7 RCR, which I treated as both a farewell lunch and, without the prime minister's knowing it, a birthday party for Alaka.

1 October 2012, Monday

I joined the World Bank today. My office is on the fourth floor of the Main Building of the Bank on Pennsylvania Avenue. In terms of square footage, this is the largest office I have ever occupied. I tried not to feel good and proud about such trivial things but I failed. This used to be Joe Stiglitz's office. Joe's secretary, whom I used to occasionally stop by to chat with, was fond of me, and insisted that one day I would be in this office. This was so far-fetched that I treated her remark as that of a person wishing me well. It was not something I thought twice about. Strange indeed is fate that here I am sitting in that very office.

As I mentioned before, during the 1998–99 visit, I had the opposite experience, of getting to use the smallest office I ever had. There was a shortage of space in the Bank that year, the regular, permanent staff had grabbed all the decent offices and so I had to take a cubby hole with no windows.

Within minutes of my arrival in my new job, Vivian Hon, who was effectively my chief of staff, and Laverne Cook, my main administrative assistant, reminded me that I was to launch the 'World Development Report on Jobs'. I had agreed to do this because the report was led by Martin Rama, whom I knew well before joining the bank and whose work I admired, and also because I was told firmly by Vivian that this was my job. I had barely glimpsed through the report, but I had no choice.

Vivian and I walked down to the auditorium where the launch would take place. It was packed with Bank staff, outsiders, the press. I began speaking and soon realized that my experience in the world of Indian politics had trained me well to speak without content. I managed well enough. I was now a part of the World Bank.

6 November 2012, Tuesday

The last week was a whirlwind tour. It began with one of the most beautiful places in the World, Izmir, in Anatolia, in southern Turkey, where the Turkish Economic Association's Annual Congress was being held. I arrived on 1 November, just before dusk. There was little time to indulge in jetlag for I had a late evening meeting with Erdem Basci, governor of the Turkish Central Bank, and Mehmet Yorukoglu, deputy governor of the Central Bank. Turkey's Central Bank is run by some of the most academically established economists. This is good for Turkey because these people are able to experiment intelligently with new policies which most emerging economy central bankers are too timid and without adequate research curiosity to try.[12] As a result, I was able to have detailed and instructive discussion on the role of monetary and fiscal policy in stimulating the economy and to learn about Turkey's experience. Though I am now a World

---

12. This would change soon with Erdogan's growing power and consequent retreat of professionalism in these technical jobs, which has deeply hurt the Turkish economy.

Banker, conversation also kept veering to India and my experience as chief economic adviser there.

The World Bank allows the president, senior vice presidents and two or three other senior-most people to be accompanied by an assistant when they go on international missions. This is expensive at one level but an expenditure that is well worth it. It enhances my efficiency during these travels hugely. With all appointments, minutes and logistical negotiations being delegated, I can literally go from meeting to meeting, without a break. Vivian accompanied me on this mission and she is quite extraordinary. Among other things, she keeps reminding me that though, given my recent India experience, people naturally drag conversations to India, I now have to act the World Banker.

The next morning it was a meeting with the finance minister, Mehmet Simsek. He seems like a person with little pretension or ministerial pomposity and we got along well. We discussed World Bank–Turkey relations and also the economic policy challenges for Turkey and India. He is Kurdish and I was curious about whether and how that affects the way other politicians in Turkey relate to him. I dangled some leading questions to get a hint on this but he is seasoned enough as a politician not to take the bait.

My formal lecture was on the Indian economy. My Indian experience is so recent that I can speak off the cuff, even though, as I am already aware, the World Bank's communications department is very cautious about what we, senior people in the World Bank, say or write in public. Last week Merrell Tuck-Primdahl, who is the senior communications officer in my division, told me gently that while on this mission I should try to not speak on Spain and Greece. She also said that when Bloomberg TV's Hande Berktay interviewed me, she would try to draw me into discussions on India. I was to gently steer away from that (but not by replacing India with Spain and Greece).

The Ministry of Finance in India was much more relaxed

concerning communications. There was a communications department in the Ministry that did keep track of what I was saying and how, and occasionally gave me advice. But India is innately anarchic. So I never felt restrained by the communications folk.

The next morning, I left for a one-day trip to Ephesus, on the coast of Ionia. It is a stunning Hellenic city, with the ancient Library of Celcus and the Temple of Artemis. One of the most moving stops for me was at Meryam Ana Evi, the house of Mother Mary, Jesus' mother. It is believed, not authenticated, that Mother Mary spent the last years of her life in Izmir in this house. The belief is strong enough among Catholics that there are lots of visitors, creating an atmosphere of an ancient house of worship. Maybe because I went to a Jesuit Catholic school in Kolkata and was brought up on stories of Jesus and Mother Mary, this lovely old home and the sight of so many people praying, filled me with a spiritual feeling of awe and wonder.

But it was all too short. Late in the evening I flew to Istanbul and then to Delhi. On 5 November, I gave a lecture on labor and labor laws at the IZA-World Bank Conference. I met the World Bank's dashing Country Director, Onno Ruhl. I am staying at the Oberoi. It is disorienting to be in Delhi and to live in a hotel.

After the lecture I went to visit Manmohan Singh and later in the day I met Rahul Gandhi at his residence and chatted about the Indian economy and especially how policies can be better directed to those who are relatively poor. Rahul has frequently come under political and journalistic attack but I quite like him. I agree with his critics that he is not a natural political leader. He certainly does not have the rabble-rousing instinct. Even though I share his ultimate goals—development with greater economic equality, secularism, freedom of speech and rejection of narrow identity politics—I do not agree with all his policy ideas. Despite this, I think he will be a good leader because of three qualities. He is honest and transparent, which is rare in a politician. Next, he is willing to listen. The world today is too complex for any leader to determine on his or her own what is best policy. You need to listen to expertise and be ready to delegate decisions, even if that means someone else will steal some of the glory. Finally, he satisfies one attribute, which is so important that it should be a basic qualifying criterion for anyone wanting to lead a nation. You must be willing to gracefully give up power if the popular mandate runs out. Rahul Gandhi does not have this infatuation with power. (The importance of this criterion has become more evident, in retrospect, after we saw the damage Donald Trump did by his craze to hang on to office at all cost.)

After my conversation with Rahul Gandhi I made a brief visit to meet with my former boss, Pranab Mukherjee, who is now the president of India, at the Rashtrapati Bhavan. It is clear that, as a job, being president is nowhere nearly as exciting as being finance minister. But I hope he realizes that the square footage of his housing compensates for that.

22 December 2012, Saturday

Having just come to India, on 21 December, soon after 7:30 am I left Kolkata by car with a team for Para Block, Purulia District, on the edge of West Bengal, abutting into Jharkhand, to visit various projects concerning health (eye hospital for villagers), education and the raising of agricultural productivity, managed mostly by the NGO Nanritam, run by two remarkable women Ranjana Sengupta, an IT professional, and Bharati Bakshi, a doctor. This part of Purulia is largely tribal, inhabited mainly by Santhals, Kumis and Savars, but also upper caste Hindus and Muslims.

We left Kolkata by the second Howrah Bridge, got on to National Highway 2 that runs here on the west of and almost parallel to the famous Grand Trunk Road, that goes all the way to Delhi and beyond, with colonial history and even Moghul history markers all along the way. We drove past a desolate Singur where the abandoned Tata Nano factory gives it a look reminiscent of Fatehpur Sikri, past Shaktigarh, with its sweetmeat shops, a veritable diabetes trap, and towards Durgapur, a journey I had made so many times as a school kid with my father. Immediately after Asansol we left NH2 to head south. The quality of the road deteriorated rapidly and when, after crossing Damodar River, we entered the Purulia District, the road literally became a ribbon where the slightest lurch to the left or the right would land us on the dirt tracks that skirt the road.

Purulia, barren and undulating, is a picturesque district that reminded me of scenes from Buddhadeb Dasgupta's surreal films.

We arrived at Para Block at 2 pm, lunched, rested and went out to see the premises of the eye hospital with its surgery facilities. This is extremely impressive. It demonstrates what a few good people can do. Villagers, bedraggled and poor, come from great distances for routine eye checks, glaucoma treatment, retina surgery and cataract surgery. The doctors and nurses seem to be a dedicated lot. They tell us that, though this is a Maoist-afflicted area, with occasional bursts of revolutionary violence, the Maoists do not trouble them because they recognize the value to the villagers of the work that Nanritam is doing. They tell us they are sure that among their patients there have been Maoist revolutionaries who came incognito and got themselves treated. The eye hospital is undergoing an expansion and we reviewed the new building.

I then had conversations with local teachers, agricultural scientists, and social workers about the potentials of the region. They told us about their wish to start a regular school, all the way to Class 10, in that area. Several retired teachers from the Ramakrishna Mission school in Purulia town have volunteered to work if such a school comes up. I met some of them and it is impossible not to be impressed by their zeal. Ranjana and Bharati, the main spirit behind Nanritam, are also raring to go but they have to raise funds, Rs 10 crores minimally to create a viable school.

Seeing their dedication and the bleakness of the region, I feel such an effort will be well worth it. What is impressive about this group is that they are well meaning and passionate and, at the same time, they seem endowed with entrepreneurial skill and a sense of reality about the financial challenge. Despite their association with a Hindu Missionary movement, like much of Ramakrishna Mission, they are totally secular, with no religious or caste discrimination.

14 February 2013, Thursday

I went to meet Madeleine Albright in her office, Albright Stonebridge Group, at 5 pm. It turned out to be a wonderful meeting. We talked about world affairs and the role of politics in development. We also spoke at length about North Korea. She said she was the highest level US government official who had been there. It was a slightly chilling feeling, once there, to be completely in their charge, since USA did not have an embassy. I prodded her about how it was interacting with Kim Jong Il. She said, at an individual level she found him quite personable.

Kim had organized a special dance program for her in which a group of Korean women dancers wearing red dresses would huddle together. When they broke out of the huddle, the clothes, which probably had Velcro straps, would be turned inside out and they would all be in green dresses. Then after another round of huddling they would be in red again. On one such round, the velcros probably got stuck and one girl came out half red and half green. Kim Jong Il got so angry that Madeleine Albright had to calm him down assuring him that these things happen. Good training in diplomacy has its uses.

She said that her only disappointment was that the agreement they reached was not carried out by Kim. She felt that the North Koreans were gaming her. I pointed out that it was possible that no one among the North Koreans were individually gaming her, but they were caught in a trap. It is possible that Kim wanted to carry out the agreement but he himself was in a trap. If he did do so, his generals might have turned against him and that could be dangerous for him. And his generals may have behaved the way they did because they were in turn caught in their own trap.

She thought a bit and said that that is possible because the intricacies of foreign policy can be so complex. We got along well. I asked her to come to give a public lecture at the World Bank and she promptly agreed.

9 March 2013, Saturday

I never thought I would descend to being the kind of person who reads budget speeches for pleasure. I was therefore alarmed when, *en route* to Johannesburg, from Washington via Dakar, I found myself reaching out for Finance Minister Pravin Gordhan's Budget Speech that he had just delivered to the South African parliament. Worse, I soon found myself reading it with pleasure. The pleasure came from two sources: the eminent sensibility of the speech, and comfort from the realization that the problems we contend with, wherever we are, are fundamentally similar. South Africa is wrestling with keeping its fiscal deficit under control, its flagging growth rate up and yawning inequities in check. Musing about these problems I dozed off. When I woke up the cabin was dark. Curious about who was going to Dakar I looked around. Of the passengers in my cabin, around 30 per cent were Black, 70 per cent were White, and 80 per cent were watching *The Best Exotic Marigold Hotel*.

When I alighted in Johannesburg on 2 March, the air was

bracing, the sky clear, as only the African sky can be, and the warmth and smiles of the people switched on in my head the opening lines of Rabindranath Tagore's famous poem in Bengali, called 'Africa'. Tagore wrote it in 1936, one year after Mussolini's invasion of Ethiopia, a poet's protest against the savagery of the powerful.

Officials from the World Bank's Pretoria office were on hand to receive us. There was Asad Alam, who is the country director for the World Bank. A charming woman came and shook hands with me; I was told she is Anneline, the Bank's security officer, who will be with me during my stay here. Jacob will be driving me around for the next two days. He is the font of wisdom. Every time we are stuck on a question, be it one pertaining to street directions, South African politics or history, we would just have to lean over and ask Jacob. As we drove to my hotel in Pretoria, cruising down well-maintained boulevards, past magnificent homes, at a street crossing, we see two luxury cars that have come to a halt and two well-dressed men, presumably occupants of the cars, wrestling on the road. It was a disturbing scene. I ask Jacob what was going on. 'They are having a fight,' he said matter-of-factly, making it impossible for me to pursue the investigation any further.

There are few countries in the world that carry as big a burden of history as South Africa. The brutality of apartheid weighs down on not only the pages of the nation's history books but contemporary policy debates, and statistics. Unemployment among Whites is at a manageable level; unemployment among Blacks would make the worst performing economy in the Eurozone crisis look good. The story is similar for health indicators, poverty head counts, and per capita income. South Africa today has impressive people at the helm of policy; but the challenges are equally impressive. History can be a difficult adversary. Colored and black people do not have to leave the precincts of the main cities before dusk as they once had to under apartheid law, but thanks to poverty and housing costs many of them still do. They return to their townships, where land is cheap and housing affordable. In fact, the percentage of Blacks living in townships has gone up in the last ten years from 30 to 37.

The next morning, I had breakfast with the Indian high commissioner to South Africa, Virendra Gupta. After that, with Celestin, who has traveled with me from Washington, Asad and Sandeep from the local World Bank office, my security officer, Anneline, and a special security person for going into the township, two visitors from Brazil, Anaclaudia and Eduarda, who are experts on the problems of the favelas, Xiabo who is an expert on China's village enterprise (and was once a student of mine) and some local people, I headed out to Diepsloot, a township half way between Pretoria and Jo'burg and home to around 200,000 people. There is so much crime and violence that this visit would have been impossible but for the help received from Pravin Gordhan. I was told the fully armed personal security, with the bulge of their guns showing, was essential.

One enters Diepsloot via a modern shopping mall, and there, the mall's affable manager, Mzo, showed us around proudly showing how well the mall is run. But as soon as one enters this sprawling township, the scene changes sharply.

Diepsloot was created out of nothing, in 1994, as a residency for displaced people and low-skilled workers. Over time, through lack of work, the low skill has, for many, sloped off into no skill. The terrain is rugged—iron and asbestos, roads that are potholed and undrained. Even the homes of the poor are protected with barbed wires and the artless cubism of grills.

We walked into a couple of homes, talked to street vendors and local businesspersons. I was assured that there would be no way to do this after dark when people bolt their doors and the streets wear a deserted look and crime is rampant. As often happens in crime-infested areas, there is something lovely about the people at an individual level; and the disarming honesty of the residents take me by surprise. A cheerful young man from Mpulanga runs a modest local eatery—an open stove and some ramshackle chairs. He explained that he has no right—ownership or tenancy—to the land where he runs his 'restaurant'.

A vegetable vendor said that at all times she is ready to run with her wares when the police come, because she has no rights to the shop and the space on which the shop stands. An impressive woman who owns a hardware shop, when queried if she could be asked to leave the land since she has no titles to it, tells me without a moment's hesitation: 'That can happen tomorrow.'

With such an acute property rights problem, it is easy to see that only those with an extraordinary appetite for risk would set up business here. Not surprisingly, entrepreneurship is spare and sparse. Few people from Diepsloot go to nearby cities like Jo'burg and Pretoria to work because transport is meager and costly. Those who do, end up spending on average 20 per cent of their income on transport.

Late in the afternoon we had lunch with some local business people at a restaurant called Mome's. We discussed the economics of townships. The pressing policy needs are not difficult to fathom. The property on which people live and run business operations has to come with tradeable rights that allow people the freedom to sell those rights and move on when they need to. I cannot help recalling a paper I wrote with my student Patrick Emerson (published in 2000 in *Economic Journal*) where we demonstrated the power of well-specified property and tenancy rights. Secondly, the state needs to step in to provide minimal public infrastructure, including the soft infrastructure of law and order.

At the conference on the economics of townships, the next day, I heard about the work done by the World Bank's regional office collecting data on Diepsloot and analyzing the challenges the township faces. We engaged not only with researchers but also with local administrators, mayors of different towns and several senior politicians, including the finance minister. Talking to policymakers and the media at the conference and in other fora, the Eurozone crisis keeps coming up. Above all, they want to hear and believe that the worst is behind us. This is always a difficult conversation. It is easy to see why there is so much distrust of public statements. Responsible policymakers are supposed to calm markets by assuring people that the crisis that just occurred—in Greece, Cyprus or wherever—is an isolated event and will not spill over to larger economies. That being so, when leaders tell people that the crisis that just occurred is an isolated event and will not spill over to larger economies, no one believes them. The net casualty is that when that is indeed the case, there is no language to convey it. This is the reason one must try to speak the truth even on touchy and difficult topics.

South Africa is plagued with low growth, high inequality and record unemployment (25 per cent in 2012). These problems are reflected in and made worse by the existence of a dual-economy structure, with an advanced urban economy coexisting with a Third-World one in the peri-urban townships, informal settlements, and former homelands. While growth prospects may be limited for the advanced part of the economy that is already at the technological frontier, there is big potential from the less-developed township economy—provided that the right economic development strategy is adopted and implemented in a way that accommodates political sensitivities.

In the evening I had dinner with Pravin Gordhan at Mythos Restaurant. Unlike in India, where a meal with a minister would involve a lot of fanfare and bowing and scraping by the restaurant staff, it was refreshing to see that there was none of that here. We sat in one quiet corner and talked. Pravin is one of the most remarkable politicians I have met. An activist, a naturally egalitarian person with a revolutionary past, and deeply interested in the world of ideas. At dinner, he talked about ANC history, his own involvement in the revolution against apartheid, his solitary confinement for five months. He talked of Nelson Mandela with great admiration. We also discussed South Africa's huge income and wealth inequality and the challenge of monetary policy in emerging economies.

My lecture on 5 March at the University of the Witwatersrand Business School on 'Emerging Market Economies in a Changing World' was received well. I noted that since 2007 the global economy has been hit by recurring crises, and argued that these are not independent events but reflect tectonic shifts beneath the surface. I argued that the world will come under increasing strain from a potential jobs crisis that can be destabilizing, and that there is need for collective action to avert such a crisis. The audience was engaged and argumentative and seemed to take a genuine interest in the exchange of ideas.

In the evening I flew to Cape Town, staying at the Taj. I had heard so much about Cape Town but had never been there. On the 6th morning I explored this fascinating city, which could have been somewhere in Europe. I participated in a Cape Town University Roundtable and left in the evening for Senegal.

I have never been to West Africa before. Luckily I have Celestin Monga, my colleague at the World Bank, with me on this trip. He can speak and write in French. While I cannot judge his French, I know that he speaks and writes English with a writer's flair, maybe better than anyone else in the World Bank. If his French is anywhere close to this, he is a great asset on this mission.

We arrived at 1:30 am, 7th March at Dakar. The head of World Bank's resident mission, Vera Songwe, received me along with Philip English, the lead economist, and Mademba Ndiaye, the senior communications officer. We were driven to our beautiful hotel, Radisson Blue.

The visit to Dakar began with a tour of the Slave House on Goree

Island and its socio-cultural center (a historical monument). The World Bank is involved in the rehabilitation of key institutions on the Island—including the health care center. It is painful to hear about the history of slavery and human trafficking. Slaves would often be captured in these regions, chained and brought here and then be sent off to America in ships. I was told that when President Obama came here and heard this story he shed tears. This is not hard to believe. One has to hold back tears as one listens to this devastating history and sad commentary on what human beings are capable of.

Senegal aspires to become a higher middle-income country by the next decade. Like other countries in the West African Economic and Monetary Union, it has had sub-optimal growth performance over the past ten years—about 1 per cent more than the population growth rate of 2.6 per cent. I discussed with Finance Minister Amadou Kane the challenges of policymaking in a context of large social demands and the difficulties of pursuing fiscal consolidation without jeopardizing growth. Minister Kane raised some of the policy challenges posed by the CFA (Communauté Financière Africaine or African Financial Community) Zone arrangements, especially in the aftermath of the Eurozone crisis, and the difficulty of debating possible options without fueling capital flight and political speculation.

On CFA, my lips are unfortunately supposed to be sealed. The CFA Franc is a currency peg that the French had arranged with its former colonies in West and Central Africa. Despite the switch over of France from the franc to euro, the peg, now vis-à-vis the euro, continues, which gives the ECB an enormous amount of power over these West African economies. The peg cuts down on currency risk but handicaps this region in terms of trade and exports capacity. However, this is treated as a topic that you cannot even mention in West Africa because it may give ideas to nations, like Senegal, to break out of the peg. Before I set out on my West Africa mission I was advised by my senior colleagues in Washington and also by the Communications department not to ever bring up this topic when in Africa. To me this smacks of colonialism—don't even plant ideas in the minds of the colonized. I violate this stricture and raise the topic in my conversations with ministers and central bankers. However, and this I regretted later, I did not raise this when the media was present because I did not want to get a phone call from Washington.

I also had a meeting at the BCEAO (Central Bank). Deputy Governor Mamadou Diop who presided over the meeting was quite optimistic in terms of the growth prospects for the region. But, as is often the case, my most satisfying meeting was with civil society leaders.

One of the high points of my Dakar visit was the time I spent at the Dalifort neighborhood (Pikine District) where recent floods have taken a heavy human and economic toll. The site remains flooded several months after the rainy season. Floods affect the poorest city dwellers who already suffer from a lack of basic services. One of the three elementary schools has been closed and living conditions there are dreadful. The World Bank is working with the government to prepare a Storm-water Management Project, which aims to address the cause of floods (the lack of functioning storm-water drainage systems, increased groundwater levels, uncontrolled settlements in flood-prone areas, absence of urban planning, and weaknesses in the natural disaster risk-management system). I visited some homes in this area, wading through knee-deep water in many of their front yards. These are lower middle class homes, the kind I am familiar with in Delhi, Mumbai or Kolkata. Indeed, the people are very similar—charming in a simple, unaffected way, the way the rich rarely are. They remind me of some of my relatives in Kolkata. But their lives are a mess because there is water and slush everywhere, often in their ground floor rooms. I felt reassured by the energetic leadership of the local authorities, the resilience of the population, and the effective collaboration between the government and the World Bank team. These are some of the World Bank initiatives that make me feel good.

I gave a lecture to a huge audience at the Cheikh Anta Diop University, on 7 March on 'The Social and Moral Foundations of Economic Development'. I made the case that economic development depends on economics but also, and in a critical way, on the social norms, customs, habits and even the moral norms that prevail in a country. The traditional neglect of these social factors behind development has done a great disservice to economics. I suggested that there is need for research to understand how good norms are formed and dysfunctional norms can be rooted out. I was delighted to find the audience was not shy. Listeners asked aggressive questions and contested my claims. This is true all over Africa and rather akin to India and also, in my experience, to Israel.

Yesterday, my last day in Senegal, I had a lunch appointment with some of the leading local artists at The Lagoon. This, of course, has nothing to do with the Bank mission. But knowing of my interest in art, Vera and Celestin organized this. The Lagoon is a beautiful restaurant in a lagoon, and my lunch companions included Amadou Dione and Aissa Dione. They seemed wonderful and engaged. I had a lovely conversation with Aissa Dione, a well-known artist, who is also an entrepreneur promoting the art and textiles of that region. We talked about the art of Senegal and Togo. After that, along with Vera, I visited the home of one of the artists, a woman, who also deals in art. Her home is like one of those fashionable homes in Defence Colony, Delhi, and the walls are full of art from Senegal, Togo, Mali and Cameroon.

If I recall right, I first met Vera Songwe in Delhi a few years ago in the home of Roberto Zagha, along with Ngozi Okonjo-Iweala, who was then finance minister of Nigeria. Charming, intelligent and keyed in to the local scene, Vera had planned and ensured that this would be a memorable visit for me.

13 March 2013, Wednesday

A few days ago, completely out of the blue, I got an invitation from Bill Gates to attend a dinner with him and a few others at the Taj Restaurant in Washington's Georgetown area, a walking distance from my home at The Plaza. I was very excited.

I knew the restaurant well—just an ordinary Indian restaurant, not bad, but nothing fancy. Was Bill Gates trying to make a statement of simplicity by choosing this as our watering hole? Thinking about this I walked up to the restaurant. There were six of us there, at a table near the window on the first floor. They included Melanie Walker (who was at the Gates Foundation and was doing some short-term work at the World Bank), Makhtar Diop, Rachel Kyte, and Pamela Cox. There seemed to be no fanfare in the restaurant about this special guest. It was interesting that the ground floor of the restaurant was full of people but the upstairs all empty, except for our table. My guess was that Bill Gates had booked the full floor for the six of us, for reasons of privacy, and maybe also security.

It was an exciting evening. It is not always that one gets to spend an evening with the richest person in the world. I wanted to size him up. Had the wealth messed up his mind and thinking? Was his huge financial success because of some special talent he has or was it luck? I believe much of what one achieves in life is luck. Being in the right place at the right time matters. There are so many decisions one makes in life without a thought. Some of those decisions can set one on the course to the top of the world—in terms of money or fame or power. It may have little to do with the person or his or her talent.

I may add that I believe, in the ultimate analysis, *everything* in life is luck. Even if it is your hard work that gets you to the top, why did you work hard and not the other person? It has to do with your genes and your environment, neither of which you chose. But here I am not talking of this fundamental philosophical matter but simply asking a more basic question: Is Bill Gates special and that explains his success? Or is he like me, Makhtar, Pamela, Rachel or Melanie, and just happened to have hit the jackpot?

So for me, it was a Sherlock Holmes evening. Throughout the conversation and the meal I tried to observe him closely and make as many deductions as I could. I have to confess I did not get any clear answer. I would need to get to know him more to get a full answer.

He certainly seemed a somewhat unusual person but I could not make out if he was innately so or had become so having to live the life of the richest person. There was a certain child-like, nerdy quality to him. He was evidently a guzzler of facts and statistics. Throughout the evening he kept asking me questions about India and South Asia, and Makhtar questions about Africa, and he, in turn, was comfortably spewing out facts and numbers. The names of Indian politicians he, on his own, brought up that evening were Rahul Gandhi, Akhilesh Yadav and Nitish Kumar. At one point, talking about Nitish Kumar, he added, 'My favorite person.'

Whether he has a good, deductive brain I could not make out, but he clearly has very high intelligence of a particular kind. He guzzles books and seems to have an extraordinary memory. Not too many American leaders can say 'Akhilesh Yadav' without choking over their tandoori chicken. I was also trying to size him up in terms of ethical standard. Had money corrupted him so he cared for little else? My conclusion was that the answer to that was no. My hunch was that he is a nice human being, with the right ethics and secular values. He spoke courteously with the waiters and made no demand to be treated specially.

Overall, it was a pleasant evening with little small talk but friendly conversation about the world, developing countries and how to make the world a better place. Towards the end of the meal, I told Bill Gates that I liked the restaurant but I wondered why he chose it. He said he loved Indian food and this was the closest Indian restaurant to his hotel, the Four Seasons. I had made exactly that deduction as I walked up to the restaurant earlier in the evening.

As we bid good-bye and started to walk away, I realized that Bill Gates was going to walk across Pennsylvania Avenue, to Four Seasons, which was also what I would have to do to walk back to The Plaza. So the two of us walked the few minutes together, chatting. About twenty feet behind us two men in suits walked with a sharp eye on us. I realized these must be his security personnel who go everywhere with him. They were not visible during the dinner but were probably there downstairs, having a drink and waiting for him.

Is it worth being the richest person on earth? I concluded the answer was no and I wished I could have asked Bill Gates the same question, as I said good-bye and walked away.

7

Nomadic Days

6 April 2013, Saturday

I was in Moscow for two days, 1 and 2 April, for a few meetings and to participate in the Higher School of Economics (HSE) Conference. I spoke in the opening plenary session of the conference on the Global Economic Crisis and the Russian Economy, alongside Alexei Kudrin (former minister of finance), Mikhael Abyzov (minister for open government), Andrei Fursenko (aide to president, and former minister of education), Alexey Ulukaev (deputy chairman of the Central Bank), Alexander Shokhin (HSE president), Evgeny Yasin (HSE academic supervisor) and Marek Dabrowski (former deputy minister of finance and member of the Polish Parliament). Sitting with these kinds of names I was overwhelmed with, paradoxically, a romantic feeling, as though I had walked into one of those Dostoyevsky or Turgenev novels that I used to wallow in when I was in school in Kolkata.

Over the years, the HSE conference has become a landmark event with broad international participation. My talk on 'Emerging Market Economies in a Changing World' is a bit of a canned lecture, Russianized for the occasion. It is a rather uninspiring lecture that I give.

At the conference I was interviewed by Russian TV on the

Russian economy and its dependence on oil, the BRICS bank, and the impact of the Cyprus bailout on the global economy. I argued for greater competitiveness and diversification of the Russian economy, pointed out the international space for development finance has increased, and expressed the view that with decisive moves toward banking union in the Eurozone, the repercussions of the Cyprus crisis will be contained.

I also gave a lecture at the New Economic School (NES). NES's rector, the brilliant economist Sergei Guriev, wanted me to blend my talk with some theory. This is an unusual request in policy circles. I was delighted and spoke on 'Economic Theory and Implications for Policymaking in Emerging Market Economies'. Established in 1992, NES is an elite, privately funded graduate school, ranked by the Social Science Research Network among the top 100 economics departments in the world. It is a relatively independent institution and is viewed with some suspicion by the Russian government. My lecture became rather theoretical and I was concerned that it would leave my audience perplexed. I was wrong. Being a school of excellence, the audience was good and understood my arguments. The lecture was followed by a lively discussion with the students.

I had dinner at a beautiful, bourgeois restaurant—the kind you can find only in communist and former-communist countries— with Mikhael Rutkowski, World Bank's Country Director for Russia, and Sergei Guriev. Sergei had been an adviser to the 'Doing Business' Review Panel, which had been set up before I joined the World Bank and I was using the report to revise some of the 'Doing Business' work. We discussed 'Doing Business' over dinner, with Sergei emphasizing its importance as an instrument for policy analysis in Russia and a tool for policy reform.

On 3 April, I set out from Moscow for Dushanbe, the capital of Tajikistan, with Aristomene Varoudakis, one of my most gifted advisers at the World Bank. Aristomene and I were both excited and a bit nervous. Till my briefing sessions before I set out on this trip, where I learned a lot about the economics and politics of Tajikistan, my only familiarity with the country was a reference to the minarets of Dushanbe in one of Bhupen Hazarika's Assamese songs about his own nomadic life. Adding to the nervousness was the fact that the only airline we could get was Somon Airways and that just ten minutes into the flight Aristomene turned to me and said, 'So far so good.' I was trying to calculate how many slices of ten minutes of good luck we would need over the three days for this trip to be considered a success, when a flight attendant—a young Tajik woman—came to me to lay out the table and made small talk. On discovering that I was not Tajik, she looked nonplussed and asked, enunciating each word, 'Why, may I ask you, are you going to Tajikistan?' The query hinting at faulty decision-making on my part was not comforting.

As it happens, the Tajikistan mission turned out to be one of my most memorable ones at the Bank. It was a country that was a mish-mash of Russian communism and Islamic culture. People were friendly, inviting me to go to their homes and joining me on walking tours in the city. And at an informal dinner, after some rounds of whisky, the deputy prime minister sang 'Dost, dost na raha' to me. As an Indian, I found it easy to relate to the people and the country.

Tajikistan is a small, remote, landlocked nation, vulnerable to natural disasters and the influence of external economic and political shocks. Despite strong growth, poverty remains widespread (28 per cent of the population in 2009 lives on less than $2 a day) after the end of a post-independence civil war in 1998. Poverty reduction has been faster than in other low and lower-middle income countries, helped by the large remittances from Tajik workers who are immigrants in Russia. Total remittances were 47 per cent of GDP in 2011, the highest proportion in the world. Despite prudent macroeconomic management, poor transport logistics, electricity shortages in winter and a weak business environment contributes to low private investment. Achieving broad-based high growth by stimulating private investment and diversifying the economy is Tajikistan's main medium-term challenge. Also, the huge dependence on remittance from Russia meant that if anything went wrong with that one link, the entire Tajik economy would spiral downwards.

One of my first meetings was in the stunning palace of the president of the nation, Emomali Rahmon. The meeting was with President Rahmon and his economic team: Davlatov (first deputy prime minister), Najmiddinov (minister of finance), Rakhimzade (minister of economic development), and Khamraliev (economic adviser to the president). President Rahmon, first elected in 1994 and seeking a new mandate in November, expressed strong appreciation for the twenty years of partnership with the World Bank including support for the WTO accession. He reiterated the commitment of the Government of Tajikistan to the reform agenda for sustained growth and poverty reduction. He emphasized that the economy is still vulnerable in the aftermath of the global economic crisis and underscored Tajikistan's difficult external environment—Uzbekistan's blockade of gas supply and traffic to and from Tajikistan in the context of the two countries' dispute over the Rogun hydropower plant. He also expressed concern over the volatile situation in neighboring Afghanistan. Absent these external constraints, Tajikistan's growth could have been significantly higher in the president's view. In this context, he pleaded for higher budget support and IDA allocation to help offset the impact of these adverse external factors. The president also underlined the World Bank Group's main contribution in the current juncture would be to help improve regional cooperation in Central Asia.

I emphasized that the work on reforms needs to continue despite the difficult external environment and emphasized the need to enhance the quality of education, especially higher education, arguing that this would also help strengthen domestic policymaking capacity and improve ownership of plans for poverty reduction.

The president became very friendly and asked me to keep some extra time on my next visit so that he could take me to a part of the country from where 'you can see the Valley of Kashmir'. I thought to myself that must have been like one of the vantage points from which the Moghuls came into and conquered India. He told us how their Muslim names had during the Russian period been Russianized. His Rahmon, during the Russian period was Rahmanov. He presented me a book of photographs of him with various global dignitaries. I flipped through it as we talked. All the photos seemed with presidents and prime ministers of various nations, with one exception—President Rahmon with Amitabh Bachchan. He said he could not leave that special picture out of the book.

I had follow-up meetings with Davlatov, Najmiddinov, Rakhimzade, Shirinov (Central Bank chairman), Saidov (chairman of the Committee for Investment and Privatization) and Tagoimurodov (head of the Antimonopoly Committee), where we discussed in more detail the macroeconomic and development policy issues that are relevant to the reform agenda. I argued that remittances have played an important role in reducing poverty but the challenge now is to develop other economic sectors, including manufacturing, energy, banking and education. The economic team explained that remittances are mainly spent on consumption, often on imported goods, with little intermediation through the financial system. I argued, a bit *sotto voce* so that my World Bank colleagues would not hear, that they should not need so much advisory support from the World Bank. They must promote higher education and research so that for most matters they have expertise enough in their own country.

The conversation also covered issues pertaining to competition policy and the poor quality of commercial bank loan portfolios.

The next day I went on a visit to Nurek secondary school and Nurek Dam. The visit to the school in Nurek was a high point of my visit and I was touched by the warm reception from the students, staff and local officials. The Nurek school facilities have been renovated and expanded recently with donor support and the teaching conditions are good. However, school infrastructure remains poor across the country and most schools require major rehabilitation. The World Bank has supported textbook provision and the introduction of per capita financing to increase the efficiency and transparency of resource use in education—a reform that has generally been successful.

My visit to the Nurek dam served as a useful background to understand the energy challenges faced by Tajikistan, including for the construction of the Rogun dam and the hydro power plant, which is a high priority of the Tajik government and an emotional matter in the entire country. The Rogun dam and quarrels with neighboring countries come up in formal and informal meetings everywhere. The World Bank has undertaken an assessment of the Rogun project and its regional impact, including a study of environmental and social impact and a techno-economic assessment. Uzbekistan is concerned about the downstream impact of the project on water management and the environment. The process is complicated by the complete lack of trust and dialogue between Tajikistan and Uzbekistan, including unilateral blockade actions from Uzbekistan of gas supply and traffic and threats of possible escalation to military conflict. The process will move into a more sensitive period this summer with the finalization of the Rogun project assessments, the November presidential election in Tajikistan, and the 2014 NATO withdrawal from Afghanistan.

While the Rogun project will clearly help address Tajikistan's energy needs, it is essential to move toward a regionally negotiated solution to share the costs and benefits of the project through appropriate compensation schemes. In my closed-door meetings with the World Bank staff, I argued that the World Bank should play a more active diplomatic role to bring key partners (UN, USA, Russia) to persuade the two governments to refrain from unilateral actions and engage in dialogue and a negotiated solution.

I gave a public lecture at the Ismaili Center, one of the landmark venues in Dushanbe on 'The Challenge of Extreme Poverty', where I addressed the evolution of global poverty and poverty in Tajikistan and drew lessons from international experience on policies to protect the poor through the direct provision of goods, price subsidies or cash transfers. The lecture was followed by a question and answer session on economic issues relevant to Tajikistan, though repeatedly I was taken back to the topic of Rogun dam. After that I did a press conference centered on energy policy, energy tariffs, remittances and, of course, the Rogun dam.

The entire mission was crowded with meetings with me trying to flee every now and then to walk in the streets and to talk to local people. I had a substantial meeting with Tajikistan's donors, which included the Agha Khan Foundation. There was a meeting with the Bank's Country Office staff, with others joining in via video conference from Almaty, Asthana, Bishkek and Tashkent. We discussed the status of the World Bank's changed management process, and the new strategy and targets for poverty reduction and promotion of shared prosperity. The World Bank has many faults. It's offices in Washington are over-bureaucratized but every time I visit some of these far away countries and meet the local staff I come away impressed by how much commitment members of the local staff have.

3 May 2013, Sunday

It is now more than seven months that I have been in this job. It is lucky I fit in easily in most surroundings. This is a totally different setting from the life I have lived thus far but it feels like home. Summer Sundays in office are especially nice. I walk down from home, The Plaza, along roads basking in the early summer sun, with few cars, and with flowering trees leaning out from people's yards on to the pavement. Washington at this time has a southern feel which I have only read about in books and novels. I manage to get some quiet work done in office which on other days is impossible amidst the mayhem of decisions and delivery deadlines. I draw and sketch a little on the white board in my meeting room contiguous to my office.

One reason I am enjoying the World Bank is my immediate staff, who run my office and carry out my day-to-day work—Vivian and Laverne. When I was about to take up my new job I consulted Martin Ravallion, who advised me to keep Vivian, who was already working under him, as the chief of my staff. I agreed, fully prepared that I would review this after a few weeks and move her out and bring in someone else if that were needed. Vivian turned out to be a terrific decision. Temperamentally, I like to have people whom I can trust so that I can leave everyday work to them and turn to the projects and ideas that excite me. I realized soon that I could do that with Vivian, as also with Laverne, totally. At times, Vivian was a bit too aggressive in defending me and my turf, which offended others. But I'd rather have her defend my turf than other people's. And in any case, Laverne did some of the smoothing of other people's feathers. As someone born in a cricketing country, I also related easily to Laverne, given her West Indian background and loved hearing her descriptions of growing up in the West Indies. I had helping me two other wonderful people—Grace and Bintao. Diligent, efficient and with a quiet sense of humor, these four individuals made a big difference. All of them were people I could trust with my computer, emails, and all things personal, and even gossip about others in the Bank without fear of the stories spilling out. (At the end of my four years, the four of them gave me one of my most treasured farewell gifts. Bintao had kept photographs of my Sunday sketches on my whiteboard. I have sufficient good taste in art to know that my own art is subpar but still I was thrilled then they gave me a 'book' that they had printed out with my whiteboard sketches.)

I also like my space. I have managed to do up my enormous office, private meeting room and large waiting area for guests the way I want. The World Bank has a treasure trove of art that senior officers can borrow for their office. I have picked up some stunning art for my walls. The prize piece is M. F. Hussain's Mother Teresa in outline. I was instructed that this was among the specially valued pieces of art in the World Bank's collection, and I should take special care so that the sun does not fall on it. I have in addition brought a beautiful art by Kazi Anirban from Kolkata. Anirban is the grandson of the great Bengali poet Nazrul Islam. After a chance meeting with Kazi Anirban in Delhi I had visited his home in Hindustan Park, Kolkata, and bought some of his paintings. His art has a touch of oriental fauvism.

Another reason for my happiness is the cultural diversity of the World Bank. You get into the elevator and it is a mélange of races, skin colours, religions and languages. I love that. This is the way the world should be. It is a reminder of humanity's common origins and the need to banish hatred, divisiveness and discrimination.

All this is not to deny that there is a lot to criticize about the World Bank, which, as an insider, I cannot publicly air. I feel a majority of the people at the Bank are instinctively conservative— or at least more so than I am. Big countries have too much voice in what the Bank does; while the poor small nations that need the Bank the most, have little say. Much of this is caused by the fact that the Bank's system of voting on major decisions is weighted by how much money the nation gives to the Bank. Thus USA alone has 18 per cent of the vote share. USA, Japan, UK and a few

European countries can command a majority in most matters. In short, the Bank has democracy of the kind you would have in a nation in which the number of votes each person gets to cast depends on the person's income level.

I also think the World Bank salaries are too high. This includes my own salary. I would not give up my money unilaterally but would prefer a system where no one had such high salaries as long as some people were so badly off.

As you enter the Main Building of the World Bank there is a big board that reads, 'Our dream is a world free of poverty.' Indeed, the World Bank's central mission is to create policies to banish poverty from the world. But given that the continuation of our jobs and salaries depend on trying to fulfil this objective, I often wondered if that board should not be changed to 'Our dream is a world free of poverty, and our nightmare is that the dream will come true.'

26 June 2013, Wednesday

My travels to Malaysia begin at the distant eastern edge of the country, in Sabah's capital, Kota Kinabalu, the strange name a reminder of the distance I have traveled from home. Meeting local folks, regional politicians, and masters of local arts and crafts, it quickly becomes evident that this ancient island, Borneo, symbolizes all the mysteries and romance of human movement through history. The people who seem settled here forever arrived one day after traveling great distances, braving the wilds and the seas. They were then the modern people who had come to an ancient land. They would soon be absorbed and become the natives in the eyes of the next wave of arrivals and modern-day visitors like us.

Frederico Gil Sander, Vivian, Kup (a senior officer of the Ministry of Finance) and I are received at the airport at Kota

Kinabalu by a charming young woman, Intan. She is tall and has a head-scarf carefully draped around her head covering her hair. Intan looks a mixture of Bangladeshi and Indian but explains she is part Arab, part Chinese, and part Bajau, an ancient tribal people, smiles, and adds that she considers herself Bajau.

Sabah seems a melting pot of cultures and peoples of different kinds. From my hotel window I can see the ocean and on the edge of it a canopy of irregular blue rooftops. I am told this was originally a bazaar run by Filipino immigrants. Two men sit comfortably on their haunches and chat, thereby revealing that the middle income status of Sabah is relatively recent. I am most impressed by the complete comfort with which two obviously transsexual students sit among the boys and girls at the art school, Kolej Yayasan Sabah, laughing, chatting and painting. This is what civilization should be judged by.

Coming into Kuala Lumpur from Borneo, the first thing one notices is the haze. Peninsula Malaysia is shrouded in a haze from burning wood and smoldering peat in Indonesia. When we arrive the 'API haze count'—an index of the intensity—hovers around Italy's sovereign debt-to-GDP ratio. Make what you will of that. This gives rise to a gentle smoky aroma from which there is no escape. I deal with it by persuading my mind that someone has spilled a bottle of single-malt Laphroaig whiskey in the vicinity. It works; I enjoy every moment of my visit.

My visit to Malaysia is to witness the country's economic challenges first hand, launch the Malaysia Economic Monitor (MEM), address the Prime Minister's Economic Council, explore the scope for greater interaction between the World Bank and Malaysia and meet with policymakers who've had their hand on the tiller guiding the economy, which is now expected to grow by 5.1 per cent for both 2013 and 2014.

According to the MEM, resilient domestic demand is spurring a recovery from a slow first quarter in 2013. Higher consumer and business spending is expected to boost GDP and the country's external sector will be a key driver, offsetting the impact of tighter fiscal policies on the domestic economy.

Malaysia's trade is dominated by crude oil, palm oil, natural gas and rubber and we all know that putting all of one's eggs in the proverbial commodities basket isn't a good idea. With the demand for commodities dampened by weak growth in key export markets such as China and Europe, and an abundance of global supply, Malaysia needs to accelerate structural reforms to ensure that its economy remains diversified and dynamic.

Malaysia's sound policy choices thus far ensured that revenues from resource extraction were reinvested in the economy in the form of machines, buildings and education. This supported high rates of growth, the benefits of which were shared among the citizenry, raising the average incomes of the bottom 40 per cent of rural households by 7.1 per cent a year over twenty years, while poverty fell quickly.

Given the Bank Group's two new goals of getting extreme poverty down to less than 3 per cent by 2030 and of promoting real income growth of the poorest 40 per cent of each country's population, I am convinced more than ever that we have much to learn from Malaysia. What I did not know earlier is that Malaysia had set itself the goal of focusing on the poorest 40 per cent of its population well before the Bank adopted this as a target.

What is most impressive about Malaysia is its effort to transform its business ethos. Government bureaucrats are repeatedly reminded that their aim is to help citizens and enable entrepreneurs to do business efficiently. One can see palpable manifestations of this in several areas of governance such as during our visit to the Urban Transformation Centre in Malacca. Passports are now issued within two hours of receiving applications.

Malaysia has formidable challenges. It is a multi-cultural, multi-ethnic society and will have to address the tensions and fissures that all such societies have to deal with. It has to continue to diversify and modernize its industry and, above all, build human capital and promote research and innovation.

Nevertheless, I come away with optimism and hope for Malaysia. I had a memorable meeting with Prime Minister Najib Razak, in his office in Putrajaya. As we drove up in the haze, Putrajaya looked like a Company-period watercolour painting of some magic kingdom from a Satyajit film, covered in fog.

With the prime minister and his team, and with our own small team from the World Bank, which includes Vivian and the Malaysian executive director to the World Bank, Annamalai Sundaram, we discussed Malaysia's economic challenges. One topic led to another. The conversation ranged from strategic decision-making, through Henry Kissinger's diplomacy and British colonialism to the constraints under which even the most well-intentioned political leader has to operate and how these constraints can compel unwanted compromises. At one point Sundaram broke into the conversation to tell the PM that he heard me give a lecture at George Washington University's Elliott School, on game theory and the Cuban missile crisis. Much to my surprise (the ED clearly already knew this) Najib showed great interest in this and we talked at length on the 1962 crisis. He may be a crook, as some people say, but his erudition is that of a professional historian. I asked him how he knew so much about the Cuban missile crisis. He said he has a special interest in military strategy.

The Government of Malaysia is keen to have World Bank presence on the ground. This was expressed by the prime minister in his earlier meeting with Axel von Trotsenburg, and again in my closed door meeting with him. This was further substantiated when the Central Bank officials showed us the impressive office space reserved for the World Bank in their new building, fully equipped with state-of the-art technology.

I made opening remarks at the discussion of the skills study with the recently appointed minister of human resources. I met with the Federal Land Development Authority, a government-linked cooperation that was initially established to assist with the resettlement of the rural poor into newly developed areas and to organize smallholder farming.

At the Ministry of Trade and Industry, we discussed the 'Doing Business' report. The Malaysian government is a strong supporter of 'Doing Business'. They currently rank 12th overall. A few years ago, they were ranked 96th and used this poor showing to motivate reforms in the various sectors, both at the federal and state levels.

From Kuala Lumpur, I traveled south by road to meetings in Melaka and Johor, on the North-South Expressway, the longest expressway in Malaysia connecting nine states, from Kedah, on the Malaysian–Thai border to Johor Bahru, at the southernmost tip of Peninsula Malaysia to Singapore. This expressway has significantly reduced the travel time and improved the connectivity within Peninsula Malaysia and connectivity to its southern and northern neighbors. We passed a lot of palm oil plantations on both sides of the expressway.

Malaysia is making a lot of effort to make its bureaucracy citizen-friendly and enable entrepreneurs to conduct business efficiently. Manifestation of its business ethos was evident at the Urban Transformation Center in Melaka, the first of four planned in the country, where passports are issued within two hours of receiving applications

My last meeting was in Iskandar, Johor, a new southern development corridor that has been identified as one of the catalyst developments to spur growth. The idea is to offer fiscal and other incentives to attract key clusters to the corridors. One such effort is 'Educity' which is positioned to be a regional education hub and destination for quality world class education for major Asian cities. The 600-acre education enclave that we saw was planned to be an academic hub encompassing all levels of education, from pre-school to tertiary. It thus far has managed to attract Newcastle University, University of Southampton and Raffles among others. We were impressed by the state-of-the-art facilities—hotels, theme parks such as Legoland and Hello Kitty—which were financed by Khazanah Nasional (strategic investment fund of the Malaysian government) and private funds.

From Iskander I travel to Singapore and then leave for Washington.

24 August 2013, Saturday

On 23 August, with Jimmy Olazo, one of the most dependable administrators from my World Bank office, accompanying me, I set out for Samoa, better known by its earlier name, Western Samoa. Going to a tiny island in the midst of the Pacific, made me feel a bit like Paul Gauguin setting out for a new life. Well, for me it would be just three days and with Jimmy continually by my side, it would not match up to Gauguin's adventure but still it felt exciting. To get myself into the right mood, I pushed aside the thousand briefing notes my office at the World Bank had prepared and instead read Margaret Meade's *Coming of Age in Samoa*.

For the last three hours of the flight you see nothing but a blue ocean outside the window and then, after the descent begins, two specs of islands appear. We landed on one of them, in the airport of Samoa's capital city, Apia. We were received at the airport and taken to our simple but beautiful, sprawling one-story hotel called Tanoa Tusitala.

Samoa has a population of 194,000, which means that for every twelve Samoans we can assign an exclusive World Bank staff member in charge of them. We have not done that but the World Bank is engaged in several projects in Samoa and I felt I should learn the challenges of a small, remote island state with limited natural resources and vulnerable to natural disasters and unusual risk management challenges.

As a result of global warming and rising sea levels, Samoa is susceptible to natural disasters, such as the Pacific Tsunami (September 2009) and Tropical Cyclone Evan (December 2012) which devastated the country's agriculture and infrastructure and slowed down the economy significantly. The country remains vulnerable to natural disasters and has asked for World Bank support in managing risks to natural disasters.

I toured the cyclone and tsunami affected areas of the main island of Upolu where widespread destruction occurred and witnessed the high level of reconstruction that has taken place, thanks in part to IDA loans from the World Bank. We are active in supporting the building of roads and other infrastructure in the two main islands of this nation, Savai'I and Upolu. I saw the long strip of beach and homes next to the beach where the 2009 Tsunami had struck and there was devastation with many lives lost. The problem was that a few hundred yards from the sea front was a wall of steep hills and mountains. So by the time people became aware that a tsunami was coming, they were trapped with no escape routes.

Often, big problems have small solutions. The World Bank's engineers came up with a simple idea. We should have loudspeakers to be able to announce future tsunamis as soon as there was knowledge of one coming and we should build narrow paths for people to run up the slope of the mountain to be above the height of most tsunamis. These projects are in the process of being implemented. But more needs to be done. The Government of Samoa is seeking assistance to upgrade its submarine cables. We shall be discussing the government's needs and ascertain support by other partners such as the Asian Development Bank, and the governments of Australia and New Zealand.

I met with Prime Minister Tuilaepa and Finance Minister Faumuina Luiga. We have good discussions on the economy. It is fascinating for me to think of an economy that is so small that it's viability depends critically on 'globalization'. It has to buy many things from abroad, as it just does not have the size for getting the economies of scale to produce for itself. Also, a major prop for the economy is the remittance that come in from Samoans settled in New Zealand and Australia.

There was a fascinating discussion on monetary policy with the governor of the Central Bank, Maiava Atalina Enari. A lovely and gracious person, she told me about the difficulty of trying to manage inflation and aggregate demand when the bulk of the liquidity comes from abroad. I learned a lot. Given the size of Samoa, it was like discussing monetary policy for Nizamuddin East in Delhi where I used to live.

I also had a meeting with senior officials of the health ministry, impressively, seven loquacious women and one man looking uncomfortable. They raised concerns about shortage of doctors and the lack of fully functioning hospitals; and the increasing number of cases of non-communicable and lifestyle-related diseases like diabetes. The Government of Samoa is receiving support from China to build hospitals and the government is supporting the Open University of Medicine to address the shortage of doctors. A major problem was that of ensuring that the medical students stayed on in Samoa after graduating.

Since the early 1990s, growth underpinned by prudent fiscal policy, has averaged 3 per cent per annum, well above Pacific and Caribbean comparators. Extreme poverty affects only about 3 per cent of households. However, based on the national poverty line, one in five households is considered poor. The adult literacy rate is 99 per cent but there is a shortage of teachers in science and mathematics. Strong policy initiatives for almost two decades have resulted in some favourable outcomes and economic performance well above the average for comparable island economies. However, the government's attempts to narrow the fiscal deficit will be impeded in the next two years by the need to finance reconstruction. Moreover, the economy remains narrowly based and vulnerable to shocks, with tourism and remittances representing 20 per cent and 24 per cent of GDP respectively over the last few years.

Samoa is a beautiful country with beautiful and friendly people. At first sight, the Islanders seem overweight. But that is simply a reminder that many of our perceptions are socially conditioned. The natural grace of the people soon obliterates any awareness of this. As the local newspaper, the *Samoa Observer*, noted pithily about the beautiful Miss World contestant from the island, Penina Maree Paeu, she 'defies the beauty pagent stereotypes'.

Walking up early in the morning in the quiet Tanoa Tusitala, with the sound of leaves rustling outside, I remembered the lines from Margaret Meade's book: 'The life of the day begins at dawn, ... the shouts of the young men may be heard before dawn from the hillside. Uneasy in the night, populous with ghosts, they shout lustily to one another as they hasten with their work... As the dawn begins to fall among the soft brown roofs and the slender palm trees stand out against a colourless, gleaming sea, lovers slip home from trysts beneath the palm trees or in the shadow of beached canoes, that the light may find each sleeper in his appointed place. Cocks crow negligently and a shrill voiced bird cries from the breadfruit trees.'

It is easy to understand why Europeans like Paul Gauguin tried to settle down in these Pacific Islands. Robert Louis Stevenson spent his last years in a sprawling estate just outside Samoa's capital 'city', Apia. On the last day, before catching my flight out, I, along with Jimmy, and Maeva and Antonia, from the local World Bank office who were our local escorts, attempted to climb the peak where the great writer lies buried. From the slopes of the hill one gets a majestic, panoramic view of this impossible kingdom and a sense of what lured Stevenson.

There are contemporary examples of outsiders settling down here. One morning we go to meet Vanya Taule'Alo a short drive from Apia. Vanya is a remarkable woman who came from New Zealand in 1976, married a local—I assume that's how she got the Taule'Alo—and made her home in this village. She now spends her time painting and running an art gallery, displaying the handicrafts and arts of local Samoans. Her own art is remarkably original and imaginative and her home, which she opened up to us with a little persuasion, is itself a work of art.

On Sunday morning, Jimmy and I head out to the fish market. There are men and women—women with flowers in their hair—selling and buying stuff. As one man moves away from a shop with some purchase, a man leans over and tells me that that was the prime minister. 'He often comes here on weekends to buy fish.' I tell the man that it is surprising that I did not recognize him, since I met him the previous day. He responds that I may not have recognized him 'because he was wearing a hat'.

My last evening's meeting is with local business people in a restaurant. I am in a daring mood. Before the meeting, much to Jimmy's disapproval and entertainment, I go and buy myself a lava-lava—a one-piece skirt, which I have seen lots of men wear, and a bright red, short-sleeved shirt. Dressed in this, with sandals, and with Jimmy alongside me, I head out to the formal meeting. I enter, self-conscious about my attire, but there is no shock in anyone's face. What else would a man wear but a skirt to a formal meeting? We discuss the challenges of the local business people; the shortage of credit; the lack of the advantage of scale; the big dependence on the policies adopted by Australia and New Zealand and what the World Bank can do to help.

At the end of it, tugging my lava-lava down to my knees, I bid them good bye and Jimmy and I return to Tanoa Tusitala, talking and making a list of things we need to do for the island economy once we are back in Washington.

But there was one more job remaining. I was curious to check if there were any Indians settled on the island. It is always fun to hear of their experiences. Having made some inquiry, I learned from Antonia and Maeva that there were no more than four or five. I learned of a Bengali mathematics teacher in the local school and a man from Mumbai who ran a restaurant called Tifaimoana. Much to my regret I did not have the time to meet the school teacher. Who was he? Why did he come here? Was he married to a local person? I never found out.

But Tifaimoana was nearby and we could have late night dessert there. So Jimmy and I decided to walk down there from our hotel. It was late. The roads were deserted, barring a few stragglers and stray dogs. I was curious to find out who this romantic soul was who had travelled so far to set up a restaurant. Its manager turned out to be a young man from Kalyan, Mumbai. Three years ago, his brother-in-law who has some business in Fiji came here and did a back-of-the-envelope calculation about the financial viability of an Indian restaurant in Samoa. They brought in two cooks from Dehradun, one to run the tandoor and the other everything else. They hired local helping hands and Tifaimoana was founded, and judging by the fingers that were being licked and the slurping sound of the seven or eight late night diners, it was serving what till its founding was a latent, Nurksian demand.

While walking in the street one day, I had asked an inhabitant of Apia, 'Why is there so little crime and burglary in Samoa?' His answer came pat: 'That is because our homes are completely open, with no walls and no doors. That's why no one dares to go in and steal.' I have to admit that as I walked up the tarmac to the plane waiting to fly us over a vast expanse of the Pacific to Auckland I tried to dissect the logic of that answer and had to contend myself with the thought that this was a logic that worked only in Samoa, a country after my heart.

When you have travelled so far from home, in my case Washington, you want to pack in as much as possible in the region. On 25 August I travelled from Samoa to New Zealand.

In Wellington, I met with key government officials, including Prime Minister John Key, Graeme Wheeler, the governor of the Reserve Bank of New Zealand, and Bill English, finance minister and deputy prime minister. My meeting with the prime minister was meant to be primarily on World Bank New Zealand collaboration in the region. We talked about that, especially since I had just come from Samoa, which relied so hugely on trade, exchange and other forms of interaction with New Zealand. He seemed to have wide interest in the global economy, and we ended up covering a range of topics beyond the planned ones. The country name that came up most frequently was China. There is concern in New Zealand with China's economic slowdown. China has become one of New Zealand's major trading partners, particularly on agricultural products. New Zealand's growth is expected to slow marginally to 2.3 per cent this year as weak external demand weighs in on the economy. While no one is talking—at least openly—about any dramatic slowdown in China, one senses a concern between the lines. Not in this but in another meeting I heard about an internal report of the government doing the rounds that discusses the impact on New Zealand and also on the world of a sharp slowdown in China, in particular, of annual growth dropping to 3 per cent per annum. The idea is for New Zealand to be prepared with policy options to deal with that.

At the end of the meeting Jimmy whispered into my ear that we should have a photograph. It is not every day that you get to meet the prime minister of a major country, he added. I thought this was indeed a good photo op and said yes. Jimmy got all excited and asked Prime Minister Key if he would stop for a moment for a photograph with me. He graciously said yes. Not wanting to waste the PM's time, Jimmy ran and took a quick photo, wasting no time on posing and focusing. I now have a nice photograph of me with the prime minister of New Zealand, with a lot of empty space above our heads, but no wastage of space below. The photo starts from our knees.

With Graeme Wheeler I could burrow deeper into economics. Sensing my interest in exchange rate management, he provided me a detailed perspective on the NZ dollar which has come under pressure lately but has outperformed other commodity-exporting economies, including Australia.

Finance Minister Bill English spoke about the costs of the devastating earthquake that hit Christchurch in February 2011. Spending for reconstruction is providing a boost to the economy but has also resulted in the government's fiscal deficit soaring to over 9 per cent of GDP in 2011. Over the past twenty-five years, New Zealand has done well with market reforms and is one of the most open and flexible economies in the world.

At the Treasury and the Ministry of Foreign Affairs and Trade, I lectured on the World Bank's twin goals of reducing poverty and building shared prosperity and participated in roundtable discussions on New Zealand's living standards framework and the Pacific island economies. New Zealand collaborates closely with Australia and other partners, including the World Bank, on the Pacific Islands. Concerning the Pacific islands, we agreed that despite being small or maybe because of that, the challenges are complex. Some of these challenges are social and political, such as the low representation of women in government, a long history of conflict, integration problems because of the multiplicity of dialects being spoken, land ownership where it is mostly communal, and land registration, access to credit and infrastructure.

I also took advantage of being in New Zealand to deliver the keynote address at the opening of the New Zealand India Research Institute, which is a collaborative effort between the Government of India and a consortium of six New Zealand universities, including Victoria University, which hosted the conference.

From New Zealand I travel to Hong Kong. The main purpose here is to deliver a lecture to the 59th World Statistics Congress of the International Statistics Institute, I give the keynote address as the president's invitee. I speak of the World Bank's twin goals, yes yet again, but because it is an academic conference decide to dwell on the second goal of shared prosperity, which is actually based on my own early research, which I had done in response to an invitation from Joseph Stiglitz during my visit to the World Bank in 1998–99. I take them through some of the axiomatic properties of that goal. The audience being quite nerdy, relates well to it and the lecture tumbles out comfortably, and generates a lot of interest among the statisticians.

I met later with the outgoing and incoming presidents of the International Statistics Institute, Jae C. Lee and Vijay Nair, respectively, and discussed a potential collaboration between their institute and the World Bank for improving statistical data for better poverty measurement.

In Hong Kong I also met with the IFC staff and had a luncheon meeting with various representatives of banks which are active in Asia, including Citigroup, ANZ, HSBC, and JP Morgan. Concerns were expressed about the market turbulence caused by the US tapering of Quantitative Easing, in particular, on the exchange rates in Emerging Market Economies. It must be my interest in exchange rate movements that cause this but many of my meetings end up veering to this topic. We also discussed the slowing down of the Chinese economy, which would have effects on IFC investments. IFC wanted to discuss engagements with India and so on the following day I had a phone meeting with Jin-Yong Cai and Karin Finkelston on this.

From Hong Kong on to South Korea. On 31 August I reached Seoul. I am here at the invitation of the Institute of Economic

Research of the Seoul National University (SNU) on the occasion of the 21st Seoul Journal of Economics International Symposium on Understanding Economic Growth in India: Implications for India-Korea Cooperation. I lectured on the 'Social Foundations of Economic Development and Remarks on Asia's Growth Experience'.

I met the finance minister and deputy prime minister, Dr Hyun Oh-Seok, the former prime minister, Dr Han Seung-Soo, and the US Ambassador to South Korea, Mr Sung Kim, and my brother-in-law, K. Ramakrishna, who heads UNESCAP in East Asia, at a small private dinner. As always happens in East Asia, it was a bit more formal than what would happen in Europe or North America, and certainly Samoa. But, through the veneer of formality, it nevertheless turned out to be a warm and engaging meeting. We discussed a range of topics, mainly to do with the World Bank's activities in the region, and at some point I managed to steer the conversation to my favorite topic—North Korea.

The following day I met the governor of the Bank of Korea, Kim Choongsoo. We discussed the current state of the global economy and lessons learned from the Korean development experience. The Korean economy is resilient despite the slowing of growth. The economy is expected to expand by 2.8 per cent in 2013, up slightly from 2 per cent in 2012, but still lower than the potential economic growth rate of 4 per cent (though, as my World Bank colleagues know from my interjections in meetings, I am skeptical of the concept of 'potential growth' that some economists compute using methods that I consider suspect). Economic expansion will be driven primarily by domestic private consumption growth, given continued subdued demand from some of Korea's main export markets, including Europe. With the Central Bank governor we also discussed the central bank's role as well and the differences in monetary policy responses in countries like Korea, India, China and New Zealand.

At the Korea Development Institute, I met President Joon-Kyung Kim, and Sang-Woo Nam, the dean of the School of Public Policy and Management. I gave a short lecture and discussed collaboration on local research capacity building, research in areas such as impact evaluation, and staff secondment. On staff secondment, the idea is to have two to three staff from my division of the World Bank, DEC, who will be assigned to the office in Seoul to work alongside local researchers from the Korea Development Institute and the universities on research topics of mutual interest to the World Bank and Korea. The office could serve as the research hub for the East Asia Pacific Region. I do feel that if we are going to decentralize a little of our Research Group by opening a regional office with some local researchers, South Korea should be one of the top choices.

With Kyunghoo Choo, first vice minister of strategy and finance, we discussed the current global economic situation, including China, and the effects of QE tapering, and World Bank-Korea strategic collaboration. On the latter, we discussed how DEC could deepen its collaboration with Korea on research topics pertaining to shared prosperity and distilling the lessons learned from the Korean development experience and staff exchange program where Korean staff could be seconded to DEC. The minister reiterated his government's support for the Knowledge for Change Program, a multi-donor research program that is being managed in DEC, and confirmed that he is seeking ways to deepen the cooperation.

Mr Jong Lok Yoon, vice minister of the Ministry of Science, ICT and Future Planning, shared President Park's new economic paradigm, the 'creative economy', which included innovation of the country's industries based on imagination, creativity, science and technology, and ICT, as well as the re-creation of industries and markets as new growth engines. I stressed what I do believe, that Korea also needs to invest in arts and humanities in a big way, not just in science and technology, to further stimulate creativity, which is a long-run driver of economic growth. I assured him I would push the World Bank to support and collaborate closely with the Korean government to realize the vision of a creative economy.

At the Korea Institute for International Economic Policy (KIEP), the government's advisory think tank on international economics and the impact on the Korean economy, and a sister institution of Korea Development Institute, I talked with Mr Heunchong Kim, director of research. We talked of potential areas of collaboration. Currently, the Bank has limited engagement with KIEP. Given the high quality of KIEP staff, there is huge potential for collaboration with DEC, the division of the World Bank under my charge, in the areas of trade, macroeconomics and international economy, international finance.

During this South Korea mission, ever since the dinner with the finance minister, another idea had begun to take shape inside my head—that of getting the World Bank engaged in research on North Korea. North and South Koreas are completely like Satyajit Ray's two kingdoms in *Goopy Gyne, Bagha Byne*. And North Korea is as mysterious and unknown as one of those two kingdoms of Ray.

Currently, the IMF and the World Bank have no contact with North Korea. My feeling is that if we can begin a soft engagement with the region, this can help North Korea and the world. Research is the best way to do this. It would allow us to make some inroads into this mysterious kingdom—may be send envoys to collect data, and also send them our report which could help them with their own policymaking.

In addition to these good intentions, I feel that studying North Korea can be fascinating as an end in itself. During this trip I met a researcher who has been tracking how North Korea is doing in terms of nutrition by keeping a record of heights, weights and other health measures of those who escape from North Korea to South. He said these data provided some evidence of deterioration of health in North Korea over time, and there was indirect evidence that 'stunting' was increasing. Of course, to do any major research I would need data based on satellite pictures of North Korea and would need to contact the CIA to get some of these. I quietly consulted several individuals on this matter and find that there is a lot of support among South Koreans for me to do this. I am resolved to follow up on this when I am back in Washington.

(After returning to DC I floated this idea with the World Bank president, Jim Kim. Jim's father had left North Korea at the age of nineteen. So Jim had a natural interest and gave me the go ahead. I had several meetings with senior colleagues at the Bank and also with the US Treasury. The US Treasury was keen but worried that China would not take kindly to the World Bank engaging unilaterally with North Korea. A few days later, as I was getting ready to start this study, I got a message from Jim Kim asking me not to pursue this idea. I do not know what happened—whether the Chinese objected or the US government objected or if it was Fiji. But sadly I had to abandon this exciting project.)

12 September 2013, Thursday

After the long trip to the Pacific and East Asia I barely get to catch my breath in Washington and have to travel to Nicaragua and Guatemala. Nicaragua is a nation that has long fascinated me. Since the time when I was a student in Kolkata and Delhi in the late 1960s and early 1970s, and later in London, I used to read about the Sandinista revolutionaries who overthrew the brutal regime of Somoza Debayle in 1979. The late '60s and early '70s were revolutionary days all over the world. Somoza was a tyrannical dictator who, behind the cover of nationalism and patriotism, exploited the nation with a few of his cronies. My friends, especially those who were members of the Communist Party in Kolkata, Delhi and London, admired the Sandinistas, and their leader Daniel Ortega, who was famed as a revolutionary and was also a poet. Their commitment and courage to take on such a powerful dictator was admirable indeed. We had disdain for the IMF which was lending money to Somoza's government all the way till 1979, even when it was clear that Somoza was looting the country. Somoza fled from Nicaragua in 1979 to Miami. Later he found refuge in Paraguay, which was then controlled by another dictator, Alfredo Stroessner. Somoza had plundered enough wealth to live in luxury, till he was assassinated at the age of fifty-four, in 1980, just outside Asuncion.

Mine is a quick, two-day visit and I am keen to pack in as much as I can and make up a little on behalf of one Bretton Woods institution, The World Bank, for the historical wrongs of another Bretton Woods institution, the IMF.

In recent times, Nicaragua has successfully established macroeconomic stability and avoided the extreme crime and violence problems that have affected other countries in Central America. The themes of my visit were the current macroeconomic context, the Bank's development goals, and the role of crime prevention in supporting human development. I am aware that there are charges of authoritarianism and high-handedness against Daniel Ortega and his wife, Rosario Maria Murillo Zambrana. I do not know enough detail to form my own opinion. I remain convinced that when he led the revolution, he was a genuine idealist. And it is possible that he still is. Rosario Murillo too was a colorful person, once upon a time a revolutionary, who later worked for La Prensa. She is known for her intelligence and command over several languages.

But we all risk getting caught by the slow drift of the ground beneath our feet, and we change, often unwittingly. The charge of brutality against Daniel Ortega (and Rosario Murillo) could well be right. I do not know enough. If so, this is tragic for a person, once so admirable.

The political, economic, and social landscape changes and we have to make small compromises and often there comes a point from where there is no turning back even if you realize that this is not what you had set out to do. There is yet another problem. In politics, you often face a choice. You have to do something that is morally wrong (at least in deontological terms, such as having to tell a lie or collect illegal money which you want to put to good use) because of a good consequentialist concern. You do not want some evil politician or party to come to power. Once you take these little steps and your evil opponents take similar steps the one who stops loses out. So even with ultimate aims which are moral you may fall into the trap of evil actions.

In any case, those are not my immediate concerns and there is no easy way to answer these questions. I want to play my advisory role for which I have come here, and also indulge in the joys of meeting different people and seeing some of their day-to-day lives—and fulfil some of my curiosity of history—meet some of the leaders to hear first-hand about what had happened in this nation that I had watched so closely in my youth.

Amidst policy meetings, I managed to slip in some ground-level visits. I visited a youth center administered by the police that was impressive. Police identify youth at risk—either through arrest history or observed behavior—in one of Managua's poorest neighborhoods. Transportation is provided for them to the center where traditional courses are complemented with vocational training and counseling. It is a good example of the outreach to local communities that is part of the policing 'model' that has been established.

I also visited a special police unit that attends to domestic violence and sex trafficking problems in one police district. It is a small unit for the approximately 250,000 people in that district;

however, the central unit is complemented by 200 volunteers who engage in community outreach. The unit has specialized staff, including psychologists and social workers, who are trained in the special needs of victims of domestic violence. It seemed to me to be an important initial attempt to dedicate specific resources to a longstanding problem.

There is a section with former sex workers who were being rehabilitated by the police. There were lots of uniformed police running this center and, at the same time, the women inmates—the one-time sex workers there were almost all women—seemed happy and relaxed. They laughed and joked with us and talked about the horrors of their former lives in the back streets and alleyways of Managua, and their current safe haven. I commented to the officers running this center that what I saw was truly rare. Male police running a unit for women sex workers would in most developing countries—and why only developing?—be very different. The women would be taunted and teased, and be uncomfortable. How come this 'almost missionary' sense of purpose in the police here? I asked more than once. And on several occasions I heard officers mention the head of police in Managua and how she—yes, it was a she—was a remarkable woman. A lot of the efficiency and goodness I was seeing in the police force was because of this person at the top, I was told. Her name was Aminta Granera Sacasa. The best way to describe her, a junior policeman told me, was as a Christian socialist.

I decided I would use my World Bank clout and try to meet Aminta Granera in the remaining day of my mission in Managua.

The local World Bank office sent a message and I was lucky I did get to see her. It was a memorable experience. The chief of police, Aminta Granera, is a remarkable individual. She came from a very wealthy background but while growing up she became disillusioned by Nicaraguan society and politics and the exploitation and poverty all around. As a result, she decided to become a nun. While she was training for this the Sandinista socialist revolution had started, and she joined the Sandinistas in the fight against the dictatorship. The Nicaraguans are quite proud of their success in establishing themselves as a regional 'shield' against the proliferation of drug trafficking and gang violence and she is mentioned everywhere in a tone of reverence.

At a personal level too she seemed like a good person with empathy and humane concerns. I told her about the praise I heard about her from the local police, and she described to me how she tried to do what she did. We talked about Nicaragua's many problems. She asked me about my background. I told her about my current work in the World Bank, my years of working and teaching in Delhi, and also my childhood in Kolkata and how in Kolkata's revolutionary days we heard a lot about Nicaragua. She got visibly excited when she heard about my being from 'Calcutta'. She said that wherever she goes she keeps close to her one memento, and that is from Kolkata. She walked up to her desk to bring it and show it to me. I guessed right. She returned with a little picture of Mother Teresa.

She said Mother Teresa's kindness and compassion went well with her own belief in socialism. This felt wonderful because I too hold Mother Teresa in high esteem. One of my sisters, Nandini, in Kolkata worked closely with her. And so I have the kind of information on Mother Teresa, first hand, which Christopher Hitchens and other critics of Mother Teresa did not have. My sister said she used to feel guilty because Mother Teresa would, at every turn, say how she did everything for God, for Jesus. My sister felt guilty because she is an atheist. One day my sister felt she would have to come clean on this and so told Mother how, while she loved working with her and admired her, she herself did not believe in God. At that, Mother Teresa held her head and said that my sister should go on with whatever her beliefs were, and that Mother Teresa would do the praying on her behalf.

During the meeting with Aminta Granera, the deputy chief of police proudly reported the declining incidence of homicide and violent crime. His presentation was also laced with political references to the 'police model' that was established following the Sandinista triumph in the 1980s, the deterioration in crime statistics during the 'neo-liberal' interlude that was followed by improved crime numbers when Daniel Ortega and the Sandinistas returned to office in 2007. The improvement does indeed seem to be important and Managua is a relatively safe city by Central American standards. But, as so often with cases of success, I do not think they fully understand why they have had the level of success they have. To put it down to their politics is too easy to be convincing.

I also had to do some meetings with ministers. There was one with the finance minister of Nicargua, Ivan Acosta, whom I already knew well and liked. He was accompanied by the deputy minister of foreign affairs, Valdrak Jaentschke, other government officials and I had my World Bank team. I led the meeting by highlighting my longstanding interest in Nicaragua, since the country's political developments in the 1970s and 1980s were covered with great interest in India. I congratulated the economic team on their successful macroeconomic management during these recent years of global turbulence. I also reminded them of the two targets that are guiding the World Bank Group's Strategy.

Ivan Acosta noted that since 2008–09 there is a broad political consensus that macro stability has to be maintained as an underlying foundation for social progress. He then laid out the main pillars of their economic strategy, which he said fit well with the Bank's goals. The first pillar is to focus on education and technology. The second is to improve productivity in the agriculture and ranching sectors that remain key export sectors. Third is to enhance competitiveness through improved transport infrastructure and logistics—with a special focus on the underdeveloped North East region of the country where transport links to the rest of country are very poor. Fourth is to develop renewable energy sources to reduce dependence on oil imports.

Despite the steady growth on the order of 5 per cent and inflation under control, there are risks from a persistently large current account deficit. Financing has been secured in recent years, but a large share comes from Venezuelan bilateral aid and capital flows from Venezuela.

The officials discussed the models of community participation that are a key part of the social fabric in Nicaragua. One area where local participation is working well is in controlling the spread of gang violence that has plagued other countries in Central America.

I managed to slip in a dinner with political and business leaders, and a lunch with just local business leaders. I learned about the private sector's concerns and heard the views of some opposition politicians to get a broader sense of the development challenges facing Nicaragua. Guests for the dinner included former vice president and renowned author, Sergio Ramírez, former Central Bank president, Antenor Rosales, the transport sector businessman, Manuel Hernández, opposition political leader, Edmundo Jarquin; and the executive director of the FUNIDES think tank, Carlos Muniz. For the lunch meeting, there was a major coffee exporter, Dania Baltodano, former minister of economy and former Central Bank president, Mario Arana; CEO of INVERCASA Bank, Raul Amador, general manager of Banpro bank, Luis Rivas (one-time favorite student of mine at Cornell), vice president of SINSA (building materials group), Nestor Silva, and IMF Resident Representative Juan Zalduendo. In terms of the discussion, there is the general sense that the business climate has improved in recent years, and relations between traditional business interests and the government have improved. That said, burdensome regulations and corruption still limit the scope for growth of small- and medium-sized enterprises.

Testing my capacity for handling endless meetings, the country office also enlisted a local think tank to help organize an informal chat with young, local economists. They had many questions about the evolution of the global economy and challenges facing the developing countries. They also asked about the World Bank and its role in the development community. It was an excellent and enjoyable opportunity to reach out to the community of future economic policy thinkers. I was very impressed by the quality of the questions and the ensuing discussion.

Finally, among my formal commitments was a keynote address to the annual conference of the Human Development and Capability Association (HDCA)—an organization founded by Amartya Sen, and of which I was a former president. I used the event as an opportunity to present and discuss our World Bank Group goals, the data issues and scenarios developed for setting the poverty target, as well as some more academic considerations for development strategies. The conference was well attended with over 600 registered participants from around the world.

Right on arrival in Managua I had told the head of the World Bank country office there to send a message to President Daniel Ortega's office saying that I was extremely keen to meet him. She told me she would, but not to expect a positive response because Ortega did not much care for World Bank officials. I told her not to stress my being the chief economist of the World Bank but to let the president's office know that I had grown up in Kolkata and since then and also during my student days in Delhi and London had closely followed the Sandinista revolutionary movement, and was for that reason keen to meet him. But nothing seemed to come of all my effort to see Daniel Ortega.

On my last afternoon, when I was doing a meeting with the World Bank staff in the World Bank office, suddenly someone came in and interrupted me with a slip of paper. It was a message saying that Daniel Ortega could see me right away. It felt like a historic opportunity. I interrupted the meeting, apologized and went with the chief of the World Bank's country office to meet the president.

On arrival, we were taken to a strangely beautiful meeting room. It was like an enormous sun room, with large glass walls, and a garden with flowers and plants all around us. It felt a bit like being inside a glass coffin. Daniel Ortega walked in with his finance minister, Daniel Acosta, greeted me cheerfully and sat down to talk. I told him right at the start that I had no serious World Bank business to talk to him about. My interest was in hearing a little first-hand about the Sandinista revolution. He believed me and was visibly relaxed. We talked about Nicaraguan history, about my years in Delhi and Kolkata. He did not go into details but made it clear how hard it is to live up to the idealism of a genuinely progressive revolution. I would have loved to have asked him about reports of his fall from grace. But how could I?

He then moved on to talk about the global economic situation and pounded me with questions. I was taken in by his keen interest. He was engaged and asked about my views, in particular, on developments in the Euro zone and the US economy. He also discussed the need now to bring more foreign investment into Nicaragua. It was almost as if he had taken a page out of Lula's tenure in Brazil—he was keen to combine social welfare engagement along with stable macroeconomics performance. I also congratulated him for Nicaragua's remarkable performance in terms of the World Bank's shared prosperity goal (indeed, Nicaragua is among the best performers in the world in recent years). Given my Indian origin, though this visit had nothing to do with India, he told me how he valued foreign direct investment from India, especially in the motor vehicle and two-wheeler industry, where the Mahindra's had made important investment. He appreciated India's contribution to the generic drugs industry.

This was a memorable meeting because it was almost like

academic friends sitting and having a leisurely, free-flowing conversation about the state of the world, about Nicaragua, America and India. I thanked him, thanked the finance minister, and left.

The next day, 11 September, I travelled to Guatemala for two days of meetings. Somehow my mind kept drifting back to this momentous day in history—the attack on the Twin Towers. I vividly remembered my mother on that day in 2001. She was already too old to understand what had happened. Hearing all the commotion and everybody talking about 9/11, she told some people how she was proud that her grandson (my son, Karna) was born 'on this important day'. As often with my mother's conversations, I had to do some damage control after that.

Thanks to prudent macroeconomic policies, Guatemala has been experiencing slow, but steady, economic growth in recent years. The country faces huge challenges: in particular, deeply entrenched poverty among indigenous populations in rural areas (including depressing rates of malnutrition) and a growing threat to social stability from the rising influence of drug trafficking and gangs. Unlike in Nicaragua where we could freely walk in the streets, here we were strongly advised not to. In fact, the crime situation, I was told, was so bad that the World Bank staff would not allow me to walk even one block on the streets. This takes away half my pleasure of travel and the Guatemala visit, which I had been looking forward to for a long time turned out to be a disappointment.

I had a meeting with the minister of finance, Pavel Centeno. I congratulated the minister on the strong fiscal performance in Guatemala and then gently turned the conversation to the need for tax reform and the need to generate additional revenues. I emphasized that Guatemala's tax-GDP ratio was too low. They need to collect more taxes. The Bank's team that came with me also used the opportunity to discuss health sector reform that might be supported by an upcoming lending operation. The government is anxious to rehabilitate key health facilities that are in disrepair—something that needs to be done; however, the Bank's team is expanding the dialogue to look at other key areas of health system reform that could benefit from support from the Ministry of Finance.

There is, as always on these missions, the meeting with local World Bank Country Office staff. We did this over lunch, I gave them the usual pep talk about how we in the Washington headquarters value the work of the local office and I explained to them, as I do *ad nauseum*, the World Bank Group's twin development goals. A lot of this is a formal lecture but at the same time it is true that when you belong to the same organization a family feeling develops, and I feel a lot of genuine affection for the local staff and their excitement at what they are doing.

I was fascinated by the transformative efforts of a local agricultural cooperative in Chimaltenango that was supported by a Ministry of Economy project financed by the Bank. The local cooperative in Chimaltenango is comprised of traditional indigenous farmers working relatively small plots. The project provides grants for producers to build simple plastic and wood greenhouses that facilitate cultivation of non-traditional crops—in this case, tomatoes. This was allowing farmers to devote some of their land to cash crops while they continued to produce traditional subsistence crops (corn and cabbage). In addition to increasing incomes, the new techniques were opening up new opportunities for accessing markets to further increase incomes in the future.

At my meeting with private sector representatives, many expressed the view that growth needs to accelerate to 6 to 8 per cent (from the current 3 to 3.5 per cent) in order to generate the jobs that will improve Guatemalans' well-being. They cited business regulations, corruption, public safety and lagging infrastructure as key barriers to investment. They noted that one result of these problems is that many of the 'maquila' manufacturing assembly jobs that grew rapidly following the DR-CAFTA trade agreement (that is the free-trade agreement between Dominican Republic and Central America) have disappeared. I was struck by a strong tone of perhaps excessive conservatism in fiscal matters. Businessmen never like to pay taxes; however, Guatemala's tax take to GDP is very low by international standards and the public debt to GDP is low as well (on the order of 25 per cent). It seems to me that there should be a way to reach a consensus for improvements in the business regulatory environment to be accompanied by higher infrastructure and social spending to launch a faster economic growth path. The latter could be financed by some combination of increased tax revenues and modest borrowing. The meeting included prominent corporate personalities such as Felipe Bosch, president of Foundation for the Development of Guatemala think thank (Fundesa), Jaime Díaz, executive director of Pronacom (National Program for Competitiveness), Santiago Molina, president of the Coordinating Committee of Agricultural, Commercial, Industrial, and Financial Associations (CACIF), Guillermo Gonzalez, president of CECOMS (Chamber of Commerce), Fernando Safié, director of Burger King Group, Manfredo Topke, manager of Fruta del Motagua, and Roderico Anzueto, manager of Nutrifrutas.

I had a separate meeting with the commissioner for competitiveness, Juan Carlos Paix. Mr Paix is a businessman with a company that provides baked goods to twenty countries in Central and South America. In his role as commissioner, he advises the president on competitiveness issues. We discussed the 'Doing Business' report, which Mr Paix reported is tracked closely by the president. We also discussed the need for creative approaches to public private partnerships. In addition, we talked about the possibility of doing a case study on competitiveness of Guatemala.

Overall, the Guatemala mission, while useful from the point of view of World Bank work, was personally disappointing. I could not walk in the streets. I did go to beautiful Antigua but only for a dinner and had no time to see it. The politicians and policymakers seemed to be unthinkingly right-wing. There was not enough sensitivity to the problems of poverty and deprivation, and the dismal conditions of the native population. It was quite a contrast to Nicaragua.

20 November 2013, Wednesday

I came to Seattle yesterday for a day-long meeting with the Bill & Melinda Gates Foundation. It began at 8:45 am today and was a packed day discussing various World Bank programs and the possibility of cooperation between the World Bank and the Gates Foundation. I had lunch with their Development Policy and Finance Team, and separate meetings with the Program-Related Investments people, and the Integrated Delivery team. I met and talked to several very impressive people—Dan Kress, Ankur Vora, Rodrigo Salvado and Gargee Ghosh—so many that this will soon be a blur. I am usually good at remembering names and also good at remembering faces. My handicap is that I forget how these are paired—that is, which face belongs to which name.

The high point was my meeting with Bill Gates from 9 to 10 am, earlier today. The taxi driver who drove me this morning was excited to hear that I was going to meet Bill Gates. Being a Seattle resident, he said he had seen Bill Gates on a few occasions and told me what he liked about him was that Gates did not have a chip on his shoulder. He interacted with people like anybody else.

For my meeting with him, Bill Gates had Gargee Ghosh with him and I had Vivian with me. It was an informal meeting but enormously useful. We discussed a host of topics where the Bank could collaborate more with the Gates Foundation. At one point he said that in the Bank publication what he found most valuable was our annual 'Doing Business' report. I seized the opportunity and launched into an idea I had been carrying in my head. 'Doing Business' studies how easy and efficient it is for small businesses to get various permits and clearances that they needed to run a business efficiently. That is, how long does it take to acquire all the permissions to start a business? How much time does it take to clear customs when they have goods coming in from some other nation? How efficient are the courts to resolve disputes concerning contract violation? And so on. Having lived in India, the USA, the UK and other European countries I am acutely aware that the challenge of interaction with the government or departments of the government arise not just for small businesses but also for ordinary people. How much paperwork does one have to do to get a driving license? When you file your tax return how much bureaucracy do you have to encounter to get this done? And so on. Having lived in different countries, I was aware that there can be huge differences in these and that can make ordinary people be more or less productive. If you have to wait in queue for hours to get food, as used to happen in Eastern Europe, you will be less productive. I had also given this a name—the Living Life Index. This would measure how much transactions cost ordinary people encountered in living their daily lives, just as the Doing Business Index measures the transactions cost faced by small businesses.

I tried to get Bill Gates interested in this. He evinced special interest in health and agriculture. How difficult is it for people to get the health services that the government provides for them? How difficult is it for farmers to interact with government?

We discussed this and other topics. It was decided that we would keep in touch with Gargee and take some of these ideas forward.

(I did meet Gargee a few more times in Washington and the

ongoing work between the Gates Foundation and the World Bank progressed well. But the Living Life Index never took off. It was meant to study bureaucratic hurdles faced in everyday life. It never took off because of bureaucratic hurdles in the World Bank.)

8

Pausing to Ponder

29 December 2013, Sunday

A year is drawing to a close. I have enjoyed it but in a rather different way from my experience in the world of policy in India. In India, there were more chilling moments because we had to take decisions which we knew would immediately affect markets and could cause political turmoil. I had to deal with politicians almost every day. In the World Bank, the tricky part is the bureaucracy, and internal rivalry. At times, I am caught by surprise at how strong people's allegiances are to their own division or unit. I feel grateful to some individuals, who helped me navigate this complex organization in my early days. The Ghanian economist Yvonne Tsikata stands out for her combination of sharp intellect and natural warmth in relating to people. Because of her connection to New York University we discover lots of common friends from the academic world. The Peruvian economist, Jaime Saavedra, quickly becomes a person I can rely on for honest advice. But all said and done, it has been a year of joy.

The division under my charge is DEC—the Development Economics group, with about 500 staff members. Our primary charge is research, the collection of statistics and all knowledge work. There is continuous pressure from other units to chip away at DEC and a lot of my time, when I am in Washington, is spent on defending the importance of the knowledge sector. Luckily, it has gone fairly smoothly. I seem to enjoy managing and mediating in other people's conflict. I must now resist the urge to create conflict in order to manage it.

One part of DEC which is critical for the Bank's knowledge work is the Research Group with around 70 economists. Because of my background in the university I relate to them easily. But even outside this, scattered through the Bank, there are immensely talented research economists. I do not have enough time to interact with them as a researcher because of my administrative workload. But I feel grateful that I have had some research interaction with and even the opportunity to write papers and reports with some of the finest minds here, such as Francisco Ferreira, Tito Cordella, and Aristomene Varoudakis.

As chief economist, I get to have a high-powered, external advisory team. Done well, this can be a source of strength, both in getting new ideas and starting up new initiatives, and also as armour against infighting within the Bank. After a lot of thought and getting ideas from friends inside the Bank—I remember getting some excellent tips and suggestions for names from Shanta Devarajan—I set up a team of twelve advisers for the Council of Eminent Persons (CEP): Amartya Sen, Joe Stiglitz, Michael Spence, Eric Maskin, Montek Singh Ahluwalia, Francois Bourguignon, Heba Handoussa, Justin Lin, Ory Okolloh, Maria Herminia T. de Almeida, Pepi Patron and Finn Tarp.

This turned out to be extremely useful to me. Our plan was that we would meet once a year and I should feel free to reach out to them at other times. On 13 and 14 April this year we had two full days of consultation with this group in Washington. DEC has to continuously deal with tricky, politically sensitive matters. Calculate purchasing power parity in one way, country x becomes richer than country y. Do it another way, they reverse rank. We know these things can cause furor and anger in nations. I wanted to do such calculations as honestly as possible and using the best methods and ideas. CEP has been invaluable to me for this, both to actually get ideas and to use the Council as a cudgel against detractors.

There are two important areas of knowledge where I have managed to push through initiatives that please me. Jim Kim told me, soon after I joined the World Bank, that he wanted me to develop some 'mission goals' for the Bank; so that we could think of the entire work of the World Bank as organized around these large ambitions. The World Bank has long been considered the Bretton Woods organization that carried a special responsibility towards developing countries and emerging economies. And since Jim Wolfenson became its president, it has had a focus on poverty mitigation. So one goal had to be related to this. I wanted to put in another mission goal which was focused on mitigating inequality in the world. After a lot of consultation and calculation, I and the big research team working with me decided that ending extreme poverty, that is, those living on less than 1.90 dollars (PPP-adjusted) a day, by the year 2030, while not easy, is not impossible. So we agreed that one mission goal should be the end of extreme poverty in the world by 2030. To get consensus in the World Bank on this was not difficult.

The goal for mitigating inequality however ran into heavy weather. Mitigating poverty is a nice distant goal that virtually everybody finds easy to agree with. As soon as you talk of inequality, it is clear that something has to be taken from the rich and given to the poor; and this pinches our own pocket. But I was determined that the World Bank had to openly speak out against inequality and the need for greater sharing. One simple measure of sharing that I had earlier published a paper on and had plenty of discussions on with my friend, the economist S. Subramanian (Subbu) in Chennai, is to simply evaluate a society in terms of how the bottom segment of the population fares. This had a nice Gandhian ring and was rooted in the philosophical work of John Rawls. I formalized it as follows. The Bank would gather data on each country's poorest 40 per cent of the population. How much per capita consumption the bottom 40 per cent has and other indicators of their welfare. We should learn to evaluate societies in terms of the performance of this bottom segment. We called this the target of 'promoting shared prosperity'.

There was a lot of opposition to this in the Bank and I was told that the US, the biggest stakeholder in the Bank, as well as China and India—all three countries where the poorest sections of society do relatively poorly—would object to this 'left-wing' target since these countries would lose rank when the focus was on the bottom 40 per cent.

I am not good at confrontation but at the same time I hate retreating on important matters like this. In many a cantankerous meeting I would remind myself that I must not make the mistake so many make of fighting and shouting. My aim should be not to get my say but to get my way. And I did. I used a lot of the academic writings of people like Amartya Sen, Joe Stiglitz and Francois Bourguignon. I marshalled support from the Council of Eminent Persons. And I felt that if I got the US government to be supportive of this, I would get my way. Fortunately, the World Bank has an excellent US executive director on its board—Sara Aviel. Sara had become a friend of mine and, more importantly, she was a fine economist and instinctively progressive that I knew she would support me. I also went to the US Treasury, met with Tim Geithner and others and made the case that, while it is true that USA would not show up well in global rankings based on the bottom 40 per cent of society, surely USA was confident enough and had other great achievements to be able to take this in its stride and admit that this was a weakness in its economy. I got a clear nod and I knew I had got my way. (This would not have happened if it were a Trump administration instead of Obama. One defining feature of authoritarian political leaders and the kind of people who surround them is that, deep down, they lack self-confidence and so they cannot tolerate any criticism. This new mission goal of the World Bank will highlight a weakness of the United States. It needs a strong leader and not a school-yard bully to face this without getting ruffled.)

The twin goals were adopted by the World Bank formally and we have made a commitment to publish data every year comparing how nations fare in terms of the bottom 40 per cent of their populations. Of course there were technical debates—such as why the focus on 40 per cent and not 20 per cent or 60 per cent. Subbu was strongly in favor of what I had suggested in my original paper, namely, 20 per cent. There were people in the Bank suggesting 60 per cent. I did not want the proposal to get derailed on this and we agreed on 40 per cent.

The other contested project was the next 'World Development Report'. The World Bank's WDRs, which are analyzes of global development built around a special theme chosen each year, are celebrated the world over. The Bank takes the report writing seriously. A team is selected to produce each report, drawing on research from around the world. We move the whole team—some ten or twelve people—to a specially demarcated set of offices in one of our buildings. There they sit and work for a year.

I wanted the first full WDR under my charge to be a signal that economic development depends on much more than just economics. To understand economic development, we must be prepared to trespass disciplinary boundaries, to use Albert Hirschman's expression, and look at the other social sciences. But this is anathema to mainstream neoclassical economists. I had written on the importance of this in some of my books and papers and wanted to nudge the Bank in this direction. The first job was to persuade the president, Jim Kim, that we needed a report on the broader foundations of economic development, on the fact that economics is embedded in other disciplines. There were two talented social scientists who could lead this— Karla Hoff and Varun Gauri. I had known Karla when she was a student in Princeton and I was a visiting professor. I decided to sit in on some lectures by Stiglitz and there was this young girl in class interrupting Stiglitz at every stage but with fantastic questions. That was Karla. She later became a good friend. She has an enviable body of research, is irreverent, totally honest, and takes a normative line on matters which is similar to mine. I could see her leading a great report. Varun was a later discovery, after I joined the Bank.

Once again getting a consensus on this topic in the World Bank, where a substantial number of economists are orthodox, was a grueling task. But in keeping with my instinct that lots of matters in life are not worth fighting over, but some are, I decided that, given my position, I owed this to the policy world. I decided I would not fight with anyone but would get my way. I did. And the 'World Development Report: Mind, Society and Behavior' is now rapidly progressing.

These were some of the important battles, and perhaps for that reason, fun. But there are the pressures of everyday bureaucratic battles—mostly turf wars inside the Bank. I have managed to deal with them with equanimity but I did not enjoy them. What has been unblemished enjoyment is the travel and engagement with people and policymakers in different parts of the globe. I have done quite a bit of that. I just tried to list the countries I have travelled to this year. I may have missed out one or two but here is the list: India (thrice), Nicaragua (twice), Guatemala, New Zealand, Australia, Samoa, Senegal, South Africa, France, Germany, Sweden, Russia, Tajikistan, Hong Kong, Malaysia, Singapore, Mexico, Canada, Italy, Switzerland.

9 February 2014, Sunday

It is time for the Infosys Prize ceremony. I took the British Airways flight, Washington to London and London to Bangalore, landing in Bangalore at 4 am the day before yesterday. The first person I ran into at the airport was Amartya Sen. A smart young man from the hotel where we would stay, ITC Gardenia, rushed up to us with a broad grin of familiarity, turned first to Sen and said, 'Kaushik Basu?' and, before he could answer, turned to me, showed greater respect and said, 'Amartya Sen?' He had clearly tripped up on his Google research. Before I could say, 'Yes,' Sen said, 'Could have been, but no.'

I was a bit jet-lagged the first day, gave a groggy speech at a nondescript Price Waterhouse event, and went for dinner to the home of Rishi and Julie, my grand-nephew and his wife. It is always such a pleasure to see them and their cute daughter, Niharika.

Yesterday was the big Infosys event, always done with great efficiency and also attention to aesthetics. I planted a tree at the Infosys Campus. I feel quite thrilled at the thought that there will be a tree well after I am dead and gone with a plaque saying, 'Planted by Kaushik Basu'. Though, given a choice I'd rather be there myself to show people the tree.

I met Kofi Anan at the ceremony and got to sit next to him at dinner. What a charming person.

It happened to be a dinner without drinks; so Amartyada suggested the two of us could go somewhere 'for a little indulgence'. We headed to the open square in the middle of the hotel and Sen asked the waiter what Grover Reserve red wine he had. When the bottle arrived, he began to read the label carefully. The waiter picked up the wine list and was about to leave when Sen said, politely and patiently, like in a lecture to a student, 'The fact that I want to read the bottle label first suggests there is a possibility that

I will not order that wine, in which case I will need the wine list to order another. So you should leave the wine list behind.'

We chatted for over an hour—about Narendra Modi, Rahul Gandhi, Sukhamoy Chakravarty, Jagdish Bhagwati, Ashok Mitra, Buddhadeb Bhattacharya, Mamata Banerjee and many others. It was a session of free-flowing gossip, which seemed to go very well with Amartyada's Grover Reserve and my more-pedestrian Campari on ice.

On gossip, years ago, Amartyada had told me about a rule he followed. You can gossip with people who are in your inner circle about people who are outside that circle. In other words, if you think of concentric circles of friends, such that the smaller the circle, the closer the friends, then in any group you cannot gossip about those in an even smaller circle. Once you think about it, this 'concentric gossip rule' is quite a reasonable one.

4 May 2014, Sunday

I was recently off to a part of the world I had never been to earlier. For nomadic souls, these World Bank missions are pure balm. I do have a nomadic soul but not the nomad's guts to rough it out. So the World Bank, with its country offices, own travel department and staff to travel with the chief economist, is the ideal way to indulge in the nomadism. I know I am using the word incorrectly. Almost two weeks ago I left Washington for Vilnius, Lithuania and then from there to Warsaw. It was a packed program, with lectures, meetings with politicians and policymakers and also some with researchers and intellectuals.

Giedre Balcytyte, alternate executive director to the World Bank, representing this region, accompanied me during the three days in Vilnius. Over the last months Giedre has become a good friend, she grew up in Vilnius and so it is wonderful to have her as my local guide. This meant, I could walk around in the bylanes and explore the city between meetings. We went to the homes of some local artists, visited some galleries and also saw some rundown hip areas. I needed those breaks because in many ways this was a tense mission, taking place against the backdrop of the political tensions in Ukraine, which were on everyone's mind in the neighbouring countries. This created tensions but also provided an opportunity to hear the assessments and concerns of political leaders and elites on broader regional and global issues.

Political leaders in transition countries take pride in their status as new donors and would welcome help from the World Bank Group in strengthening that image, positioning themselves in the aid industry, and shaping their policy agenda. Top-level leaders in the Polish Presidency and in the Lithuania Foreign Ministry expressed the desire to develop their presence in Eastern European countries, Latin America, and Africa. They wish to tap into the World Bank's experience to make this happen. One possibility discussed is to have them set up Trust Funds, which would fund some analytical work in Ukraine.

In both countries the legacy of decades of difficult relationships with Russia is striking, even among the elites, which could be seen as Cold War hysteresis. The crisis in Ukraine has sparked (rational and irrational) fears of civil wars and Russian intervention in other Eastern European countries where there are sizable Russian populations—even those that are NATO countries. This is generating calls for higher levels of military spending at a time when fiscal consolidation processes that protect the most vulnerable segments of the population are badly needed. As a result, the World Bank's advice and expertise on tax and public spending policies was well received.

Lithuania is doing well, with real GDP growth of 3.3 per cent, one of the highest in the EU. Two decades of currency board arrangement have prepared the economy to operate well without an independent monetary policy. This should make it easier for Lithuania's planned adoption of the Euro next year.

I gave a public lecture on 'Human Behavior and Economic Development', met with senior government officials, like Rimantas Sadzius, the minister of finance. I had a one-on-one breakfast with him which made it easy to discuss sensitive topics. There were also meetings with Vitas Vasiliauskas, Central Bank governor, and Rolandas Krisciunas, vice-minister of foreign affairs. There were deliberations with central bank governors from several Baltic countries, and academics, like Ramunas Vilpisauskas.

I had a particularly good meeting with the former prime minister and currently an opposition leader—Andrius Kubilius, and Giedre over lunch. The euro adoption and Ukraine would come up in every meeting. For these small countries the World Bank is a source of support not so much for the money as for global political economy. The policymakers are worried about the still high level of unemployment (11 per cent) and the problems with the current growth model in the context of an aging population, out-migration, and low birth rates.

Drawing from the experience of previous EU accession countries and from the global crisis, participants at the conference on 'Convergence Dynamics in the European Union after the Economic Crisis' highlighted some lessons for the Baltics: the multidimensional nature of convergence (nominal, legal, institutional and economic); the need to see convergence as a continuous process that should take place both before and after euro adoption; the importance of having realistic expectations, and understanding that euro adoption can either bring benefits (through trade, FDI and lower borrowing costs), or vicious circles of housing bubbles, fiscal profligacy, low productivity and deteriorating competitiveness.

There was broad consensus that the country still needs several structural reforms, maintaining macro stability, especially counter-cyclical fiscal and macro-prudential policies to ensure that fiscal buffers are bolstered in good times. It needs to reduce the size of the shadow economy; and address the country's energy issues. An energy terminal is currently being built by Korea and should become operational early next year to free the country from dependency on Russian gas. Having served on the Security Council for two years and held the EU Presidency, Lithuania also expects negotiations to join the OECD next year.

Of the occasional escapades with Giedre, from these interminable and often tense meetings, to explore this beautiful city, the most exciting was the visit to the home and painting studio of the artist Algis Griskevicius. Giedre knew him a little and organized the meeting. He sits in a studio cluttered with art—finished, half-finished, abandoned, with paints spattered all over. The studio is basically a large room, in a quiet, surreal East European looking apartment building. It reminds me of the film *The Lives of Others*.

I had never heard of Griskevicius, but seeing his art it is immediately obvious that he is a person of rare talent—comparable to some of the great artists in the world. His paintings are best described as a kind of magical surrealism. The landscape and cityscapes of Lithuania and Eastern Europe are real enough but for the colours. The colors capture beauty and anxiety in a way that is difficult to describe. As I chatted with him, it was quickly clear that he lives for art alone. He had an unusual route to becoming a full-time painter. In his youth, he was part of the USSR army. Sensing his deficiency in battle and his interest in sketching and doodling, he was made to do some 'ideological art'. He felt he fooled them by doing meaningless art. He quit the army to work as an artist's assistant at the Opera and Ballet House. Soon his talent was being spotted and he quit everything to become a full-time painter. I felt like buying his art but he seemed awkward about all practical matters and did not pick up my hints. Also he seemed to have little interest in selling. So I let it go. (I did later buy one of his paintings by writing to Giedre from Washington and making her do the talking to him.)

Walking out of his studio, stepping out of the sets of *The Lives of Others*, on to the streets of Vilnius, I felt a mixture of sadness and joy; and I was glad to have slipped out of the world of economics, the challenge of joining the euro, currency risk, youth unemployment and counter-cyclical fiscal policy for a little bit of art.

On 25 April, I traveled to Warsaw, my first visit to Poland. Alaka had gone to Stockholm for some meetings and we had planned that she would join me in Warsaw. I had therefore extended my visit with two free days. Since we both enjoy gallivanting in cities, we did a lot of that. Seeing Polish art, walking around the Jewish residential quarters, and taking in the tumultuous history of this city.

I gave a public lecture on 'Human Behavior and Economic Development', with Governor Marek Belka chairing it. I drew on my own research and on some of the work that Karla Hoff and others were doing at the World Bank. The lecture went off exceedingly well. I am impressed by the interest that Marek Belka takes in such an academic talk. I also had meetings at the National Bank of Poland with Marek, members of the Monetary Policy Committee and central bank board members. I met up with leading academics and young researchers from various ideological backgrounds, from Leszek Balcerowicz to Grzegorz Kolodko, Witold Orlowski and Andrzej Slawinski; Olgierd Dziekonski, chief of staff of the president; Adam Jesser, president of the Office of Competition and Consumer Protection; and some other policymakers, bankers, and the media. I managed to slip in a visit to the World Bank office and meet up with friends and Bank officials. Mamta Murthi happens to be in Warsaw. We chatted and caught up on India, Poland and the World Bank.

2 July 2014, Wednesday

I came to Delhi yesterday after a packed few days in Vietnam—Ho Chi Minh City and Hanoi—and then Hong Kong. At Hanoi, I, along with the World Bank's country director, Victoria Kwakwa, had a very useful meeting with Vietnam's Deputy Prime Minister Vu Duc Dam. He was keen that the Bank produce a report on Vietnam the way we were doing China 2030. He was concerned about bureaucratic inefficiency in Vietnam and the inadequacy of infrastructure. When I praised Vietnam's performance in the PISA tests, he said he was glad about that but education has to be about more than just taking tests. He worried about whether they were training themselves well enough to handle our globalized world. It was overall a very interesting meeting with a remarkably thoughtful politician. This augurs well for Vietnam.

I managed to slip in a trip to the Bac Giang province and met a cross-section of people from farmers to politicians. In conversations at the top and at the grassroots level, it becomes clear that Vietnam's biggest worry is China.

The last two days in Hong Kong were intense. Among the many people I met was Benny Tai Yiu-ting, legal scholar and professor at the University of Hong Kong. He is a practicing Christian and a pro-democracy activist for democracy, who has caused displeasure in Beijing. (In 2019, he was charged with conspiracy and sentenced to sixteen months in prison.)

As I was picking up my luggage at Delhi airport my phone rang. It was the Indian prime minister's office. They were calling in response to my call from the World Bank requesting a meeting with Prime Minister Narendra Modi. He would be happy to meet me the next day.

So this morning I was there at 7RCR, waiting in the same waiting area where I had been umpteen times for my meetings with Manmohan Singh. I was called in within a few minutes. As I entered the prime minister's chamber I thought I recognized one of the paintings on the wall. There are few developing countries where the transition of power takes place as smoothly. I did not like the direction of the transition but felt good about the smoothness of the process. I began with a 'Namaste' and went on to tell the prime minister that it was nice to see that most of the décor was unchanged in this room and that this well-functioning democracy was something for Indians to feel good about. He nodded and showed me to my seat.

It was a thirty-five-minute conversation. He briefly wanted to talk about World Bank–India relations but then conversation quickly shifted to the Indian economy. I told him about the imperatives, about what I was working on during my last months, about fiscal and monetary policy management. I also briefly explained to him the need for the Indian rupee to be more of an international currency and about some intricate strategies for strengthening India's economic ties with other emerging economies. At one point I felt I was getting too much into the weeds but he seemed to listen with attention. I felt it was important for him to have some understanding on these matters so that some of the seedier characters in government would not be able to mislead him.

Then we turned to a more casual conversation on politics and India. He talked about the Ganga clean up; he asked me what was happening in Bengal. I said I was not in touch with day-to-day matters but I felt bad about the erosion over the last two decades of the outstanding higher education system that Bengal had. Restore that and Bengal, as an economy, would turn around. He went on to make some of his own comments on this.

Finally, I hesitated a bit on this and then thought I had come here as an outsider and so could step on sensitive topics which his own advisers might not be able to do. I said that India's strength was its diversity and inclusiveness. India was treated as a global model on this and we must make every effort to uphold this tradition. He said that he too wanted this and went on to talk about the far eastern edges of India and how to make the people there more a part of the nation. I wanted to steer the conversation to Kashmir but did not.

I left his office feeling good. Despite my ideological differences with his government and misgivings, I felt maybe, now that it was in power, the BJP would not go the divisive route it had so often adopted. Time will tell if I am right.

Later in the day I went for a quick visit to Pranab Mukherjee, now in his grand presidential home. We reminisced about our time in the Ministry of Finance and talked about current economic policy challenges for India.

4 July 2014, Friday

Yesterday I met Dr Manmohan Singh, now in his post-prime-ministerial home. We talked at length about India and the world. He was deeply concerned about the way India's economy would go. I am worried about the economy but not quite as much as him. My bigger worry, which Manmohan Singh also shares, is the politics of divisiveness that is likely to be unleashed. The economy depends primarily on professionals and experts, and unless the political leaders make big blunders, the economy is reasonably insulated. Politics, on the other hand, is in the hands of politicians and can go haywire. We also discussed Iraq and its possible fall-out, the World Bank and India's prospects.

Today I met the new finance minister, Arun Jaitley, in his grand North Block office. As I entered the building, the security guards were thrilled to see me after such a long time. It felt nostalgic walking past my old office. With Jaitley we talked about the World Bank. He was also interested in some nitty gritty issues pertaining to fiscal policy and the Budget since I had worked earlier on them and he was in the final stages of work on his Union Budget.

I asked him if he had met the erstwhile prime minister since he took office. He said he had not. I said, gently, that it would be nice if he did. Also, Manmohan Singh was such a font of knowledge, it would be useful for him in his new job. This was going beyond what advisers typically tell ministers and I wondered how he would take it. As I was finishing my gentle admonishment, he rang the bell for his secretary. As the secretary came in, he asked him to set up a time with Manmohan Singh within the next two or three days for him to go and see him at his residence. As always, Jaitley could be extremely gracious.

18 October 2014, Saturday

Last week was exhausting—the usual Annual Meetings of the IMF and the World Bank, during which finance ministers and central bank governors from all over the world descend on Washington. There are gala events, public lectures and a seemingly endless stream of closed-door meetings, of policy discussions, and of financial negotiations, for grants and other financial support. I have begun to get used to these and participate in these meetings fairly effortlessly. What was unusual this year, and memorable, was my meeting with an LGBT group from around the world that had come to the Annual Meetings to make a case against homophobia in international organizations and other walks of life, and to show that this has economic costs. There was a panel discussion on 'The Cost of Homophobia'. I was asked very hesitantly by a gay colleague of mine at the World Bank if I would like to participate in the panel discussion. Some of the people playing a role in organizing it were Satu Santala, executive director of the World Bank, from Finland, Fabrice Houdart and Chad Dobson. They were bringing in top researchers who were working on the economic consequences of anti-LGBT discrimination, such as Melissa Minor and Lee Badgett. Satu is one of my favorite EDs, I had heard of Fabrice's admirable activism, and my own view that homophobia is repugnant were reasons enough for me to agree to participate in this roundtable and address the group, even though this was quite outside my brief as chief economist of the World Bank. I was also keen to hear Melissa and Lee present some of their research.

The activists who had come for this meeting included Simran Shaikh (India), Georges Azzi (Lebanon), Bisi Alimi (UK and Nigeria), Jonas Bagas (Philippines), Tamara Adiran (Venezuela), Altin Hazizaj (Albania), Njeri Gateru (Kenya), Mmapaseka Letsike (South Africa), David Masengesho (Rwanda), Ying Xin (China), Xiaogang Wei (China), Odile Ndoumbe Faye (Senegal), Clare Byarugaba (Uganda). These were courageous people, many of them had come from countries which treat homosexuality as a crime.

I was a bit nervous about the meeting because this was so outside my area of expertise. I told them that I have had an interest in this because I have seen the meanness and discrimination that hijras and those belonging to LGBT groups in India face. I know that homosexuality is treated as a crime in many places. In my view, treating it as criminal is criminal. I told them that I had written against India's penal code 377. After the little chitchat at the start and my opening remarks I felt I had established enough of a rapport with the audience to risk a funny story—a real-life one.

I told them: Sixteen years ago, when I lived in Washington, my mother came from India to stay with us for a few weeks. One day, my wife and I were going to meet a gay couple, friends of ours—two men—and I thought I would take my mother along to this couple's home. My mother was a traditional, abiding, Hindu woman, but instinctively liberal. We took her along, a bit nervously, aware that older people have a capacity to blurt things out that can cause awkwardness. She entered the home, and being social, was thrilled to meet them. She chatted with them, and with a lack of shyness that comes with age, she said she wanted to see their entire apartment. 'Where is your bedroom? Oh, the two of you sleep here?' My wife and I were impressed by my mother. We were proud that she was engaging, so the evening went fine. When leaving, at the door she turned around and said, 'I'm feeling so happy about your great life. All you need now are two women and your lives will be perfect.' Fortunately, my friends also were very good natured. They laughed and virtually assured her of their readiness for the new women in their lives.[13]

I told them we were lucky today to have a Pope with the moral courage to take a stance against homophobia, I told them about the wedding of my friend Ruth Vanita to Mona in New York, before same-sex marriage was legally recognized by the state. After a lot of difficulty, they found a rabbi willing to preside over this unconventional marriage. The words of the rabbi still resonate in my ears, when at the end of the short and beautiful ceremony, with recitations from Rabindranath Tagore's poems, the rabbi said, 'Now I declare you married in the eyes of all enlightened human beings.'

I told them about the poor plight of hijras in India, who were so totally boycotted by the mainstream that they were forced into livelihood in the margins and crevices of society. It is not just good enough to be neutral. We need affirmative action.

At the end of the panel and again later in my office I got to meet Simran Shaikh, who lives in a hijra colony in Delhi. A person of great dignity and obvious leadership quality, I got to hear about her life story, of rejection and survival. She was born into a middle-class Parsi family in Mumbai. But as 'he' grew up, 'he' was a source of jokes and ridicule that, he, could not take and left

---

13. This paragraph is a transcript (with minor editing) of my speech. This and one or two details I share below were not in my diary. Fabrice Houdart had the transcript and shared it with me.

home, worked as a sex worker, living in slums, and was rescued by a hijra. She later moved to Delhi and became a voice for the LGBT community. What I liked about Simran was her empathy. Her parents rejecting her was clearly a deep wound but she did not blame them. As for her own life, she refused to describe it as one of exploitation and coercion. But she was determined that we need change—India and nations around the world.

7 November 2014, Friday

On 29 October, I travelled to Dublin, Tallinn, and Berlin, for a packed mission. On the agenda were efforts to raise funds for the World Bank's Knowledge for Change Program (KCP), which I chair; consultations on economic policy, the Eurozone crisis and also a meeting with the Advisory Panel for the next World Development Report. But, let me not inflict on you any more of these mission details, which are rather similar, but just some of the highlights.

Travel to Ireland has to be special for any Indian. Ever since India's fight against British colonialism began, there has been a special bond—more emotional than political—between India and Ireland. Also, growing up in Kolkata with its active literary scene, and later at Delhi's St Stephen's College, the two countries, outside of England and America, whose writers we were most exposed to were arguably Russia and Ireland. Dostoyevsky, Tolstoy, Turgenev, Joyce, Yeats, Beckett were part of our consciousness. I was never a voracious reader but there were many in my school and college who were and I grew up with them. Interestingly, I also read and heard some of these writers' and poets' in Bengali translations. My first exposure to Tennessee Williams, whose writings would later grip me, was listening to *The Glass Menagerie* in Bengali on radio in Kolkata. I did not even realize the writer was an American, I took it to be a local playwright. As for Ireland,

I have long had a special interest in the art of Francis Bacon. Also, growing up in India, we had all heard the story of Yeats's critical role in discovering and introducing Rabindranath Tagore to the West. Yeats and Tagore first met in 1912 in the home of the photographer William Rothenstein. Soon after that Yeats had given readings of translations of Tagore's *Gitanjali* to literary groups in London.

Landing in Ireland was exciting. In addition, I was excited that I was to receive Trinity College Historical Society's Gold Medal for Outstanding Contribution to Public Discourse. I am not completely sure Trinity College made the right choice but I was not going to correct them. It turned out to be a grand event in the stunning Trinity College. I also gave a lecture on the role of social norms in driving economic development, as part of the award ceremony. I discussed the importance of trust, altruism and integrity in economic development and how norms can change in the long run, illustrating with examples from Japan and India.

I had meetings with the deputy prime minister, Joan Burton, the second secretary in the Ministry of Finance, Ann Nolan, and gave a lecture to a group of Irish policymakers at the Institute for International and Economic Affairs. But my two most memorable meetings were with Patrick Honohan, the governor of the Central Bank, and with Michael D. Higgins, Ireland's president.

Meeting Patrick was special for personal reasons. We were students around the same time at LSE and knew each other a little. It was wonderful to meet up after so many years and in such different circumstances. We had a formal meeting discussing the European sovereign debt crisis, the global slowdown and the plusses and minuses of Ireland's demographic dividend, given that India was headed to a similar 'dividend'. But we also met up, Patrick with his wife, and Alaka and me, for dinner for banter and to reminisce about our college days and then to go to the theater.

The meeting with President Michael Higgins will go down

in my memory because he is one of the most unusual political figures I have met. President Michael D. Higgins has been in office since 2011. He has also been one of the most active politicians in Ireland in relation to issues of international development and human rights.

Alaka came with me to see him. President Higgins came in and said he knew of some of my more popular writings. He knew I was a student of Amartya Sen and spoke with obvious admiration for him. It was soon clear that his politics was left-wing and liberal. Since I sympathize with such politics, we hit it off. What was surprising was how openly and honestly he spoke, criticizing politicians freely. The World Bank communications department would have thrown a fit if the Bank's president Jim Kim spoke like that.

At our lunch meeting with President Higgins and his adviser, Liam Herrick, we discussed a variety of issues, from the methodological assumptions of econometrics to the poetry of Dylan Thomas. We also talked about his forthcoming state visits to Africa. I found him to be one of the most colourful, interesting and progressive political leaders that I have met. And Ireland went up in my respect for a head of state like him, and for letting him speak the way he did.

From Ireland, Alaka and I went to Estonia. This is exciting for me. I had visited Tallinn once before in the late 1980s, taking the ship Georg Ots, from Helsinki. I had gone alone, as a tourist, but broke away from the tourism agenda to do some fact finding on the economist Ragnar Nurkse, who was from Estonia. I had discovered the work of Nurkse as an undergraduate student at St Stephen's College in Delhi and was fascinated by it. To learn about Nurkse's early life, and following some leads I had been given, I visited some strange homes and research institutes. At the end of the visit to Tallinn, I realized I had missed out on all of tourist Tallinn and managed to get zero information on Nurkse.

A big World Bank team met me in Tallinn, where I had to chair two meetings. One for fund-raising for research in the World Bank and the other for the Advisory Panel for the 'World Development Report 2016'. This report was on 'Internet for Development'. Traditionally the chief economist of the Bank chairs these reports. But this was such a technical report that I felt I needed a co-chair. So at the suggestion of Indermit Gill, I had asked Toomas Ilves, president of Estonia, to join me as co-chair. This was, in retrospect, a great decision. Toomas turned out to be a slightly eccentric and brilliant mind, with total commitment to the project. It is largely under his stewardship that Estonia has become one of the front-runners in the world in the use of digital technology. I also wanted India to be well-represented on this World Bank project since India was among the front-runners in the use of digital technology. I was glad that I could persuade Narayana Murthy, who is the pioneer of India's information technology revolution, to join the Advisory Board. In addition, the Advisory Board has as members, Carl Bildt, former prime minister of Sweden; Yessica Cartajena, Dimension Data, Chile; Dorothy Gordon, Advanced Information Technology Institute, Ghana; Richard Heeks, Institute for Development Policy, Manchester; Monica Kerretts-Makau, Communications Commission of Kenya; Feng Lu, Peking University; and Hal Varian, Google.

I have a soft spot for Hal Varian. In my early years as an unknown economist working in Delhi, I submitted a paper to *American Economic Review*. Research economists know how difficult it is to break into the top three or four journals in the world, especially, if you are not in one of the hotspots of research in America or England. But in a few months a reply came with two referee reports, one moderately positive and one asking for an outright rejection. The surprise was the editor's letter from Hal, saying that he had read my paper and was overriding the negative referee report and accepting the paper. This is so rare in the journal world, especially for young authors not located in Stanford or Cambridge—I mean Cambridge, MA. Cambridge, UK, does not work as well any more.

There is a little background to this story, of possible interest to researchers. I had first submitted that paper to the journal *Manchester School*. The paper was a theorem on adverse selection and technological stagnation. Sitting in Delhi, having worked on that paper alone, I thought it would be impossible to get it into a major journal and so sent it to *Manchester School*, which by then had lost its earlier reputation. Several months later I heard back from the journal. One referee gave some useful suggestions; the other asked for it to be rejected. The editor, understandably, rejected it. I felt depressed, tossed it into my office drawer and thought of it as an abandoned project. Many months later, I thought, the journal world is not perfect. It is one person's judgement versus another. The fact that a paper is rejected by *Manchester School* does not mean it is impossible to get it out in AER. Almost as an experiment, I took the paper out from the drawer and without changing a word, sent it off to AER. And it got accepted and had a big impact on my career. In retrospect, I feel so thankful not to the good referee but the nasty one of *Manchester School*.

Finally, Berlin. This visit is for meetings hosted by the Federal Ministry for Economic Cooperation and Development. The German government has been collaborating with the Bank since 1997 in hosting this workshop which had been providing a valuable forum for the Bank to consult with policymakers and academics, as well as representatives from the donor community and civil society. Two days of this and it is back home to Washington.

6 January 2015, Tuesday

Landing at Paro in Bhutan involves making a question-mark shaped maneuver while dropping altitude rapidly to avoid making wing-contact with the Himalayan mountains surrounding the Paro valley where Thimphu, the capital, is also situated. Alaka insisted she would not miss out on Bhutan and is traveling with me. As we chat, a fellow passenger leans over and informs us that there are only nine pilots in the world who are trained to make this landing. I use up one of my rare prayers to request that it be one of those flying us now. It is, I think, the infrequency of prayers that makes them so effective. God is not irritated by me. Our plane descends smoothly and tiptoes on to the tarmac.

During my four-day visit, I start by meeting with and lecturing to economics students from Bhutan and the neighbouring countries—India, Bangladesh, Sri Lanka, Pakistan, Nepal and Afghanistan—brought together as part of a program to build intra-regional intellectual cooperation and understanding, sponsored by the World Bank. This is an annual program that was started by the economist Debkusum Das, after the two of us went to Lahore together in 2002. It has been a great success for a region where inter-regional interaction is woefully slim.

I conclude my Bhutan visit by dining with and engaging in a roundtable conversation with policymakers, thought-leaders and corporate heads from around the country.

Between those opening and closing events, I have several meetings. There is an informal dinner that Alaka and I have with Prime Minister Tshering Tobgay, who seems to be an extremely agreeable person, engaged and interested in the world and in everyday life. I later have a more detailed meeting with him on the challenges facing Bhutan and the region. I meet and consult with the finance minister as well as with officials of the Central Monetary Authority, and have an excellent conversation with the director of the Center for Bhutan Studies, Dasho Karma Ura.

Finally, there is the meeting with the king. I have never met a king before and so am quite excited to meet up with one. Alaka is keen not to miss out on this opportunity and so I send a message asking if it can be both of us to see him. The answer is yes and we get to see him at the king's palace. It feels like a fairy-tale meeting. There is no formal agenda for our meeting. Maybe because of that, it turned out to be a most memorable conversation with His Majesty, the fifth King of Bhutan, Jigme Khesar Namgyel Wangchuck. It is impossible not to be impressed by his dignity and courtesy. We discuss the world but also talk about home and family. He spoke about his wife, the queen, and his other family members. He told us about his sister studying in USA. That encouraged us to talk about our family backgrounds—mine from Kolkata, Alaka's from Baroda and Mumbai.

Bhutan is an amazing country, embodying simultaneously tradition and modernity rarely seen elsewhere. There is a deep-seated heritage of Buddhism and innate simplicity that marks all aspects of life. This is combined with a striving for high environmental standards, organic farming and an attempt at a smoking ban not just in buildings and parks, but in the nation.

We are staying in the majestic Taj Tashi Hotel. The occupancy is rather low and that makes the stay even more wonderful. We are in the vicinity of the capital but the stillness and silence of the nights is quite magical. The only sound that breaks the silence is the occasional barking of dogs—in the stillness of the dark, all the dogs of Bhutan bark.

A highlight of the trip was a visit to two urban infrastructure development projects in the Thimphu suburbs, with the mayor of the capital, Kinlay Dorjee, and Genevieve Boyreau, the Bank's resident representative and senior economist. The projects are being supported by the World Bank Group. Amidst all of this I also manage to walk up, with the World Bank's Joe Qian, to the beautiful Cheri Monastery and come down after two hours, feeling as though I had spent a week at a meditation camp.

Much of Bhutan's challenge for development stems from the twin traits of deeply held tradition and a drive towards a modern notion of sustainability. This is a nation that has had remarkable success in fighting extreme poverty. As reported in the Bank's Bhutan Poverty Assessment 2014, growth in the country has been inclusive and Bhutan is a society graced with a high degree of social mobility. Nevertheless, there are some clouds of concern. After a period of rapid development, including double-digit growth in 2011, the GDP growth rate slowed down 2.1 per cent in 2013 as a result of the global slowdown and domestic macro-structural strains, including a high current account deficit.

The nation's big business is hydro-electric power generation and export of power to India. Another sector with significant potential is tourism. The country has an interesting tourism policy, which consists of requiring, with minimal exceptions, that each tourist spend at least $250 per day. While the urge to follow a 'high value, low impact' tourism policy is understandable, it is not obvious that the method currently used is optimal. For one, I believe Bhutan can afford to charge more in the peak season and less in the lean season to improve on utilization rates and increase the revenue earned from tourism. Moreover, it can use nonlinear pricing, and possibly even alternative auction systems and increase the revenue it earns from this sector.

With its success in nurturing human capital and health, Bhutan should also be able to develop its education and information technology and digital data management sectors. These advances could help absorb its educated labor force.

Finally, there is indeed scope for huge developments in inter-regional trade, travel and tourism. South Asia is one of the least economically integrated regions of the world. Success in advancing inter-regional economic cooperation is of course not within the reach of any single country. Much will depend on collective determination and also the resolve of the big country of the region, India. This should however be treated as a priority for South Asia and maybe little Bhutan can play a neutral role in egging on the big players.

Successful and prominent cities and regions in Asia are often referred to as 'such-and-such place of the East'. After four heavenly days in Bhutan, nestled peacefully in the high mountains, with a warm and friendly citizenry, I have decided that, reversing this tradition, I shall now think of Switzerland as the Bhutan of the West.

29 January 2015, Thursday

Early this month I was working in my office when the phone rang. It was my assistant, Laverne Cook, from my front office, sounding excited and saying that there was a call for me from the White House, in fact, from President Obama's office. The caller was Salman Ahmed, special assistant to the president and senior director for strategic planning. He asked me if I could come to the White House the following week—he mentioned a specific time—to brief the president on the Indian economy and Indo-US economic relations, before his trip to India later in the month. It would be a small group with three other persons advising him on other aspects of his upcoming visit and it would last for a maximum of two hours. However, he added (quite unnecessarily), he would fully understand if I were unable to attend because it was such short notice. I said I would look into my calendar and get back, knowing full well I would cancel whatever else I had at that time.

So on the morning of 23 January, I walked out of the World Bank building, at 1818 H Street, NW, and east on Pennsylvania Avenue, to the White House, folder in hand and fully prepared for the meeting even though I had no idea how such meetings went. It must have been the fact that I was seen coming in from a distance on foot that I was taken to be a tourist trying to take a peep, and I was stopped rather curtly at one of the side gates and pointed to the more public entrance. When I insisted I had a meeting right next to the Oval office, he asked me, meeting with whom. Saying President Obama felt good and I was ushered in promptly.

There were four of us who had come to brief him and, as we waited for him, we were told he would have four or five of his advisers with him. This included Susan Rice. From her television appearances I expected her to be friendly and reached out to her accordingly, and realized the TV is not always the best guide (though it could have just been one of those bad days for her). President Obama came out, shook hands with us, and exchanged one or two pleasantries. I reminded him that we had met at a dinner at the Indian Prime Minister Manmohan Singh's residence in Delhi and I think he lied, if gestures can be classified as true or false, for he nodded as though he remembered.

He sat down flanked by Susan Rice, Caroline Atkinson, John Podesta, Salman Ahmed and two others. What I had felt on my previous meeting with Obama, in Delhi, was reinforced now. He exudes a genuineness and kindness that is rare among politicians. There is an air of inexplicable goodness about him. These fleeting impressions are important to me. He is the kind of person I would trust, even though my general rule about trusting politicians is: Don't.

It turned out to be a riveting meeting; and one of those rare meetings where my advice actually translated into action, or at least so I believe. I spoke for seven minutes, mainly a short history of Indo-US economic relations, including how totally unpalatable and immoral USA's behavior was in the early 1970s when the US tried to stop the liberation of Bangladesh. But things have changed a lot subsequently. I stressed how the closeness between India and the USA, which happened after 1991, was based on political similarities between the two nations rather than on short-term strategic interests, and could be a force for global good. Before ending I said (not exact words, I am recounting this from memory): 'Mr President, I want to take a moment on a matter that goes beyond the economy and not what you invited me here for,' and I told him that one thing that India truly had reason to be proud of was its democracy and secularism. There are few parallels in world history of a nation as poor and as young as independent India, achieving what India has on these dimensions. Yet there are genuine risks to these core values at present. So when in India, I went on to say, he should remind India's leaders of this great heritage and urge them to preserve it.

Obama broke into gentle laughter and said something like that would surely make him popular. I said I was asking him to do this out of my love for India. I felt he heard and understood me but deliberately allowed the remaining conversation to meander back to imminent geo-political matters and the economy.

At one point when the discussion veered to details of military and defense matters, President Obama said how, left to himself, he would much rather spend time talking about health and education instead of war and military, but unfortunately the latter were unavoidable in today's world. I think he said that both because he genuinely believed in it and also because he did not want to disappoint the outsiders, especially since I had spoken at some length on the importance of soft-power.

At the end of the meeting, after the president left and the rest of us did some small talk as we prepared to leave, one of his advisers came up to me and asked if there were statements in the Indian Constitution or other Indian writings that stressed these points about democracy and inclusiveness. I gave a few general suggestions and walked out to Pennsylvania Avenue, in the direction of the World Bank, feeling wonderful for having had the chance to speak to a world leader, and not just any leader—I really would not care for that if I did not respect him or her as a person—but someone who stands out for his moral leadership.

I was confident, having now been in the policy world for more than five years, that like so many such briefings, this could have some goodwill effect, but in terms of concrete effect there would be none. And indeed Obama's India trip coursed on uneventfully.

Till the last day. His last big engagement was a public lecture at Delhi's Siri Fort auditorium on 27 January. It was going on as usual, flawlessly but also uneventfully, given that Obama was both a master speaker and diplomatically skilled. Then he veered off the usual lines in such speeches and said that he wanted to remind India of its heritage of democracy and inclusiveness, and how some shadows had been cast on this in recent times. He went on to cite the Indian Constitution to reinforce his point and also so that it did not appear to be a message from a foreign super-power.

Furor broke out in India because it was treated as just that—a super power preaching to India. This speech was unexpected in this otherwise you-pat-my-back-I-pat-yours visit. India has a few hyper-nationalist social media outlets; these were furious with Obama for going off the usual diplomatic script. Much of the regular Indian media also criticized Obama for venturing beyond what is expected of a foreign leader. But I am sure there were many in India who love India and who were pleased by this because this was not a super-power preaching something in its own interest but clearly speaking as a well-wisher.

Was it my brief intervention on this subject in the White House that did it? There is no way to be sure, short of asking Obama. But my hunch is it was. Obama was clearly caught by surprise when at the White House meeting I urged him to speak on this in India. He is a moral enough person for it to have played on his mind. He did not sour his India visit by bringing it up early, but my guess is, he felt he had to mention it when all the urgent matters were done and wrapped up. Of course, nothing is unscripted on such visits, so this must have been planned in advance.

So the hyper-nationalist Indian media that screamed foul after Obama's speech should be comforted. It is possible that this was not a case of a foreign leader arrogant enough to be preaching to India, but the exact opposite—a foreign leader responsible and modest enough to do what an Indian citizen had urged him to do.

9 February 2015, Monday

Gargee Ghosh, of the Gates Foundation, had written to me suggesting a meeting with Melinda Gates. I wanted to observe first-hand what the wife of such a wealthy person is like and so agreed. I went to see her today at her DC office, along with Gargee. As I had expected, there weren't too many overlapping concerns between what she was doing and what I was doing at the Bank. We talked about possible areas of collaboration between us, talked of gender balance in the workplace, and my interest in starting something related to 'Doing Business', namely the 'Living Life' survey that I had earlier discussed with Bill Gates. This was not meant to be a meeting with an agenda to get something specific done. It lived up to being a meeting from which nothing specific to-do emerged. But I decided that she had a mind of her own, which I liked, and she had genuine concerns and empathy for people, which too I liked.

27 March 2015, Friday

A good way to fight jet-lag is to lecture on arrival. Accordingly, my kind office had made sure that in Kuala Lumpur, within a few hours of my arrival on 19 March, I had to give a lecture on 'Social Norms and Economic Development' at the Economic Planning Unit.

Malaysia is a country that I have got to know rather well after joining the World Bank. I had never travelled there before coming to the Bank but this is my second visit and because of our plans to set up a section of the World Bank's 'Doing Business' office in Kuala Lumpur, I have been having lots of interactions with Malaysia. Malaysia is also among the few nations, along with Britain and also USA, that uses behavioral economics to design government policies and interventions. Basically they have a nudge office. And because of our 'World Development Report on Mind, Society and Behavior', the Bank and Malaysia have a lot of collaboration going.

One of the joys of setting up the new World Bank office for 'Doing Business' work has been the interaction with Zeti Akhtar Aziz, the governor of the Central Bank or Bank Negara. Zeti is a person of old world charm and grace. She is modest in a regal way. I later learned she does have royal lineage. Zeti told me that her father, Ungku Abdul Aziz, who was an economist, knew Amartya Sen well.

Zeti was keen to set up this office in Kuala Lumpur. I was also keen, mainly to decentralize the World Bank work to beyond Washington. But there were huge hurdles. The most unexpected one was to do with homosexuality being a criminal offence under Malaysian law. Unlike in some other countries where such laws exist on paper but are not enforced, in Malaysia the law is actively enforced. I have moral objection to such laws but even without such objection I had to consider practical problems. If some World Bank staff in the Kuala Lumpur office were charged of homosexuality, we would be in deep trouble. Many in Washington advised me not to set up shop in Malaysia for this reason. But the trouble is that close to a hundred nations in the world have similar laws. We could not avoid them all. Finally, I took the decision that we would go ahead, set up this office, but not send any of our openly gay staff there. We did not want anyone to get arrested. Some gay staff would work for that unit but be based outside of Malaysia.

The other remarkable person I got to know was the Minister of Planning Abdul Wahid bin Omar. He combined the efficiency and dynamism of a corporate sector head with a natural simplicity, which made him an effective leader and a nice person to interact with. He had helped my team in the Bank to get a lot of data on Malaysia and I was also grateful for that. We chatted about all that and then he chaired my lecture on 'Social Norms and

Economic Development'. I drew from the messages of the 'World Development Report 2015'. I spoke about how this report broke traditional barriers in economics and illustrated using examples about the importance of psychology and sociology in understanding economic development. I also spoke about the importance of trust in societies for economic growth. The audience comprised high-level staff from different ministries, and other invited guests including UNDP. During the Q&A, there was interest expressed in the operationalization of the WDR to the Malaysian context.

We planned it such that my mission coincided with the 'Doing Business' team's data collection mission in both countries. This provided me with the opportunity to participate in a 'Doing Business' meeting with Dato Rebecca and her team from the Ministry of Trade, which went off very well. Rebecca reminded me of friends from Goa and we connected well. I discussed the new 'Doing Business' unit that we were setting up in the Bank Negara premises.

I next met with PEMANDU, and its head Idris Jala. PEMANDU is the Malaysian PM's delivery unit which is charged with transforming Malaysia into a high-income economy by 2020 by transforming public service delivery and attracting foreign investment into the private sector. Its main role is to oversee the implementation, assess the progress, facilitate as well as support the delivery and drive the progress of the Government Transformation Programme (GTP) and the Economic Transformation Programme (ETP). PEMANDU was set up in 2009 with initial assistance from Michael Barber. PEMANDU operates on 'Big, Fast Results' which uses lengthy, closed door discussion sessions with stakeholders from the public and private sector to create transformative changes within a given sector.

My trip to Penang was hosted by Khazanah, and included a site visit to the Bayan Lepas Industrial Zone and George Town, a

UNESCO Heritage site. I was impressed by the urban regeneration program managed by ThinkCity. The program (RM 20 million) which ran from 2010–13 builds on public–private partnership to revitalize the city of George Town which was accorded UNESCO World Heritage site in 2008.

Quite apart from the work, Penang charmed me like few other places. It is a mish-mash of cultures, with lots of people of Indian origin but with habits and practices a bit frozen from earlier times, as happens with migrant populations. There were bars with music spilling out—English, Malay but also often old Hindi film songs. There was a memorable dinner with Sundaram, Vivian, Pui Shen Yoong and a few others at Seven Terraces.

On 23 March, I flew into Yangon, setting foot in Myanmar for the first time. Just being there is so evocative. Growing up in Kolkata, we had read and heard tales of Myanmar. Lots of middle class Bengalis had moved there during the British colonial period, working and living ordinary lives in 'Burma'. I had relatives who had gone there, including an uncle who then abandoned his family to marry a local girl. My aunt came back on foot to Kolkata, became a nurse and made a living for herself and her children. Nihar Pishima was a wonderful person and would often come to our home. We were told that her husband returned in old age, hoping to move back into his Kolkata home. I don't know if he did but he used to be sighted in various parks in the city sitting alone.

We had also read romantic semi-autobiographical tales of Sarat Chandra Chattopadhyay. So I was raring to go when I arrived. It was a mission crowded with meetings because the World Bank was in an expansive mode in Myanmar. I launched the Myanmar Investment Climate Assessment (ICA); had bilateral meetings with senior ministers, like U Tin Naing Thein, policymakers, and political personalities, like Aung San Suu Kyi. I had roundtable discussions with the private sector, international partners, the National Economic and Social Advisory Committee, and had meetings with the World Bank's staff there. But in between these meetings I tried to escape for glimpses of Yangon and Nay Pyi Taw. I had a wonderful meeting with the Indian ambassador to Myanmar, Gautam Mukhopadhay, who clearly had an interest in Indo-Myanmar history and so I got some nice stories and glimpses from him.

The second day while traveling from meeting to meeting in Yangon in the World Bank's car, I told the Bank staff that I wanted to experience a bit of the city by myself. Disregarding their protestation, I hopped on to a local city bus. It was wonderful to be jostling with and watching regular commuters going about their daily lives. Suddenly, looking out of the bus window, I saw my World Bank car, with the attired driver and assistant, cruising alongside the bus, keeping a firm eye on what the chief economist was up to. Thereafter, certainly, I was not up to anything.

Friends had told me not to waste any time in the capital city Nay Pyi Taw, which was all built up and barren. They were wrong. It was barren, with mutli-lane highways, with no cars, large buildings seemingly unoccupied. Wide avenues where you wondered what the width was for. Clearly the city never took off. But for those very reasons, it was magic. It was a surreal experience. It could have been a cityscape in a science fiction, or something straight out of a Satyajit Ray creation for a fairy-tale.

The highlight of my visit there was my meeting with Aung San Suu Kyi, chairwoman of the National League for Democracy. She was joined by other parliament members of the National League. I began by saying that I was very happy for this opportunity to meet her and this was important for the World Bank. She said she wanted to meet me not so much for the World Bank but after hearing that I was Amartya Sen's student.

It was a rather multi-topic conversation. She expressed concerns about the state of the poor. In her opinion the poor in Myanmar are worse off today and there is increased inequality. She welcomed the World Bank's help in generating growth that creates jobs and is inclusive, and advice on equal access to education that would serve Myanmar's needs given its diverse language and ethnicity. She lamented the vanishing fauna and flora of old Burma. It was a long meeting, with some of her advisers joining in and ended with a photo session.

During my site visit to the Pyinmana Township Development Committee, I learned about the new bottom up planning process. The Committee was formed in 2011 to foster greater collaboration between townships and state or divisional governments. These committees are made up of elected members of the community with the idea that these local leaders are better able to work with the community and have closer day-to-day interaction.

In all these interactions, I was impressed by the dedication of the individuals and their commitment and am hopeful for Myanmar's future. Many have returned to Myanmar despite having achieved success in the USA and the UK. I came away also quite taken in by the World Bank team based in Myanmar. There was Abdoulaye Seck, country manager for Myanmar, the economist, Andrea Wodehouse, and several others. Ulrich Zachau, country director for both Malaysia and Myanmar was clearly doing a good job.

3 June 2015, Wednesday

Last weekend, as Alaka and I drove back to Washington after visiting James Madison's home and the birthplace of the American constitution in Virginia, Diksha called to give us the news. John Nash and his wife, Alicia, had just been killed in a car accident on New Jersey Turnpike. The tragedy of it was difficult to fathom. How could a person of such genius, after a life of so much struggle, battling schizophrenia and overcoming it, go in such a way?

I told Alaka we would have to stop. We got off the highway and stopped at a nondescript café to make sense of the news. Within minutes I got a message from Jorgen Weibull about the tragedy. It was with Jorgen and at his initiative that I first met John Nash. In 1989, I was a visiting professor at Princeton. By then Nash's schizophrenia was in remission. He could be seen strolling in the Princeton lawns for hours on end. For the residents of Princeton, this was part of the fixtures and so they barely noticed. For me and Jorgen, also a visiting professor, it felt strange. There we were in classrooms analyzing or applying the 'Nash equilibrium' and the 'Nash bargaining solution' and the man after whom these concepts were named was out there, pacing the yard, immersed in his own world.

It was through Jorgen's painstaking effort that we managed to get Nash to join us for lunch in the university cafeteria. It was exciting to be with a person who was known for his genius, even though he spoke little and, every now and then, seemed to drift off into his own thoughts. One vivid memory from that day was Abhijit Banerjee, who, seeing Jorgen and me, came over and joined us. When we introduced him to the other person with us, his reaction was like a literature student joining friends for lunch and being told that the third person at the table was Shakespeare.

The only other time I met Nash was at a conference in Mumbai, organized by Pradeep Dubey in January 2003, that brought several prominent economic theorists to town, including Robert Aumann, Roger Myerson and Amartya Sen. The audience for Nash was large, with some recognizable faces from Bollywood, who may have come expecting to see Russell Crowe. The talk was disappointing, as Nash tried to address some practical policy questions. He was too much of a hedgehog, in the sense of Isaiah Berlin, and so was good at focusing on one thing very deeply, and too unlike the fox to be able to range over many topics, even superficially. It was a poor lecture.

The next day, much to my surprise, as I prepared to give my

talk in the conference, Nash walked in and sat in the front row. I was thrilled by his attention—for the full five minutes that he was awake.

19 September 2015, Saturday

Yesterday evening the SMT, Senior Management Team, of the World Bank, including the president, Jim Kim, had dinner with a team of some of the world's top leadership coaches, with the celebrated Marshal Goldsmith at the head. All day today the SMT had meetings and advice on how to be good leaders. I find these sessions quite pointless. Management gurus remind me of India's spiritual gurus. They are a charming lot but I do not think they have anything substantial to offer.

At Jim Kim's suggestion, the senior management, including me, has taken on individual coaches to train us. I had a sweet, elderly lady who would come once every few weeks to my office and lecture me on how to be a good leader. She also tested my leadership skill by asking me questions like, 'Your junior has messed up on his task. Will you throw a fit and shout at him or explain to him what his mistake was?' When I answered I would explain what his mistake was, she would say 'Brilliant.'

During these leadership coaching sessions, she got friendly enough that she would occasionally talk about her life and troubles, and eventually, about her developing depression. I suddenly realized that the 'leadership coaching' had morphed into 'psychological counseling', with a role reversal, me being the counsellor.

28 September 2015, Monday

Ken Arrow lectured at the World Bank today. Preston Auditorium was jam packed. I introduced him by saying that this was one of those rare occasions when in introducing and describing the speaker as 'among the greatest living economists in the world' you could dispense with the 'among'. It had been my long ambition to get Ken to the World Bank. When some months ago I phoned him in Palo Alto and invited him, he reminded me that he was ninety-four years old and would be able to give a short speech, maybe twenty or twenty-five minutes long. I told him that was fine and he agreed to come. Once he got up to speak he clearly got energized and at the end of fifty minutes I had to cut him short by saying time was running out. He spoke about his discovery of the 'impossibility theorem'. He told us how, as a young man, he was struggling to establish the existence of a general equilibrium, which had remained an open question since the end of the nineteenth century, when Leon Walras had grappled with it, and how on seeing Nash's paper he realized that the fixed point theorem was the key instrument.

Alaka and I organized dinner for him in our home at the Plaza. Among guests we also had Eric Maskin, George Akerlof (Janet Yellen could not make it), Luis Serven, Hunter and Elizabeth Rawlings, Bhaskar Dutta and Italy's executive director to the World Bank, Patrizio Pagano. Among various topics of conversation, talk drifted at one point to free will and determinism, and I explained my belief that we are fully determined but we also have the ability to choose. I went on to argue that punishment must never be motivated by punitive concerns. It should be entirely driven by the consequentialist aim of making people, including observers, behave better in the future. Because this is a topic that has been of obsessive interest to me and I have thought a lot on this, it frustrates me that others do not understand my arguments clearly. What caught me by surprise was how interested Ken Arrow got. He kept cross-questioning me about my stance. He clearly had not thought enough about determinism and the moral status of punishment with any seriousness. He seemed to be troubled by the fact that he was persuaded by me.

I do actually think of Ken Arrow to be the greatest economist of the last 100 years. The span includes Keynes. I should clarify that by greatest I do not mean someone whose work has been the most useful. Clearly Keynes would beat him on that. To me scientific greatness is the ability to catch that magic pattern which eludes others, and the capacity to see through the surface and to plumb depths that others may not realize exist. Let me compare him with his co-author Gerard Debreu. Gerard Debreu's book, *The Theory of Value*, is a stunning achievement. It is a mathematical masterpiece that can, in principle, be read by anyone, including those with no background in mathematics, because it is written from the first principles, like Halmos's naïve set theory. It's entirely axiomatic, building up from little blocks all the way to big theorems about the economy. It is beautiful like poetry. But in terms of that creative insight, Arrow dominates. Arrow is to Debreu what Archimedes was to Euclid.

Fortunately for such a talented person, Ken is a very normal human being. There is something gentle and nice, almost Humean, about him. He talked a bit about his personal life, about how his wife of long years has dementia and for that reason he does not like to leave home for too long.

(His wife died while he was on his way back home from here. He wrote to Amartya Sen later that, because of her dementia, there was not too much communication between them, but nevertheless he would now have to cope with a new loneliness.)

9

Winding Down

15 October 2015, Thursday

It seems hard to believe, I joined the Bank on 1 October, barely three years ago. I am into my last year here. I have just finished my last Bank-Fund Annual Meetings, this time in Peru, which began on 8 October. I am so much more at ease with these events than I used to be—attending meetings with ministers and policymakers from different countries to facilitate partnership with the World Bank, managing the big delegation from my unit at the World Bank that has come to the Annual Meetings, and giving interviews to various media outlets, offering soundbites which say little, but hopefully inspire. Policy speak is so different from research speak. All this, coupled with the escapades, now and then, with friends to the amazing restaurants that this city has makes this a week to cherish.

I have good meetings with Rodrigo Valdes, finance minister of Chile. He is gently left-wing, educated at MIT and an economist. And I like his boss, Michele Bachelet. I think she is one of the most impressive heads of states. All this made for smooth conversation with the minister; and that is important because I am trying to set up a part of my World Bank shop in Chile. There is a useful meeting with Brodjonegoro Bambang of Indonesia. I have known him for a while and because Indonesia is such an important partner for the World Bank, there is a lot to discuss.

There are many more such bilateral meetings but the most memorable one is with Sweden's finance minister, Eva Magdalena Andersson. It is memorable because it is so non-ministerial. There is none of the pageantry that goes with politicians of so many countries. The conversation is easy-going and honest. Add to that the fact that she is progressive and openly critical of right-wing European politicians who are xenophobic and against refugees, and we cover a lot of ground, with a common vision, with minor disagreements on details, and without being weighed down by protocol.

This is generally true of Nordic country politicians. The other politician I get along with well is Norway's foreign minister, Borge Brende. I mention him because, ideologically, he is different from me—far too conservative. Yet, he has a basic graciousness and a genuine interest in the world of ideas, which makes conversations with him a pleasure. If I could wean him away to the left that would be perfect.

At the end of the mission, a few of us had planned a two-day vacation in Macchu Pichhu and Cusco. With a small group, including Haishan Fu and Jimmy Olazo, we flew to Cusco. Haishan is one of my great appointment successes in the World Bank. When a vacancy arose for the post of Director to head the large operation of collecting data from around the world and doing statistical analysis, I searched globally and appointed Haishan. Her intelligence and people skill has made her invaluable for managing a large unit. In addition, her great sense of humour makes her excellent company.

Barring the one time, soon after I began my teaching career at the Delhi School of Economics, when Prannoy Roy, Nitin Khot, Pulin Nayak, Badal Mukherjee and I trekked to Pindari Glacier (we had to turn back before we reached the Glacier because of unexpected early snow), I had never been to an altitude as high as Cusco. Macchu Pichhu is rightly famous and full of history and mysticism—the kind of place that fills you with awe and wonder about life itself.

But in terms of sheer beauty, there are few places to match Cusco. It is a strangely aesthetic blend of colonial architecture and remnants of Spanish culture, with native American homes, habitat, and market squares, with a gentleness of manners so noticeable among Quechua people. There is a simplicity to the people, which, I fear, could make them vulnerable to exploitation by outsiders, more shrewd and ruthless.

Two moments from Cusco will forever remain in my head. As we walked in a beautiful colonial part of the city, my phone kept ringing. It was coming from India. After some hesitation, I decided to take it. It was a journalist excitedly telling me that Angus Deaton had just won the Nobel Prize; he knew I knew Angus, and wanted to do an interview with me. It must have been the mountain air and inadequacy of oxygen; I agreed. No doubt to the chagrin of my companions, I did an interview while strolling the by-lanes of Cusco. I don't think I will ever again get such an exotic backdrop for an interview.

As the four of us were walking back to our hotel with dusk descending, the streets deserted, but for the occasional straggler, and homes with lights coming on in their windows, this could have been a scene straight out of an Eliot poem. Suddenly by the roadside, we saw a native girl, in all likelihood Quechua, with a ponytail, sitting alone, sweetly clutching a bag, and crying. She looked like a fifteenth century Florentine sculpture. It was heartbreaking to see her. Haishan and I tried to talk to her, to find out what had happened. But she could not follow us. Finally, with the help of a passerby, we gathered her mother had asked her to wait there, while she went back home and fetched something. She was now hungry and missing her mother; and hence the tears.

Much to our surprise, we discovered that the little bag she was so carefully guarding was full of local food and snacks. We asked her why she was not eating those. She said quite sternly those were for them to sell, not to eat. An idea struck us. We bought some of that food and gave it to her to eat. Whether she ate or not I do not know. But as we walked back home, it left me with an awareness of the human predicament that reading books and guzzling statistics cannot give.

5 January 2016, Tuesday

I just finished a long mission, with a leave—a vacation in Delhi and Kolkata—tossed in in between. The mission took me to Dhaka, Hyderabad and San Francisco.

I visited Dhaka from 12 to 15 December 2015. It began with an invitation from the governor of Bangladesh Bank, Dr Atiur Rahman, but other meetings and invitations got added on. The World Bank, meaning those at the top, were concerned about my visit because they sensed that with my experience in India and standing as an economist (Sheikh Hasina likes intellectuals but would not know that I am not one) I would have access to the top. The ostensible reason for the concern was that there was a lot of tension between the Bank and Bangladesh because the Bank had stopped a huge loan to Bangladesh for building a bridge over the Padma River because of charges of corruption. Bangladesh denied the charges. So people were worried that I might churn up the controversy. The real reason was more human. Most people do not like others to have access to the top of another country or organization, where they themselves can barely reach. So reasons are given to thwart such interaction. Luckily, I am quite thick-skinned and decided I would like to meet Sheikh Hasina. If people at the Bank got angry I could always make it out as though she wanted to meet me. It later struck me that would anger them even more.

I was returning to Bangladesh after 1992. The economic landscape of Bangladesh has changed dramatically during these intervening two and a half decades, and I was happy to see the remarkable progress. The traffic jams were a good measure of the progress and also a reminder of the need to invest in infrastructure and be mindful of the environment. During my stay in Dhaka, I delivered a public lecture, I met representatives from the garment industry, local entrepreneurs and representatives from ILO and other agencies working in the industry. I went on a field trip to visit a leading 'green' garment factory, which also uses mobile banking (bKash) to pay its workers, and a union parishad (lowest administrative unit in Bangladesh) center to observe the use of digital technology in financial transactions and provision of social services. But, let me begin with what was unlikely almost until the last minute, a meeting with the prime minister. However, finally it worked out, I am sure largely because of Atiur's effort. I suddenly got a message that the PM would meet me.

Waiting for her in her gorgeous office quarters felt strange. I have been in similar settings often enough. For one, it was South Asia and so the staff running up and down and the armed guards were rather like what I would see in Lutyens' Delhi, but at the same time there was a difference. I felt almost as though I had gone off on a time machine back to Moghul times.

There was suddenly a flutter among the staff and she came striding in, exchanged some polite words and we sat down, the two of us half facing each other, with our respective staff along the two sides of the cavernous room.

On her side, Sheikh Hasina had her economic and international affairs advisers and principal secretary (Gowher Rizvi, Moshiur Rahman, Abul Kalam Azad), ERD senior secretary (Mejbah Uddin Ahmed), Bangladesh Bank governor (Atiur Rahman) and chief economist (Biru Paksha Paul). On my team were Martin Rama (acting country director of the World Bank), Christine Kimes and Forhad Shilpi, who had come with me from Washington.

I began by telling Sheikh Hasina that my parents, if they were alive, would have been very happy by this meeting because we had all watched Bangladesh's war of independence from across the border and my parents were great admirers of her father Sheikh Mujibur Rahman. I said all this instinctively, without thought, but it eased up the conversation.

We discussed Bangladesh's impressive achievements in the last decade: strong GDP growth, substantial reduction in poverty and remarkable improvements in social indicators and financial inclusion. Sheikh Hasina reiterated her commitment to follow an open and liberalized economic policy with private–public partnerships at its center. She talked about her vision of rural development with more emphasis on crop diversification in the north and west of the country and on agro-processing at the farm and local level. The prime minister and Bangladesh Bank governor elaborated on a number of programs targeted to rural households including 10 taka accounts, rural saving mobilization program (Palli Sanchoy Bank), mobile banking and money transfer, and their 'one family one farm' initiative.

After the forty-minute scheduled meeting, Sheikh Hasina cancelled her subsequent appointment and expressed an interest to speak to me alone. So her advisers left the room, and I hesitated a bit, not quite knowing what the protocol is in such situations, and then asked the World Bank staff to leave as well. Sheikh Hasina and I switched to speaking in Bangla and the closed meeting continued for another forty minutes. My World Bank advisers later speculated what this extended meeting was all about. In reality, apart from a few politically sensitive matters concerning the Padma Bridge, USA's belief that Bangladesh may have been infiltrated by the ISIS, and one or two other matters (I shall not recount the details here), we ranged over a variety of topics, light and personal.

Taking advantage of the fact that we were both speaking

comfortably, she spoke about her father's assassination and the coup, how he heard gun shots in his home and as he rushed down to see if his sons and families were fine, he was shot at and collapsed on the stairwell. Sheikh Hasina and her sister were saved because they were out of the country at that time.

She spoke fondly of her sister's daughter, Tulip Sadiq, who is a Labor MP in England. We also spoke briefly about India's Prime Minister Narendra Modi, former Prime Minister Manmohan Singh and President Pranab Mukherjee, with whom she seemed to have an especially close relation.

Towards the end, I told her that Bangladesh and the World Bank should try to put the Padma Bridge affair behind us. For one, Bangladesh now had enough foreign exchange reserves (it was around sixteen billion dollars at that time) not to need the loan from the Bank. I assured her that as long as I was there at the Bank we would work to have a closer, more constructive relation between her country and the World Bank. She is clearly aware of the changes in the World Bank and I got the impression she was willing and happy to interact more with the 'new' World Bank.

I also had an interesting meeting with Finance Minister Mr Muhith, accompanied by Martin Rama, Zahid Hussain and Forhad Shilpi. Biru Paksha Paul also joined the meeting. The finance minister and I agreed that Bangladesh can raise its growth rate to 8 per cent per annum with appropriate policies and investments. Bangladesh will need to invest heavily on infrastructure—roads, port facilities and electricity. The current low tax revenue would have to be raised substantially to finance investment in infrastructure. We agreed that a strong partnership with the World Bank can help Bangladesh to leverage its foreign exchange reserve and secure investments in infrastructure. The finance minister's range of intellectual interests was quite amazing. We spoke about numerous historical events and personalities, from Robert McNamara, whom he knew and liked, to economists Wassily Leontief and Paul Samuelson.

I gave a lecture on the 'Bangladesh economy and the World', at the Bangabandhu International Conference Center in Dhaka. This must be the largest audience I have ever drawn. To the naked eye it looked like a sea of people. I was later told there were over 1,500 people. In introducing me the chairman said that when Amartya Sen spoke in Dhaka many years ago he was described as the Amitabh Bachchan of academics. If that be so, he added, then Kaushik Basu is the Shah Rukh Khan of academics. I tried hard not to nod but I think I did.

The second lecture was a keynote address at the inaugural session of the international workshop co-organized by Bangladesh Bank and UNDESA and chaired by the Bangladesh Bank governor. Participants included bankers and policymakers from Bangladesh and other South and East Asian countries and experts such as Vito Tanzi and Ishrat Hussain (former Central Bank governor of Pakistan). I spoke about the need to harness the energy of the private sector to continue Bangladesh's progress in economic growth and poverty reduction. With increasing globalization, Bangladesh will be exposed to unforeseen risks and dangers. Citing the example of how euro area borrowing rates for different countries diverged dramatically with the onslaught of the 2008 financial crisis, I argued for putting the brightest professionals into economic policymaking to steer the country out of those risks and dangers. The main messages of both lectures were widely reported in print, broadcast and electronic media.

The event also had a cultural program, with a dance sequence by some very beautiful women and songs by Shafi Mandal, with heartening secular, multi-religious lyrics.

The trip involved several field visits. I met representatives from the garment industry (BGMEA, BKMEA), and various organizations working on labor safety and work condition issues (Accord, Alliance and ILO). Bangladesh did not inherit the British labor regulations like India, as those regulations were repealed by

Pakistan before the birth of Bangladesh. Following the Rana Plaza tragedy, garment industry in collaboration with various national and international agencies and government counterparts has undertaken major reforms in labor safety and working conditions.

Together with Governor Atiur Rahman, Biru Paksha Paul and talented CEO of bKash, Kamal Quadir, we visited the Viyellatex garment factory in Gazipur. The factory is a pioneer in three areas: (i) its modern facility provides workers a safe and pleasant work place; (ii) its electronic payment system developed locally by bKash, an electronic payment and money transfer platform, makes it easier for workers to keep tabs on their payments and reduces the transaction costs of transferring money, this has increased worker productivity; (iii) its pledge to be carbon neutral by 2018. The factory itself is designed to use sunlight and cut electricity use and purchased an abandoned tea garden where trees are planted to offset its carbon emission. In the union parishad center in the village of Kapashia, in Joydevpur district, we saw a demonstration of a digital app/platform which will help people to access and pay for different government services as well as receive their social benefits. The portals for accessing the app will be available in post offices. We learned about a grant plus saving program that will help poor households to build up their assets under 'one family, one farm' initiative.

I had several informal meetings. The discussion with Bangladesh Bank staff centered on the green initiatives undertaken by the Bangladesh Bank, fair price for agricultural products, implementation of Stolen Asset Recovery Initiative, and how to set up and administer pension funds.

The meeting at Bangladesh Institute of Development Studies (BIDS) was chaired by Dr Morshed (Director General). I spoke about the main messages of the 'World Development Report 2015' ('Mind, Society and Behavior') and the importance of trust in society in conducting business transactions.

During these hectic days in Dhaka, I managed to give one-on-one interviews to several major newspapers or media outlets (*Prothom Alo, Daily Star, Asian Edge* and Reuters). I met with a host of people, aided by the fact that we spoke a common language even if our accents were different. I have never been to a country where I was given more books than in Bangladesh. Every other person seemed to be thrusting a book into my hand that he or she had written.

After Bangladesh, I went to Delhi and Kolkata, on leave from the Bank. Our daughter, Diksha, married Mikey McCleary in Auckland, New Zealand, earlier in the year. We had attended that. But in the grand Indian style we decided to organize another wedding in Delhi and a lovely ceremony in Kolkata. The Delhi events are a Bengali-style wedding in the Kali Bari temple in Greater Kailash and a reception in Gymkhana Club. Many of our friends from India and abroad come for this. In Kolkata, we have a reception at Bengal Club mainly for my relatives and Mikey's relatives from New Zealand. Then for all these people we have a grand idea—to take them to Belur Math, on the banks of the River Ganga. It is Christmas Eve when we are there and in keeping with tradition, the swamis of the Ramakrishna Mission sing Christmas carols. The anomaly of carols by saffron-clad sadhus is what makes it a captivating evening.

Back to earth, I head to Hyderabad for the Indian Economic Association's 98th Annual Congress. I presided over the three-day event as conference president. This is a mega-conference which hundreds of economists from all over India attend. I introduced the inaugural speaker, Pranab Mukherjee, the president of India. After his speech I spoke, mainly on India's challenges but also on the global situation. There were several other events and roundtables over the three days.

From 2–4 January I attended the American Economic Association's Annual meetings in San Francisco and spoke in a panel on the challenges faced by emerging economies in today's world, alongside Joseph Stiglitz, Dale Jorgenson and Justin Lin; and chaired by Dominick Salvatore. I hosted a reception on behalf of the World Bank, which was well attended (to the point where we ran out of food). I attended numerous sessions and this turned out to be a good occasion to catch up on what is happening in mainstream American research to which I would soon be returning.

13 January 2016, Wednesday

The last few years I have been giving a 'short course' on Game Theory at George Washington University's Elliott School, along with James Foster. I give a short course of five lectures and James the rest to make it a semester-long course. This has been a great hit and it is also a form of escape to academe for me. Somehow we missed doing it last year. Today was the first of my five lectures this year. The huge auditorium is jam-packed with lots of economists and some executive directors from the World Bank and IMF, some senior bureaucrats from the State Department and, someone told me in a whisper—though I never got to verify—one person from the FBI. And, of course, there are the students from different departments of GWU. James introduces the course with his usual flourish. Energized by the enthusiasm and size of the audience I give an inspired lecture and get the series off to a start.

14 January 2016, Thursday

The president of Estonia, Toomas Ilves, who had been advising us on the 'World Development Report', wanted to have a chat with me before its release. So I invited him for a one-on-one breakfast with me at the World Bank. We ate and chatted with his security personnel standing outside. We talked about the WDR but also other things. As usual he speaks freely about prominent politicians and leaders. In many ways Toomas is too conservative for my taste but at the same time I like his total honesty and I admire many of his values such as the way he abhors racism and discrimination.

The report is launched in the morning and then I had lunch with Toomas Ilves and some of the other advisers, including the president of Microsoft, Brad Smith, and the prominent technology activist from Ghana, Dorothy Gordon.

6 February 2016, Saturday

The World Economic Forum (WEF) at Davos is a club of the rich and the powerful, not the kind of club that we should encourage. Having said that, when I got the invitation from WEF I was excited. I wanted to see the glitz and pageant of this event and said yes. I decided Bintao should come with me to assist me deal with the multiple meetings and talks. It was all a last minute decision and when we tried to book a hotel in Davos I got a sticker shock like never before. A single room was 1,800 dollars per night. I was not paying for it myself, but I could not in good conscience allow anyone to spend that much for me. Bintao did some research and found a hotel in a neighboring town, about an hour's drive, at a much more reasonable rate. And I decided it is better to spend some money on a car and a driver and stay there.

21–23 January Davos turned out to be quite an experience. I got to meet some fascinating people, like Paul Kagame, president of Rwanda, Ericsson's CEO Hans Vestberg, the founder of the worldwide web, Tim Berners-Lee, Irina Bokova, UNESCO director-general, Jean Philbert Nsengimana, Rwanda minister of youth, and the impressive human rights activist, Amira Yahyayaoui from Tunisia. She had been exiled from her country for her activism against Ben Ali's dictatorial government. I told her about my visit to her country when Ben Ali was the president and how my hotel in Tunis was on rue Gandhi. And I got glimpses and, thank goodness, no more of political leaders like Benjamin Netanyahu.

I had a meeting with Klaus Schwab, the founder of WEF and this Davos event. The purpose was to discuss collaboration with the World Bank. But I was also keen to see him because of his phenomenal success in creating this annual Davos event. His genius is not the ideas that come out of Davos. His genius is he has created a game in which there is an event where everybody wants to be seen because everybody else wants to be seen.

The World Bank's World Development Report 2016 on 'Digital Dividends', has been a great success. It was led by Deepak Mishra and Uwe Deichmann, and there was also a lot of valuable input by Indermit Gill, one of the directors in my office (Indermit and Deepak were my students at the Delhi School of Economics). Because of that success, I had three back-to-back meetings relating to information technology and digital advances and challenges.

One of them, a private session on 'Internet for All: Connecting the Unconnected' organized by WEF, was a small closed-door meeting with Paul Kagame, Toomas Hendrik Ilves, Tim Berners-Lee, Hans Vestberg, and a few others. Since I had heard so much about Kagame, both his efficiency and ruthlessness, I was keen to meet him. I got to talk to him quite a bit.

There was a special session on Kazakhstan's 'Doing Business' report. Kazakhstan's Prime Minister Karim Massimov and I made the opening remarks. Then we had discussions with First Deputy Prime Minister Bakytzhan Sagyntaev, Minister of National Economy Dossayev Erbolat, and Nika Gilauri, former prime minister of Georgia.

I had media engagements with Reuters, and CCTV on the state of the global economy, the WDR and a wide range of topics.

One big success of my Davos mission is the hotel Bintao

chose, Hotel Scesaplana in Seewis im Prattigau. To get away from the hurly burly of the day to return at night to this beautiful, quiet hotel was bliss. Late at night, Bintao and I would go for a walk in the town, with quaint little homes with lighted windows, and not a soul in sight.

From Davos Bintao and I travel to Stockholm, for the European launch of the 'World Development Report' and for meetings with SIDA which has sponsored a lot of our in-house research. Uwe Deichmann presented the major findings of the WDR and I had useful discussions with the Swedish minister, Isabella Lovin. She is from the Green Party which makes it easier for me to connect with her.

At SIDA's request, I interviewed with Sveriges Radio. The interview focused on how digital technologies have spread rapidly in much of the world but digital dividends have lagged behind, technology's impact on labor market, as well as the challenges faced by the global economy.

While the WDR on Digital Dividends has been a huge success it has ruffled some feathers. On 15 January when I was working in my office in Washington, Jim Kim phoned from Bogota, saying that Sheryl Sandberg was very upset about our references to Facebook and net neutrality. She wanted us to make some changes. I talked to Deepak, Uwe and Indermit, looked carefully into the matter myself and decided there was no reason to make any changes and that I would not make any changes.

6 June 2016, Monday

On my return journey from Italy and the UK yesterday, I caught myself a bit weighed down and brooding. My term at the World Bank is drawing to a close. I have to take major decisions: Return to academe or think of something more in the policy world? I felt I had had enough of international organizations. I have enjoyed the World Bank—its plurality, multi-cultural ethos, and being able to give some leadership to policymaking and ideas, especially in the developing economies around the globe. But for me, doing policy is work, doing research is pleasure. Trying to change the world can be fun but once you have tried the other game, of trying to understand the world, you realize that changing is no match. I was missing that world. Maybe all this is because the UK mission I am returning from was a rather academic one. I had met Amartya Sen at Trinity College, and Tony Atkinson at his home in Oxford, and was beginning to pine for that life.

I suddenly realized that for some years now I have not done something that I did for most of my life. I would often, several times a week, go to sleep trying to solve some logical puzzle pertaining to the economy. Many of my papers emerged from this process. And also it helps with the quality of sleep that comes from such impersonal thought. The use of reason to uncover mysteries has been a source of pleasure through life. I suddenly realized that somewhere along the line I had gone off on this.

Reasoning is pretty much the capacity to use the few same axioms again and again, which often leads to beautiful recursive arguments and surprising theorems. I have always enjoyed this process. And if my mother was to be believed this propensity began early. When I was small, maybe four years old, I used to be terrified of bullies. I don't recall who exactly this was about, maybe Bunty, a wild girl in my nursery school, Loreto House, in Kolkata. I recall not the actual incident but my mother telling relatives about it. It seems I would refuse to go out to play because I was scared of bullies like Bunty. I was such a sissy that my mother felt she would have to counsel me out of such behavior. So she asked me why I refused to go out when the bully was around. With a nonchalance about cowardice which you only have when you are very small, I had said, 'Because she will beat me.' My mother countered that with, 'So what? If she beats you, you can beat her.'

My mother used to tell everybody with great pride, I thought for a moment and said, 'But then she will beat me again.' Clearly I got into the mode of recursive thinking quite early in life.

I felt almost as though I had abandoned that first love of mine. I was determined to somehow complete my remaining four months and return to the world of papers and books.

The work that put me in the mood of research nostalgia, was the long discussion with Tony Atkinson on the 'Commission on Global Poverty'. The World Bank puts out data on poverty around the world—literally how many people are poor and where. The importance of doing this work conceptually and statistically right cannot be over-emphasized. Without this, governments cannot be held responsible for poor performance. Without this, you cannot give concrete shape to progressive policy interventions. The work being done on global poverty measurement at the World Bank is absolutely first rate. We have some of the world's finest researchers here. The most prominent is Martin Ravallion. We also have Shaohua Chen, who seems to know everything about the poverty data coming out of all countries. Martin can be stubborn but it is the stubbornness that comes from being fastidiously honest about one's work.

Despite this great resource inside the Bank, there are invariably choices to be made. Exactly, where do you draw the poverty line? How do you calculate the purchasing power parity of different nations? Given that poverty has so many dimensions, should we aggregate them into a single scale or keep it as a multi-dimensional measure? I felt, given the special responsibility the World Bank has for tracking global poverty, it was time to do a major stocktaking of how we measure poverty. I set up a high-powered committee, which had twenty-four members, including Amartya Sen, Angus Deaton, Martin Ravallion, Francois Bourguignon, Nora Lustig, Stefan Dercon, Sabina Alkire, S. Subramanian, Ana Maria Ibanez and Pete Lanjouw.

To chair the Commission, I was keen on Tony Atkinson. Tony, for me, is the embodiment of what a research scientist should be—deep thinking, modest, honest, totally committed. So I phoned him last year to ask if he would do it. He told me he would love to, but he had a warning for me. He had been diagnosed with cancer and there was a possibility that he would not be there to see its completion. So it all depended on whether I was willing to take that risk. I said without hesitation that I would. I did later take a precautionary measure. I called Francois Bourguignon and asked him if he would agree to a confidential agreement with me. I told him about Tony's cancer and asked him if he would be willing to stand in as guarantor, ready to step in should Tony not be there to complete the report. The goodness of human beings can be touching. Francois agreed without pause. We did not divulge this to anybody, since it would be disconcerting for Tony to know that there was a stand-in for him.

I had gone to England last week for several meetings but the most important one was on Saturday, 4th June. He was by now confined to home, quite unwell. It was a memorable meeting. There he was in his simple, but very-Oxbridge home, sitting on a couch, amidst the clutter of books and papers. I sat next to him and talked. I felt as though I was in the home of one of the great enlightenment philosophers. Tony does have that stature. We talked at length about how the World Bank ought to make important modifications to the way poverty is measured and tracked. He talked about how he abhors the level of inequality the world tolerates, and the role that good measurement can play. It was a slow brooding conversation. Despite the gentle tone, it was clear he had strong views (luckily, views not too far from my own). We went on to talk of economics as a discipline, its long history, and tales of academics in Oxford and Cambridge. He has a quiet sense of humor. We laughed and joked about people and their foibles.

(Sir Tony Atkinson completed the Report, but died just after that, on January 1st, 2017.)

6 August 2016, Saturday

I am in wind down mode. The primary charge of the chief economist of the World Bank is to lead the huge knowledge sector of the Bank—the teams of researchers working on all parts of the world, teams of professionals collecting statistics from all corners of the world and trying to create a pathway of future policy. It is difficult to assess what one has achieved. What I do feel good about is some of the people I appointed. The World Bank's macroeconomics unit has done very well. The global economic forecasts that we put out in the form of our bi-annual Global Economic Prospects, has really improved in quality and has become a sought after publication. Since I don't do any of the work myself I cannot take any direct credit. But I chose the person who directs this unit—the Turkish economist, Ayhan Kose. His intellectual acumen and total engagement with the work helped us achieve this; and what is more, it got even me interested in macroeconomic forecasting, which is far from my own research specialization.

Research in the Bank is done reasonably well but, maybe because of my own inclination, I keep feeling the work is not deep enough. To give a nudge in that direction, and admittedly, taking advantage of being in such a major organization, I had planned a big conference and a book that will provide some guidance to the future. I decided to get two collaborators from the World Bank to organize the conference and then edit the book. They were David Rosenblatt and Claudia Sepulveda. I liked them both—an important consideration to carry out a big project. David was intelligent and such an agreeable person that we worked together on many projects in the Bank. Claudia is a natural intellectual. She seems to have read everything.

I feel good about the conference on 'The State of Economics, The State of the World' that we eventually held at the World Bank on 8 and 9 June. Because of the long title of the conference, I created a short form SOESOW, which caught on. I did get into the weeds in planning and organizing SOESOW. To make it easy to persuade the World Bank to cooperate over this big event, we needed a few Nobel laureates. David, Claudia and I conferred and we reached out to five and got a positive response from three— Ken Arrow, Amartya Sen and Joe Stiglitz. My editor at MIT Press was happy about this. (We eventually managed to give MIT Press six Nobel laureates because three of the other authors in this book, Abhijit Banerjee, Esther Duflo and Michael Kremer, got the Nobel shortly after the book was published in 2019.)

Even apart from these prominent names it was quite an all-star event, with papers by Guillermo Calvo, Hyun-Song Shin, Philippe Aghion, Nick Stern, Sams Fankhauser, Cass Sunstein, Ingela Alger and Jorgen Weibull. The formal commentators were also quite a line up: Celestin Monga, James Foster, Ravi Kanbur, Hamid Rashid, Gita Gopinath, Luis Serven, Asli Demurguc-Kunt, Maurice Obstfeld, Francesco Caselli, Aart Kraay, Michael Toman, Gael Giraud, Bob Hockett, Varun Gauri, Larry Blume, Xavier Xine, David Mackenzie and Martin Ravallion.

My own biases are of course on display in the conference and the book, *The State of Economics, The State of the World*, that would subsequently come out of it. I believe the data work and huge empirical studies that are taking place today are important for human welfare but, at the same time, economics would not be the fascinating subject that it is today but for the theoreticians of the past—their magical insights, entirely comparable to the big thinkers in the natural sciences. I am thinking of the works of Adam Smith, Augustin Cournot, Stanley Jevons, Leon Walras, Vilfredo Pareto, John Maynard Keynes, John Hicks, Paul Samuelson, John von Neumann, John Nash and a few others. I wanted this history to be captured and used to think ahead and peer into the future. In my introductory talk I suggested that to commemorate this great history we should declare 19 February the Modern Economics Day, adding to the surfeit of Days—Mother's, Father's, Teacher's, Valentine's, Administrative Professional's. This was in memory of that momentous day in 1960, when Jevons got that blinding insight into how prices are formed. As he confided in his diary, 'At home all day and working chiefly at Economy, arriving I suppose at a true comprehension of Value.' This was so stunning that the normally modest Stanley Jevons later wrote to his brother, 'I cannot now read other books on the subject without indignation.'

The book *The State of Economics, The State of the World*, did come out, in 2019, but there were some touch and go moments. On the evening of 15 February, 2017, I got two emails. The first from David Arrow, introducing himself as Ken Arrow's son, and saying that his father had been ill and hospitalised, but he was back at home and better now, and wanted me to know that he felt very guilty for not having completed the paper he presented at my conference. The next email was from Ken Arrow, who was then 95, apologising for the delay and telling me that he planned to complete it within twenty-five days. I phoned David to say that I would not dream of pushing Ken to finish his paper; it was more important to us that he gets well first. But David said that it is research that inspires and cheers up his father and so I should push Ken to work and finish it. Feeling somewhat guilty, I phoned Ken Arrow to gently nudge him to finish his paper. He sounded frail but was his usual, warm self and assured me he would finish it in the next couple of weeks. That was my last conversation with Ken Arrow. He died on 21 February. The paper was not finished but sufficiently close to that, so that with some editorial help from Larry Samuelson, who is Ken's nephew, we managed to get it in a form that it could be the opening chapter of our book. Unlike many other economists, I had not known Arrow in person for a very long time, but because of this recent interaction with him, the news of his death left me feeling strangely sad. The passing of Kenneth Arrow marks the end of an age for economics. He was among the three or four most important economists of the last century, and in my view, possibly the most.

20 August 2016, Saturday

I am glad my World Bank years are drawing to a close. I have enjoyed the four years but am also yearning for the freedom of life in academe. The thought of being back at a university with three months each year in India, as I have always done, is sheer joy. My big decision will be whether to stay on in Washington. I have got to love the city with its slightly southern feel, and Alaka and I love our home in the Plaza. Though both of us lead crazily busy lives, we have friends we treasure. In the Plaza itself there are Elizabeth and Hunter Rawlings, Courtney and Michael Singer, and Larry Pressler and Harriet. The occasional chit-chats and the evening wine on the roof top are so life affirming. But the return to Ithaca is also attractive. Cornell and our friends there, in my department and elsewhere, create the attraction of home. Well, I don't have to decide today. I have a few more weeks to decide and procrastination is fun.

There is a lot that I will miss about the Bank—the multi-cultural ethos, the wonderful supporting staff that I have which frees me to concentrate on what I enjoy most, the work to help developing countries take better decisions, and the fact that that work comes blended with travel to exotic corners of the world.

Speaking of exotic corners, last month I went to Mauritius, Ethiopia and Egypt. The World Bank has a lot of work going with Mauritius. So when I got an invitation from Ameenah Gurib-Fakim, the president of Mauritius, to deliver the first in her inaugural series of Presidential Lectures, I decided to take it. I spoke on 'Technology and Development' at the State House in Port Louis. Ameenah is a scientist of distinction—a professor of organic chemistry; so her intellectual interest is genuine. She is a charming person who reminded me of my friend from our college days in London, Zainab, when we all lived in the famous and crumbling Indian Students Hotel on Guilford Street. And, like with Zainab, the conversation with the president over dinner is nice and gossipy and not formal like with many heads of states. I wonder if her free-floating style of speaking without being cagey gets her into trouble.

What makes Port Louis so memorable to an Indian is its disorienting blend of cultures. At one level it feels like India—the people have my skin colour—but they talk with a strange accent. There are billboards with names that make me feel as though I were in Ahmedabad, Patna, Hyderabad or Kolkata. In many ways the people of Indian origin here are more orthodox than Indians in India. On the other hand, you get caught by surprise when you hear some of them speaking in French. You could be in one of the West Indian towns in Naipaul's *A House for Mr Biswas*, or in Pondicherry.

Egypt was nice especially because this time I got to visit Luxor, Qena and Dendera, on the banks of the Nile, and also because the World Bank country director accompanying me is a friend, Asad Alam. But Cairo does not feel like the Cairo I visited a few years ago as India's chief economic adviser. The winds of hyper-nationalism are blowing and the politics of Sisi has vitiated some of the lovely, old-world, open-society charm of Egypt.

One of my last missions during my World Bank job were the last four days of last month in Ethiopia. I have had a great interest in the country ever since I read Ryszard Kapuscinski's *The Emperor: The Downfall of an Autocrat*. It is a country with a long history. It has virtually never been colonised, though it came under Italian control for some years. It is a mishmash of cultures, with traces of ancient Christianity, Judaism, Islam and Hinduism. It is a cerebral country. I remember Manmohan Singh telling me, after meeting President Meles Zenawi, that he had rarely met a politician with such an intellect. In addition to all this, it is the country with the world's most beautiful women.

As an economist I have a more immediate interest. Ethiopia is a poor country, but it is now growing rapidly, at more than 10 per cent per annum, among the fastest in the world. So I packed in meetings—with the relatively new Finance Minister Abdulaziz Mohammed, the Minister of Planning, Yinager Dessie, World Bank's Acting Country Director Nicole Klingen and Africa Chief Economist Albert Zeufack. Ethiopia is at a critical juncture, with growing Chinese investment and influence. This is all very good, but it has to guard against falling into a colonial trap which it avoided so well through its history.

I visited a water project in the central highlands in the Bugena Woreda where a World Bank-financed project at Gelesot is about to provide water from a distant borehole to small hamlets living in a drought-prone part of the country which was at the center of the great famine of the mid-eighties.

Another compelling example of our work was an IFC-financed company in Ethiopia's Rift Valley on the road to Kenya called Afriflora, owned by a progressive Dutch family-run grower and distributor of cut flowers which are Fair Trade-certified. One hundred and eighty kilometers outside of Addis Ababa, the company has 400 hectares under full-time glass-house cultivation, and grows, packs, and airlifts more than 1.1 billion roses to the European supermarkets and florists every year, and they are expanding. Afriflora now supplies 25 per cent of the European cut rose market from East Africa and employs 16,000 people from local villages, the vast majority of whom are women.

It was a marvel to see this vast sustainable enterprise at work and see first-hand its development gains for the families of the local community and the wider region, including the national airline Ethiopian Airlines which delivers the flowers to European buyers in a major logistical operation.

My support staff traveling with me on this mission is Phillip Hay, who heads communications in my division in Washington, having taken over from Merrell. It is because of Phil's determination and ingenuity that I go to Lalibela. There is a lot of World Bank work there but because of its remote location, few senior members of the Bank ever visit the region. In fact, we have to take a lot of security precaution. I wanted to do the journey by road. From Addis Ababa to Lalibela would take a little more than twelve hours but the Bank's security would not allow me to travel by road for fear of ambush. So Phil and I flew there, and the World Bank, not trusting the local cars of the region—since there is a lot of trouble there, sent a car and driver from the World Bank's office in Addis Ababa.

Lalibela is in the North Wollo zone of Amhara region, a little town in the midst of a bleak mountainous landscape. It is a place of breath-taking beauty. Lalibela is famous for its rock-cut churches that go back to the seventh century. These are literally carved out of rock mountains, and are an astonishing sight. Christianity came to Ethiopia before anywhere else. It was flourishing in this region by the fourth century and the Portuguese arriving here in the fifteenth century got a shock to see that the religion they were bringing was already well established here. There is something majestic about the way religion seems to be practiced here but unobtrusively. Tall elegant men in white robes run these churches. One of them tells me that there was also some early Hindu influence here and there are symbols of that in the churches.

The World Bank has been spending a lot of money in the region to build roads and water supply channels and to contain the transmission of a variety of tropical diseases that flourish here. Studies are being done and budgetary allocations being made to increase agricultural productivity. Visiting many of these sights, I met farmers and shepherds, both men and women, elegantly draped in white shawls. They look like Biblical characters. Naturally gregarious and always with a smile, Phil also enjoys meeting people; and together we had a wonderful time talking to local residents, hearing about their woes and joys of life.

I do not know if my visit served any purpose but the people in this remote region were so visibly happy to see us that I feel gratified I went to Amhara.

(Also, in retrospect, for Phil Hay, this was almost a pilgrimage. Phil, a New Zealander, came to the World Bank after working for BBC Radio. He was one of my favourite persons. I am sorry to have to record that, soon after the memorable trip to Lalibela, Phil was diagnosed with cancer and had to take leave from the World Bank. Phillip Jeremy Hay died on 9 April 2018.)

11 September 2016

I just completed a quick but extremely fruitful mission to the Netherlands—two days in the Hague and two days in Amsterdam. Much of it was organized by Frank Heemskerk, Executive Director on the Bank's board. Frank is from the Netherlands and is a person with great interest in economics. Since early India had lots of interaction with the economists of the Netherlands, mainly because of Jan Tinbergen and his several Indian students, Frank and I have lots of overlapping interests. On 4th September I arrive in Amsterdam and am driven to Hampshire Hotel Babylon (every bit as nice as the name suggests) in the Hague. The economist and my friend, Pete Lanjouw, comes to see me and we have dinner together, talking about economics, and catching up on common friends.

The next day is packed with meetings, with a talk to the Dutch Council of State on the connection between behavioral economics and governance, lunch with members of parliament, where we discuss long-term value creation and a meeting later with government officials on migrations and migrants.

I am quite taken in by the level of intellectual interest of the Dutch politicians and policymakers. They fully appreciate when I tell them that I cannot give them all my time and need to disappear for a while to see some of the landmarks of Spinoza. It is interesting that a whole lot of philosophers who were persecuted in other countries for their free thinking found a home in Holland. Spinoza and Descartes are prominent among them.

On the evening of the 5th I am driven to Amsterdam, check into the Rennaissance Hotel, and go for dinner hosted by the Indian Ambassador J. S. Mukul. I used to have a lot of interaction with the Ambassador when I was advising Manmohan Singh's government. He seemed to know more about G-20 matters than anybody else. It was good to catch up with him. The next day again was a day of meetings, beginning with an excellent discussion with Peter van Mierlo, CEO of Price Waterhouse Coopers. The Dutch are concerned about low interest rates. They rightly perceive that the original thinking, in G-20, in the US Fed and in the ECB, that low interest rates would discourage people from saving and this would give a boost to demand for goods and services was backfiring. Persistent low-interest rates was getting people worried about how they would live off the interest earnings after their retirement. As a result they were saving more, rather than less. This kept coming up in our discussions.

In the middle of all this, Frank and I managed to slip in a boatride with one of Frank's friends down the canals of Amsterdam. I was keen to see some of the landmark places of Rene Descartes but, alas, did not manage.

19 September 2016, Monday

For more than a year I have been thinking that the World Bank ought to make a public statement distancing itself from the so-called 'Washington Consensus'—a set of conservative, extreme free-market, policy recommendations that have been used by the IMF and the World Bank to push advice down the gullets of developing countries. There were two problems with this. The original policy recommendations were developed by the wonderful British economist John Williamson for the very specific (and sensible, I may add) context in Latin America. The (deliberate) mistake was by those who converted this into an ideology, almost a manifesto, for the developing world. Secondly, it is always awkward for a Bretton Woods institution like the World Bank to take a public stance against this. It would probably cause Jim Kim some awkwardness.

But Joe Stiglitz, as chief economist of the World Bank, had prepared the ground a bit. He had used his office to do what no other chief economist had done, to criticize the other Bretton Woods institution, the IMF, for being too right-wing. This was not easy but I admired Joe for his courage and moral integrity. Once, after I took on the job of chief economist at the Bank, and Stiglitz came to give a public lecture, someone from the huge audience asked me what was Stiglitz's main achievement as chief economist of the Bank. My spontaneous answer was that, as chief economist of the World Bank, Stiglitz had managed to change the IMF. The IMF did change many of its ideological positions a few years after the East Asian crisis, that is, after the damage had been done.

The other problem was that people feel awkward to promote progressive ideas when they themselves are well off. Most people working at the World Bank are very well off. But there is no hypocrisy in saying that the world should not be the way it is. There are too many things we do just to appear correct. I feel many of my colleagues at the Bank agree with my political views but they do not say so because it does not sound right coming from a well-heeled organization.

This is the same principle involved in criticizing bad individuals who are also powerful. Most people feel scared to criticize such persons to their face. Not doing so, they then feel they should not criticize them anywhere, not realizing that this merely compounds the problem. The principle ought to be reversed. Even if you do not have the courage to criticize a bad person to his face, you must at least have the courage to talk ill of him behind his back.

After a lot of thought I decided it was time to make a public statement. I decided to invite several former chief economists of the Bank—I know almost all of them agree with me—and some prominent progressive thinkers from around the world. One or two individuals did turn me down but virtually everybody said yes.

We soon settled on the team that would work on this and draft the statement: Sabina Alkire (Oxford), Pranab Bardhan (Berkeley), Haroon Bhorat (Cape Town), Francois Bourguignon (former chief economist, World Bank, now in Paris), Ashwini Deshpande (Delhi), Ravi Kanbur (Cornell), Justin Yifu Lin (former chief economist, World Bank, now in Beijing), Kalle Moene (Oslo), Jean-Philippe Plateau (Namur), Jaime Saavedra (minister of education, Peru), Joe Stiglitz (former chief economist, World Bank, now in New York), Finn Tarp (UNU WIDER, Helsinki), and me. I had planned to have twelve signatories but later realized, I had not counted myself. We ended up with thirteen.

We needed to get together to debate, discuss and do a draft. To do it in Washington would be too much in the face. The World Bank and the IMF would get uncomfortable. I had had wonderful interactions with the Swedish government. Talking to officials in SIDA, in particular, to Chief Economist True Schedvin, I felt we would be on the same wavelength on a quasi-political document such as what we were attempting. SIDA was excited by the idea and agreed to host it. We decided on meeting in Saltsjöbaden, in Nacka country, a suburb of Stockholm. This was exciting because this is where the historic meeting had occurred between Swedish entrepreneurs and trade unions resulting in the Saltsjobaden Agreement on 20 December 1938, which laid the foundations of Sweden's welfare state.

We gathered at the venue on 14 September—the thirteen panelists, several persons from SIDA and Chorching and Vivian who had travelled with me to help organize the event and help with the drafting. The meeting was launched in the SIDA headquarters in Stockholm with a lecture by Joe Stiglitz on 'From the Washington Consensus towards a 21st Century Consensus on Development' followed by a chief economists panel moderated by Mia Horn af Rantzien, CEO of SNS Centre for Business and Policy Studies and a SIDA Board member. Charlotte Petri Gornitzka, director general of SIDA gave brief opening remarks. She spoke about the alignment of SIDA's areas of interest with that of the World Bank's which were inclusive and sustainable development.

The panel entitled the 'Changing Development Paradigms and Imperatives of the Global Economy' was kicked off by True Schedvin, who spoke about SIDA's work on multidimensional poverty, power and voice, equal opportunities and sustainability. I followed, speaking about the need for a changing nature and content of growth, concerns about the stalling and divergence of growth, and why what was often viewed as a 'labor vs. labor' problem to 'labor vs. profits' was really a problem in the global labor market. Next, Bourguignon talked about a set of postulates which allow us to better understand the functioning of an economy, and how they could be mobilized to achieve certain objectives. He viewed the development problems as stemming from the lack of recognition between the set of tools that are 'universal' and those that would require an understanding of the country context.

Justin Lin spoke about jobs and green growth. He elaborated on the possible conflict between industrialization and green growth, and advocated for low-income countries the need to adopt green technology, and the role that high-income countries could play in making such technology affordable to low-income countries. Stiglitz spoke about the important role that the World Bank can play in ushering in more balanced and equitable rules in global trade agreements.

We ended the first day with an official dinner for the participants of the roundtable, hosted by Charlotte Petri Gornitzka. We were also joined by colleagues from SIDA, the Ministry of Finance and the Ministry of Foreign Affairs where I gave the dinner address on the findings and recommendations of the Report of the Commission on Global Poverty which Tony Atkinson had chaired.

The second day of the conference was the roundtable on Development Policymaking, meant to develop an alternative to the Washington Consensus. The objective of the second day was to distill some basic principles of policymaking in today's contemporary world of global growth slowdown, growing inequality, alongside technological progress and general improvements in health and education outcomes. We had a closed-door discussion on the best policy ideas based on a preliminary list of twelve themes (later trimmed to eight) that were circulated to the group. The open exchange was extremely useful and collegial. It was agreed that the statement should be policy-driven, bold, brave and sufficiently provocative to motivate policymakers to think differently. SIDA expressed interest in disseminating the statement. It was agreed that the group would revise the statement following the day's discussion and then share it with SIDA for their consideration.

On the sidelines, I had meetings with representatives from SIDA and the Ministry of Finance, concerning strategic collaboration with the World Bank. We had two separate bilateral meetings with representatives from the Ministry of Finance. The first was an informal meeting with Karolina Ekholm, state secretary, whom I had known from years ago, before she rose to prominence in the policy world. We discussed monetary policy given our shared interest and her previous position in the Bank of Sweden, immigration and the increasing protectionism. Later that evening, I met Magdalena Andersson, joined by Joe Stiglitz and Karolina Ekholm, over an informal cocktail. We discussed a wide range of topics, mainly on Sweden's domestic challenges, politically and economically, against the backdrop of a changing EU and the implications of Brexit, both for EU and Sweden.

I also had an informal, off-the-record interview with Johan Schück, from Dagens Nyheter, whom I had met previously. It was a friendly conversation about my tenure at the World Bank.

What was most satisfying was that this deliberation led to the 'Stockholm Statement', which received wide attention, and caused some discomfort in some quarters of the World Bank. SIDA, Finland's WIDER and independent writers promoted this as an alternative to the Washington Consensus. The Statement emphasized that economics was not just about free trade, deficit control, and GDP growth. Inequality matters, for a better society and also as an end in itself. Equity across nations and peoples is essential. We want growth that is sustainable. Further, economics is embedded in society, politics and psychology, an idea intrinsic in the writings of Karl Polanyi. In crafting policy, we must be sensitive to this embeddedness. Ideas take long to have influence and one cannot but be aware that many vanish without effect. But, in the end we have little else but ideas to influence the world. I feel all thirteen of us felt very strongly that these are ideas that should encroach on mainstream thinking.

Postscript

10 December, 2020. Growing up in a traditional Indian household in Kolkata, around the time that I did, an early scientific conundrum that all children confronted was when they asked the mother how yogurt, a staple of Indian diet, was made, and were told that a key ingredient was a little bit of previously-made yogurt. Some children—I suppose the lucky ones—went away skipping, satisfied with the answer.

The typical question that arises in the world of policymaking and the answer one gets is a bit like the above secret of how to make yogurt. It is satisfying only if you are not interested in the next question. Infinite regress fascinates me, and I am interested in the next question, and the next. Trying to change the world can be gratifying, but trying to understand it is sheer joy.

It had been seven years of packing myself to the brim with observation, information and facts. I scarcely had a moment to pause and reflect on them. I was beginning to get impatient for that opportunity, and cannot deny a sense of excitement at being back in the modern-day agora, in the world of learning, questioning and debate.

Sitting in Ithaca, putting finishing touches to a diary that I stopped writing more than four years ago, with Thanksgiving behind us and Christmas round the corner, watching the few pedestrians in the deserted streets, masked and socially distanced, and taking in the news of a world torn asunder by pandemic and polarized politics, I cannot help wondering at how dramatically our world has changed in such a short time. Then, as now, we talked about poverty and deprivation, disease and well-being, and policies to combat those challenges. But today's concerns have an urgency and immediacy that we did not have then when I was busy designing policies by day, and making these hurried jottings in my diary by night. Thanks to the pandemic coming atop the dramatic advances in digital technology, we are now asking existential questions and considering the prospect of human beings facing an existential risk that we did not imagine then. It is time to ask big questions and seek answers. This is a time for exciting research and philosophical investigations.

I feel a ray of hope that this experience, especially of the past year, will mark a turning point for humankind. It will shake us out of our selfishness and complacency, spark new forms of science and understanding of how the economy works, and how societies cohere, and promote a deeper understanding of morality and ethics, which were the mainspring of economics at the time of the Scottish Enlightenment.

My expectation is that we will tiptoe past this moment of dinosaur risk. Further, after a period of negotiating this turning point, we will come out better off.

Some progressive thinkers have argued that growth has to slow down if we want to win the war against climate change. I do not agree with that. I believe this stems from the mistake of equating economic growth with more cars, more homes and more luxury boats. In reality, a constituent of GDP or the national income is anything we value. Longer life, better health, the conquest of pain, art, music, time to ponder the wonders of the universe can all be part of the GDP. Hence, rapid growth can mean growth in these kinds of consumption. Just as the world is growing much faster now than we did before the Industrial Revolution, I expect our national incomes will grow much faster in the future than now, but the constituents of that growth will be novel.

This will be predicated on and accompanied by a lot of creative research in economics and novel ways of thinking about the economy. This will also be accompanied by huge amounts of research in medicine and health care. In general, as robots and artificial intelligence displace mechanical and routine forms of labor, human beings will move more and more into research and creative activities. I also believe that our survival will depend on more radical and progressive policies, with vast redistributions of income and wealth from the rich to the poor, making for a more equitable world. Just as the hundred odd years of the Industrial Revolution was accompanied by the most seminal breakthroughs in economics, from Adam Smith to Karl Marx, and also with radical, or what at that time appeared radical, policies, such as giving workers minimal rights, and stopping children below the age of 10 from doing hard labor, and taxing the incomes of the rich, we shall see radical, or what will appear to us as radical, policies.

At a fundamental level, today's concerns are the same; the urgency is new. We need passion and determination to fight and combat exploitation, corruption, hate, and ill-will. But that is not enough. We have to combine those emotions with intellectual commitment, scientific discourse, the willingness to dissect and analyze with patience. It is for this reason that the two worlds I inhabit—those of activism and policymaking, and research and analysis—are deeply intertwined. Human beings need the intellect as well as the moral compass. We must invest in both to combat the immediate challenges that we are faced with now, and our long-term challenges of poverty, inequality and discrimination.

Index

370INDEX

corruption control 119; on An Economist's Miscellany 96; farewell lunch from 223; in honor of Venkatraman Ramakrishnan 48; on Independence Day event 149; on Independency day event 77; on inflation 160; on inflation control 25; invitation from 9, 14, 63–64, 69, 78, 137, 154, 213; letter to 139; and Obama 90; at residence of xi, 9, 25–26, 28, 49, 89, 107, 109, 119; on sugar decontrol 79; Vini Mahajan from xi; with World Bank team 254

Procope, Le, lecture at 102

public lectures 134, 200, 230, 248, 294, 298, 312, 327, 349, *see also under separate entries*

Public Private Partnerships (PPPs) 144–45, 279

punctuality 146–47

Puran 106

Purulia 227–28

Q

Qian, Joe 307

Quadir, Kamal 331

Queen's Diamond Jubilee 200

R

racism 19, 78

Radha Soamis 162–63

Raebareli 203–4

Raghavan, T. C. A. 121

Raghuram Rajan Committee 167

Rahinsunnisa 204

Rahman, Atiur 326–27, 331

Rahman, Moshiur 327

Rahman, Sheikh Mujibur 328

Rahmanov 246

Rahmon, Emomali 245–46

Raizada, Shashank 212

Raj Krishna Memorial Lecture, at Rajasthan University 178

Raja, D. 118

Rajiv Gandhi Institute of Contemporary Studies 153, 161, 177

Rajiv Gandhi Mahila Vikas Pariyojana (RGMVP) 204

Rakhimzade 245–46

Ram, N. 164

Ram, Scientist 91

Ram, Vinay Bharat 20

Rama, Martin 224, 327, 329

Ramachandran, Prof. 209

Ramakrishna Mission 228–29, 332

Ramakrishna, Anjali 112

Ramakrishna, K. 265

Ramakrishnan, Venkatraman, Nobel Prize for Chemistry 48

Ramesh, Jairam 202

Ramesh, M. 210–11

Ramírez, Sergio 274

Rana Plaza tragedy 331

Ranganathan, T. C. A. 145

Rangarajan C. 159–60

Rantzien, Mia Horn 351

Rao, C.N.R. 48

Rao, K. S. 214

Rao, Nirupama 14, 124–25

Rao, Subba 134

Rao, Sudhakar 124–25

Rashid, Hamid 341

Rashtrapati Bhavan 39, 227

Ravallion, Martin 249, 338, 341

Ravi, Vayalar 131

Ravindran, Shruti 123

Rawling, Elizabeth 321, 343

Rawling, Hunter 321, 343

Rawls, John 286

Ray, Ajoy 36

Ray, Ranjan 206

Ray, Satyajit 86, 95, 267, 317

Ray, Tridip 169

Razak, Najib 254

Rebecca, Dato 315

Red Fort 77–78, 149

Reddy, Jaipal 131

Reddy, Y. V. 145

reforms 48, 182, 196–98, 200, 205, 245, 247, 255

Rekha 196

religion 12, 19, 34, 80–81, 204, 250, 346